KT-379-513

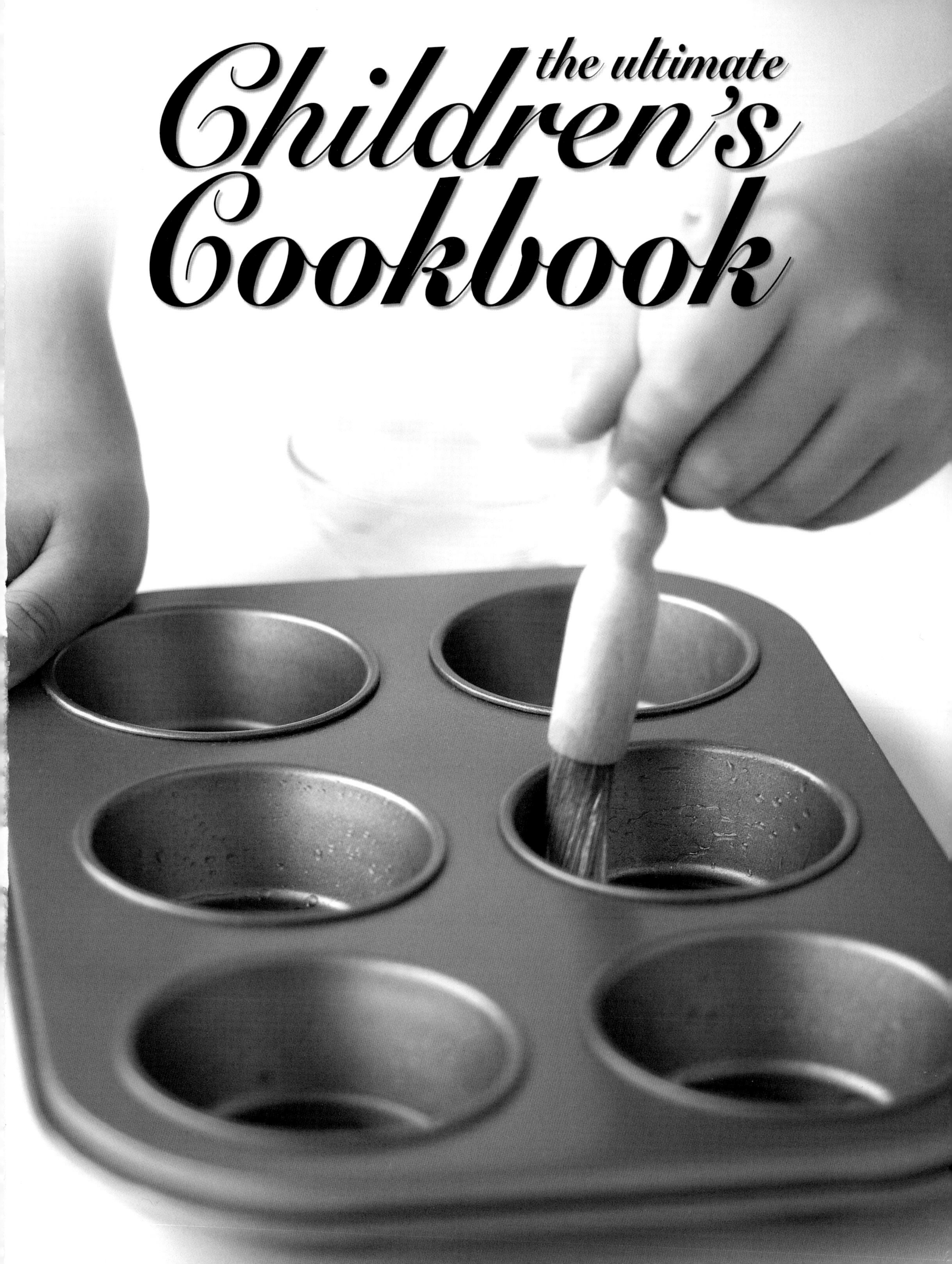
the ultimate
Children's
Cookbook

LONDON, NEW YORK, MUNICH,
MELBOURNE AND DELHI

Senior Editor Catherine Saunders
Senior Designer Lisa Crowe
Editors Heather Scott, Julia March, Elizabeth Noble
Designers Dan Bunyan, Justin Greenwood, Lynne Moulding, Thelma-Jane Robb
Home Economists Katharine Ibbs, Denise Smart
Assistant Home Economists Fergal Connolly, Lisa Harrison, Sarah Tildesley
Consultant Nicola Graimes
Publishing Managers Simon Beecroft, Cynthia O'Neill Collins
Category Publisher Alex Allan/Siobhan Williamson
Production Amy Bennett, Rochelle Talary

THE ULTIMATE CHILDREN'S COOKBOOK
Senior Designer Philip Letsu
Designer Johnny Pau
Senior Editor Julie Ferris

First published in Great Britain in 2009 by
Dorling Kindersley Limited,
80 Strand, London, WC2R 0RL

Contains content from Children's Cookbook (2004),
Children's Healthy & Fun Cookbook (2007), and Cookbook for Girls (2009)

2 4 6 8 10 9 7 5 3

A CIP catalogue record for this book is available from the British Library.

ISBN: 978-1-40535-189-8

Reproduced by Media Development and Printing Ltd., UK
Printed and bound in China by L Rex Printing Company

Discover more at
www.dk.com

The ultimate Children's Cookbook

Written by Nicola Graimes, Katharine Ibbs, and Denise Smart
Photography by Howard Shooter

Contents

Healthy Eating

Strawberry Scrunch
See page 32

Breakfast

Light Meals

Baked Potato
See page 76

Main Meals

Tuna Pasta
See page 114

Desserts

Tropical Yoghurt Ice
See page 176

Baking

Banana and
Pineapple Cake
See page 238

Spicy Potato Wedges
See page 268

Party Food

Cherry Cordial
See page 276

Drinks and Treats

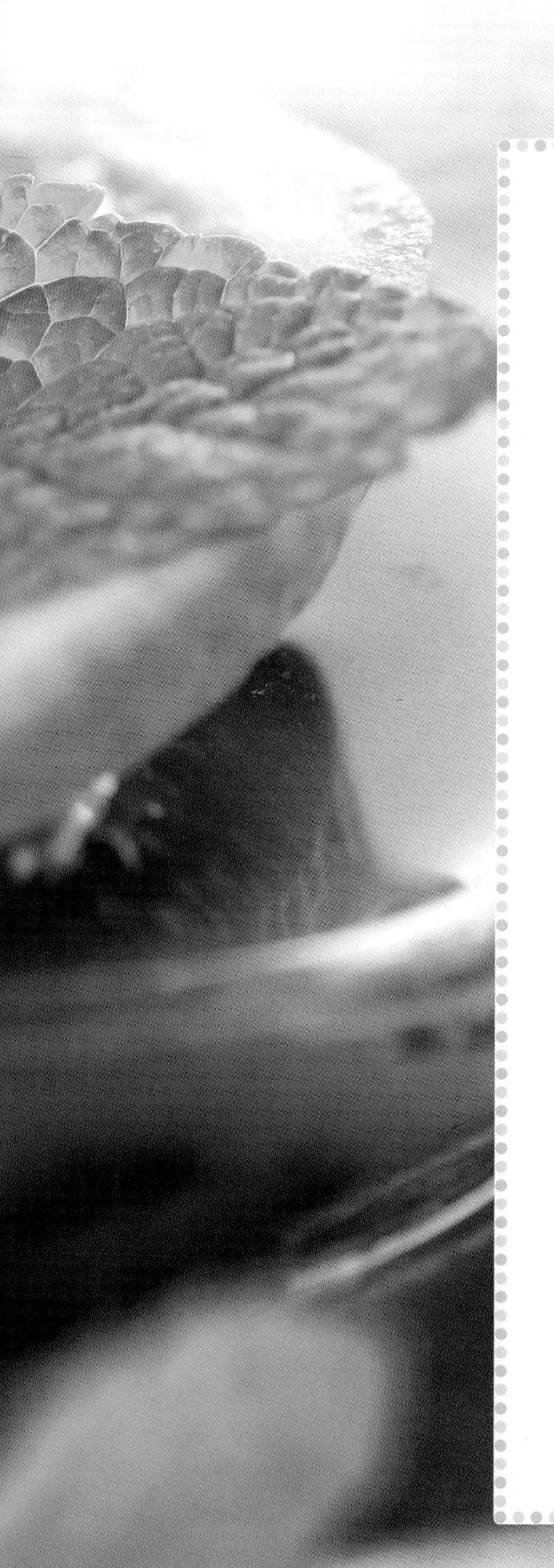

Healthy Eating

Introduction

In this book you'll find out why healthy eating is good for you and how to make your diet balanced and tasty. You will also discover lots of ideas for balanced breakfasts, luscious light meals, and mouthwatering main meals, all designed to suit even the fussiest eaters! And don't worry, there's plenty of recipes for desserts, cakes, and cookies, all with a healthy twist.

Getting Started

1. Read the recipe thoroughly before you begin.
2. Wash your hands, tie your hair back (if necessary) and put on your apron.
3. Gather all the ingredients and equipment you need before you begin.
4. Start cooking!

Be sensible! Take extra care when you see this symbol because hot ovens, cookers or sharp knives are involved.

You might need to ask an adult for help if you see this symbol. But don't be shy – ask for help whenever you think you need it!

Safe Cooking

Cooking is great fun but with heat and sharp objects around, you must always take care to be safe and sensible.

- Use oven gloves when handling hot pans, trays or bowls.
- Don't put hot pans or trays directly onto the work surface – use a heatproof trivet, mat, rack or board.
- When you are stirring food on the cooker, grip the handle firmly to steady the pan.
- When cooking on the stove, turn the pan handles to the side (away from the heat and the front) so that you are less likely to knock them over.
- Take extra care when you see the red warning triangle on a step.
- Ask an adult for help when you see the green warning triangle.

Kitchen Hygiene

Cooking is great fun but with heat and sharp objects around, you must always take care to be safe and sensible.

- Always wash your hands before you start cooking and after handling raw meat.
- Wash all fruit and vegetables
- Use separate chopping boards for meat and vegetables.
- Keep your cooking area clean and have a cloth handy to clean up any spills.
- Store cooked and raw food separately.
- Always check the use-by date on all ingredients. Do not use them if the date has past.
- Keep meat and fish in the refrigerator until you need them and always take care to cook them properly.

Did You Know?

Humans are the only creatures on Earth that eat cooked food. All other creatures (except for domesticated animals) eat their food raw and unprocessed.

Using the Recipes

There is a lot of information to take in so here's how to get the most out of the recipes. They don't just tell you how to cook the food, they suggest alternatives, give helpful advice and provide some amazing facts about the food you eat.

Fruit and Vegetables

Eating lots of fruit and vegetables is a vital part of a healthy diet and some scientists believe it could actually help you to live longer. Fresh fruit and vegetables may even help to protect you against many of the major diseases found in the modern world, including cancer and heart disease.

You should eat a minimum of five different portions of fruit and vegetables every day. One portion is roughly equal to the amount you can hold in one hand, e.g. 1 apple, a few grapes, 1 orange, 1 kiwi fruit, 1–2 florets of broccoli, a bowl of salad, 1 small corn-on-the-cob and so on.

Why are fruit and vegetables good for you?

Fruit and vegetables are good for you because they provide important vitamins, minerals, fibre, and natural plant compounds known as phytochemicals. As well as their health benefits, these phytochemicals are responsible for the colour, taste, and smell of a fruit or vegetable.

What doesn't count?

There are a few foods that don't count in the five-a-day guidelines, either because they are too high in starch or do not contain a high enough quantity of fruit or vegetables. These are:

- **Potatoes, yams, and sweet potatoes**
- **Ketchup and the tomato sauce in beans (although the beans do count)**
- **Fruit drinks, such as squash**
- **Fruit yoghurts**
- **Jam or marmalade**

Melon Fruit Bowl
p.174–175

I can eat a rainbow...

Fruit and vegetables are a colourful and fun part of any healthy, balanced diet. Different coloured fruit and vegetables provide different nutrients.

Red

Red fruit and vegetables such as tomatoes, sweet peppers, strawberries, grapes, and cherries are a great source of vitamin C, which supports the immune system and helps the condition of your skin, hair, and nails.

tomatoes

Yellow

The yellow colour of fruit and vegetables such as bananas, sweet peppers, sweetcorn, melon, and pineapple comes from carotenoids, which have been found to protect the body against cancer and heart disease.

yellow peppers

Orange

Orange fruit and vegetables such as carrots, pumpkin, squash, mango, apricots, and sweet pepper contain large amounts of beta carotene and vitamin C. Beta carotene is great for boosting your immune system and research shows that vitamin C can significantly reduce the length and severity of a cold. If you haven't already, give pumpkin and squash a try because they contain around even more beta carotene than a large carrot!

oranges

Green

Broccoli, cabbage, and sprouts have all been described as super-vegetables because they are rich in vitamins and minerals, particularly beta carotene, vitamins C and B, iron, potassium, and calcium that help to support our immune systems.

broccoli

Did you know?

It can be difficult to get the right balance with fruit and vegetables but you won't go wrong if you eat a combination of different coloured fruit and vegetables every day.

Purple

Purple fruit and vegetables, such as grapes, aubergines, blackcurrants, blueberries, blackberries figs, beetroot, and red cabbage are an excellent source of vitamin C. They also contain bioflavanoids, which help your body to absorb vitamin C and reduce pain if you bump or bruise yourself.

blueberries

Starchy Foods

Bread, cereals, rice, pasta, and potatoes are all starchy foods. They are also known as carbohydrates. These types of food are the body's major source of energy so they should form the main part of every meal. They also contain useful amounts of fibre, vitamins and, perhaps surprisingly, protein. Sugary foods are also a type of carbohydrate.

You should eat 4–6 servings of carbohydrates every day, depending on your age. A serving is 1 piece of bread, a serving of rice or pasta, 1 medium potato, or a bowl of breakfast cereal.

wholemeal pasta

Good Carbohydrates

There are lots of different types of starchy foods to choose from but choose wholegrain varieties if you can. Wholegrain foods contain more vitamins, minerals, and fibre than processed foods because many nutrients are lost during the refining process.

brown rice

Bread

The best types of bread are those made from wholegrain flour as they provide B vitamins, vitamin E, and fibre. White bread still has some vitamins and minerals but is lacking in fibre. There are plenty of interesting varieties to choose from, including:

- Tortilla
- Pitta
- Bagels
- Soda bread
- Rye bread
- Foccacia
- Ciabatta

Oaty bread see p.214

Breakfast cereal see p.22

Grains and Cereals

Grains have been grown throughout the world for centuries. These seeds of cereal grasses are very versatile and also low in fat.

- Wheat
- Rye
- Quinoa
- Millet
- Buckwheat
- Couscous
- Bulgur wheat
- Oats

Rice

Rice is popular in many countries throughout the world and forms an important part of diets in India, China, and Japan. There are many types to choose from:

- Long-grain
- Short-grain (rice pudding)
- Basmati
- Arborio (risotto)
- Sticky rice (sushi)

Jambalaya see p.136–137

Fibre

Starchy foods are also a good source of dietary fibre, which is only found in foods that come from plants. High fibre foods include wholemeal bread, brown rice, wholemeal pasta, and wholegrain breakfast cereals, which mostly contain insoluble fibre. Although the body cannot digest this type of fibre, it helps the passage of other food and waste products through your gut and keeps your bowels working properly. Soluble fibre is found in oats and pulses and can be digested by your body.

oats

Potatoes

There are thousands of potato varieties and certain types are best suited to particular cooking methods such as roasting, boiling or mashing. Vitamins and minerals are found in, or just below, the skin, so it is best to serve potatoes unpeeled, or scrubbed, if you can. The skin is also the best source of fibre.

potatoes

Protein

Eat 2–4 servings a day. A serving could be a handful of nuts and seeds, 1 egg, a serving of meat or fish, or pulses (beans, peas, lentils).

There are lots of different types of foods in this group and protein is found in both animal and plant sources. Protein is made up of amino acids, which are essential for building you up and keeping you strong. Try to get your protein from a wide range of foods for a balanced and varied diet.

Meat

Meat is a good source of vitamins and minerals such as iron, zinc, selenium, and B vitamins but it can also be high in saturated fat. It is best to choose lean cuts of meat or cut off excess fat before cooking. Poultry is lower in fat than red meat, especially if the skin is removed.

Types of red meat:
- **Beef**
- **Pork**
- **Lamb**
- **Venison**

Types of poultry:
- **Chicken**
- **Turkey**
- **Duck**

Lamb Kebabs
See p. 126–127

Tofu and eggs are two valuable sources of protein. Tofu also provides calcium, iron, and vitamins B1, B2, and B3, while eggs contain B vitamins, iron, calcium, and zinc.

tofu

Nuts and Seeds

Nuts and seeds are a good source of protein and also provide a rich collection of vitamins and minerals and "good" fats such as omega-6. However, because they are high in fat, you shouldn't eat too many and you should especially try to avoid salted nuts.

Types of nuts and seeds:
- **Peanuts**
- **Brazil**
- **Walnuts**
- **Cashews**
- **Hazelnuts**
- **Almonds**
- **Sunflower seeds**
- **Sesame seeds**
- **Pumpkin seeds**
- **Poppy seeds**
- **Linseeds**

Fish

You should eat at least two portions of fish a week, including one of oily fish. Salmon, tuna, sardines, mackerel, trout, and herring are all types of oily fish that are rich in omega-3 fats as well as protein.

Salmon Parcels
see p130–131

Pulses

A pulse is an edible seed that grows in a pod. As well as being a good source of protein, they are low in fat and also contain significant amounts of carbohydrate. Tinned pulses are quick and easy to use but try and buy products without added sugar and salt.

Did you know?

A fried chicken breast in breadcrumbs contains nearly 6 times as much fat as a grilled skinless chicken breast.

Popular pulses:

- **Lentils**
- **Dried peas**
- **Chickpeas**
- **Haricot beans**
- **Flageolet beans**
- **Cannellini beans**
- **Kidney beans**
- **Soya beans**

milk

Dairy

As well as protein, dairy produce also provides valuable vitamins and minerals, such as calcium and vitamin A, B12, and D.

Yoghurt Swirl with Dippers
see pg. 34–35

Types of Dairy

- Milk
- Yoghurt
- Cheese
- Butter
- Fromage frais
- Cream
- Crème fraîche
- Buttermilk

Alternatives to Dairy

- Fortified breakfast cereals
- Soya milk
- Tofu
- Green leafy vegetables
- Molasses
- Tinned sardines
- Baked beans
- Sea vegetables
- Sesame seeds

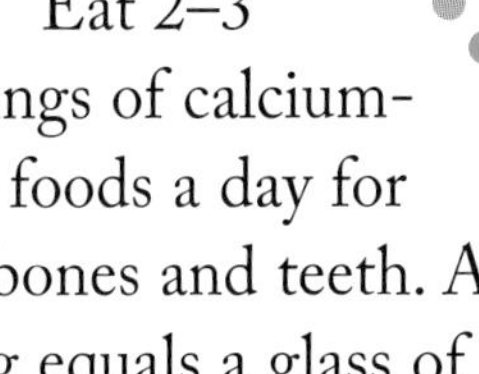

Eat 2–3 servings of calcium-rich foods a day for strong bones and teeth. A serving equals a glass of milk, a pot of yoghurt or a small portion of cheese.

Fats and Sugars

You need some fat in your diet because it provides your body with lots of energy, helps it to absorb some vitamins and provides essential fatty acids, such as omega-3. But it is important to eat the right types such as polyunsaturated and monounsaturated and to try and avoid saturated and trans fats.

Be careful not to eat too much fat. A good way to check how much fat your food contains is to look at the label. 20g (¾ oz) of fat per 100g (3½ oz) of food is a lot of fat; and 3g (⅒ oz) or less of fat per 100g (3½ oz) is a little fat. Use what you learn in this book to be sensible about your fat intake.

cheese

chips

Bad Fats

croissants

Saturated and trans fats are generally solid at room temperature and are primarily from animal sources (except fish). They are found in lard, butter, hard margarine, cheese, whole milk, and anything that contains these ingredients, such as cakes, chocolate, biscuits, pies, and pastries. Saturated fat is also the white fat you can see on red meat and underneath poultry skin. The less saturated fat you eat, the better – a high fat intake has been linked with an increased risk of coronary heart disease.

cake

Good Fats

avocados

olive oil

Unsaturated fats (polyunsaturated and monounsaturated) are usually liquid at room temperature. They are a much healthier alternative to saturated fat, helping to fuel the body, transport nutrients around the body, and also to protect your heart. Unsaturated fats generally come from vegetable sources (and some fish). These sources include vegetable oils such as sesame, sunflower, soya, and olive plus nuts, seeds, avocadoes, and oily fish, such as mackerel, sardines, pilchards, and salmon; and soft margarine. However, although these fats are healthy you only need a small amount to get the health benefits you need.

sunflower seeds

Some simple ways to cut down on bad fats:

- Snack on unsalted nuts and seeds instead of biscuits and crisps.
- Spread mashed avocado or houmous on toast instead of butter.
- Choose oily fish instead of battered fish or meat pies.
- For a change, mash olive oil into potatoes instead of butter.
- Drizzle olive oil and lemon juice over salads in place of creamy salad dressings.
- Nibble fresh or dried fruit rather than biscuits and chocolate.
- Trim any visible fat off meat and poultry.
- Buy lean cuts of meat and reduced-fat minces.
- Ditch the frying pan – try poaching, steaming, grilling, or baking.
- Swap whole milk for semi-skimmed or skimmed alternatives.
- If you use lard, butter, or hard margarine, switch to plant-based oil and low-fat spreads.

raisins

raspberries

strawberries

houmous

Sugary Foods

jam

Like fat, sugar is a concentrated source of energy. It is found in foods such as jam, sweets, cakes, chocolate, soft drinks, biscuits, and ice cream. The psychological benefits of eating these foods are obvious – they taste lovely! However, too much sugar causes tooth decay, obesity, and mood swings so it is important to limit your intake.

lollies

fizzy drink

Salt

crisps

Eating too much salt is linked to high blood pressure, heart disease, and strokes. It's not just obvious foods such as crisps and salted peanuts that contain salt, it is also hiding in breakfast cereals, bread, cakes, and biscuits. This means that it can be very difficult to tell if you are eating too much so check your food labels first to see if salt has been added. When it comes to adding salt at the table, it is easy to get into the habit of using too much. Always taste your food before reaching for the salt pot – you will find that your food tastes fine without it.

salt

Breakfast

Breakfasts

After a night's sleep you need fuel – a good breakfast to prepare you for the day ahead. Foods high in carbohydrates, such as cereal and bread, are ideal for breakfast because they are broken down into glucose which fuels your brain. Protein foods such as yoghurt, milk, eggs, sausages, bacon, and beans are important, too. They control your body's growth and development, and boost alertness. There are lots of tasty recipes in this section and here are some simple ideas to get you started.

Boiled Egg

Half-fill a small saucepan with water. Gently lower the egg into the pan and bring the water to the boil. Boil the egg for 4 minutes then remove it with a slotted spoon. Dip the egg in cold water and place it in an egg cup. Carefully slice the top off the egg and serve with toast.

Naturally Sweet

Shop-bought cereals can be very high in sugar so buy sugar-free wheat or oat flakes and add your favourite combination of dried fruit, nuts, or seeds.

Quick and Easy

Give energy-levels a quick boost. Simply add sliced banana, a dollop of natural bio yoghurt and a drizzle of honey to wholemeal seedy toast or fruit bread.

Add Fruit!

Start the day in a super-healthy way by adding fresh fruit to your breakfast cereal. It adds vitamins and natural sweetness.

Stewed Apple

Peel and core 4 apples, then chop them into bite-sized pieces. Put them into a saucepan and add 1 tsp ground cinnamon, 4 tbsp apple juice and a squeeze of lemon juice. Half-cover the pan and simmer for 15–20 minutes or until the apples are tender. Serve with a fruit muffin or stirred into yoghurt.

Cooked Breakfast

Treat yourself to a cooked breakfast once in a while, but grill instead of fry it. Use lean or vegetarian sausages and add grilled tomatoes, mushrooms, wholemeal toast, and scrambled eggs for a balanced breakfast.

Poached Egg

Fill a pan with water (about 5cm/2in deep) and bring it to a simmer. Crack an egg into a cup. Swirl the water in the pan and then gently pour the egg into the centre of the pan. Cook for 3 minutes or until the white is set and the yolk is slightly runny. Scoop out using a slotted spoon and serve with wholemeal toast.

Porridge (serves 4)

Put 200g (7oz) porridge oats in a saucepan with 250ml (9fl oz) milk and 250ml (9fl oz) water. Bring to the boil, then reduce the heat and simmer, stirring, for about 4 minutes or until creamy and smooth.

Fruit Salad

Fruit salads are perfect for breakfast, dessert, or as a healthy snack. Use a combination of your favourite fruit. Bio yoghurt also tastes great with this recipe.

Boost Nutrients

A sprinkling of seeds or chopped nuts will boost the nutritional content of porridge and other breakfast cereals as well as adding extra flavour.

- **Preparation** 5 mins
- **Cooking** none
- **Serves** 2

Carrot and Apple Juice

This fresh juice is bursting with vitamin C! But don't worry if you don't have a juicer, remove the apple cores and then use a blender or food processor to make a purée. Use a sieve to separate the juice from the pulp.

For maximum goodness, drink the juice immediately.

Helpful Hints

The lemon juice helps to preserve the vitamins in the juice and also brings out the flavour of the apple and carrot.

Ingredients

- 4 apples (stalks removed)
- 3 carrots (scrubbed)
- squeeze of fresh lemon juice (optional)

Equipment

- small sharp knife
- chopping board
- juicer

juicer

1 Scrub the carrots and cut each one into 2 or 3 pieces. Remove the stalks from the apples and carefully cut them into quarters.

2 Put the apples and carrots through the juicer. Throw away the pulp and pour the juice into two glasses. Add a squeeze of lemon juice and stir the juice.

• **Preparation** 5 mins • **Cooking** none • **Serves** 4

Fruit Smoothie

This creamy drink will give you plenty of energy for the day ahead – and it's so easy to make. Serve it with cereal or toast for a complete breakfast.

Tasty Twists

Swap the blueberries for the same weight of strawberries for a classic combination.

Ingredients

- 150g (5 1/2oz) fresh or frozen blueberries
- 3 bananas (sliced)
- 1 tsp vanilla extract (optional)
- 500g ml (17 fl oz) thick, natural bio yoghurt
- 200ml (7fl oz) milk

banana

blueberries

Equipment

- small sharp knife
- chopping board
- blender

chopping board

1 Peel the bananas and then roughly chop them into small slices. Put them into the blender and add the blueberries, vanilla extract, yoghurt, and milk.

2 Whizz in the blender until the mixture is smooth, thick, and creamy. Pour the smoothie into four tall glasses and enjoy this simple and nutritious breakfast.

• **Preparation** 15 mins • **Cooking** 3 mins • **Chilling** 1 hour • **Makes** 8–10 bars

Fruit and Nut Bars

This homemade version of a fruit cereal bar is packed with energy-giving apricots, raisins, nuts, and seeds. It makes an excellent start to the day, especially with a calcium-rich glass of milk or pot of yoghurt. It could also be a healthy addition to a lunchbox.

Tasty Twists

Any type of ready-to-eat dried furit can be used to make these bars. You could also buy a pre-mixed bag such as tropical fruit or fruits of the forest.

Ingredients

- 50g (2oz) hazelnuts
- 50g (2oz) whole oats
- 100g (3½oz) raisins
- 150g (5½oz) dried apricots (cut into small pieces)
- 4 tbsp fresh orange juice
- 2 tbsp sunflower seeds
- 2 tbsp pumpkin seeds

raisins

pumpkin seeds

sunflower seeds

oats

Equipment

- frying pan
- wooden spatula
- small sharp knife
- chopping board
- food processor or blender
- large mixing bowl
- greaseproof paper
- palette knife
- 18cm x 25cm (7 x 10in) tin

palette knife

1 Put the hazelnuts, oats, and seeds into a frying pan. Dry fry (stirring) over a medium heat for 3 mins, or until they begin to turn golden. Leave to cool.

2 Put the raisins, apricots, and orange juice into a food processor and purée until the mixture becomes smooth. Put the fruit purée into a mixing bowl.

3 Put the nuts, oats, and seeds in the food processor and whiz until they are finely chopped. Tip the mixture into the bowl with the fruit purée.

Cut into 8–10 slices and eat as part of a nutritious breakfast.

Did you know?

Hazelnuts are high in fibre, potassium, calcium, magnesium, and vitamin E so they are nutritious as well as tasty!

4 Stir the fruit mixture until all the ingredients are mixed together. Line a 18 x 25cm (7 x 10in) baking tin with greaseproof paper.

5 Spread the fruit mixture evenly in the tin. Chill for at least 1 hour, or until solid. Turn it out of the tin and peel off the greaseproof paper. Cut into bars.

Food Facts

Drying fruit is one of the oldest methods of preserving. The drying process concentrates the nutrients making dried fruit a useful source of fibre, natural sugars, vitamins B and C, iron, calcium, and other minerals. However, levels of vitamin C are lower than in fresh fruit.

dried apricots

• **Preparation** 10 mins • **Cooking** 15 mins • **Serves** 6

Crunchy Cereal

This breakfast recipe is definitely worth getting out of bed for! Create a homemade cereal that is full of important fibre and carbohydrates with a tasty combination of oats, fruit, nuts, and seeds.

Tasty Twists

Try other dried fruits, nuts, or seeds. Raisins, tropical fruits, hazelnuts, or pumpkin seeds, would all taste great in this recipe!

Ingredients

golden syrup

- 1 tbsp olive oil
- 3 tbsp of golden syrup
- 175g (6 oz) jumbo rolled oats
- 60g (2oz) Brazil nuts (optional)
- 30g (1oz) sunflower seeds
- 60g (2oz) dried pineapple pieces
- 60g (2oz) dried banana chips
- 60g (2oz) dried apricots
- 60g (2oz) toasted coconut flakes (optional)
- milk or yoghurt to serve

jumbo rolled oats

Equipment

mixing bowl

- medium saucepan
- wooden spoon
- sharp knife
- chopping board
- non-stick baking tray
- large mixing bowl
- plate
- oven gloves
- measuring spoons

sharp knife

Did you know?

Hazelnuts are high in fibre, potassium, calcium, magnesium and vitamin E so they are nutritious as well as tasty!

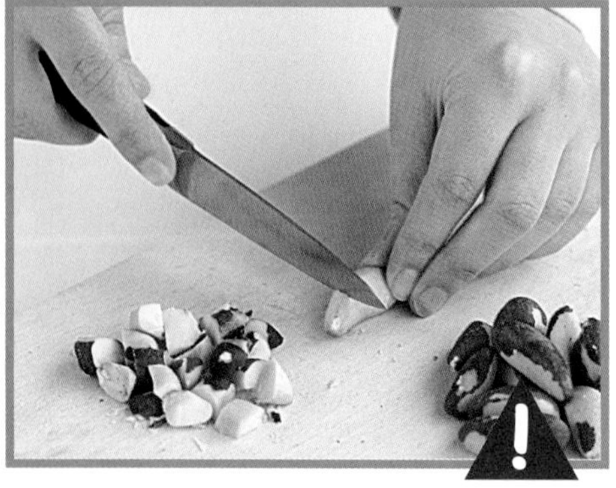

1 Chop the brazil nuts into medium-sized pieces. Remember, if you are allergic to nuts or do not like them, you can miss out this step.

2 Preheat the oven to 200°C (400°F/Gas 6). Pour the oil and syrup into the saucepan. Gently warm them over a low heat until they melt together.

3 Ensure that the heat has been turned off and then tip the oats, nuts, and sunflower seeds into the melted syrup mixture. Stir until well coated.

This cereal will stay fresh for up to two weeks if you store it an airtight container.

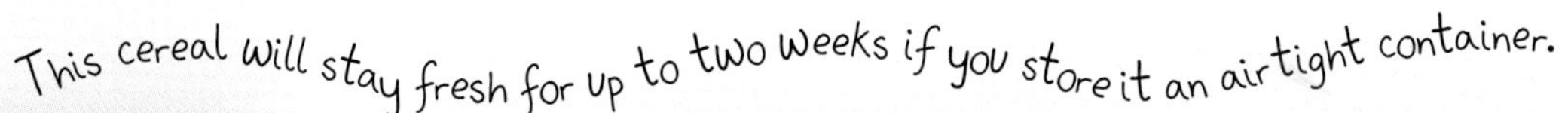

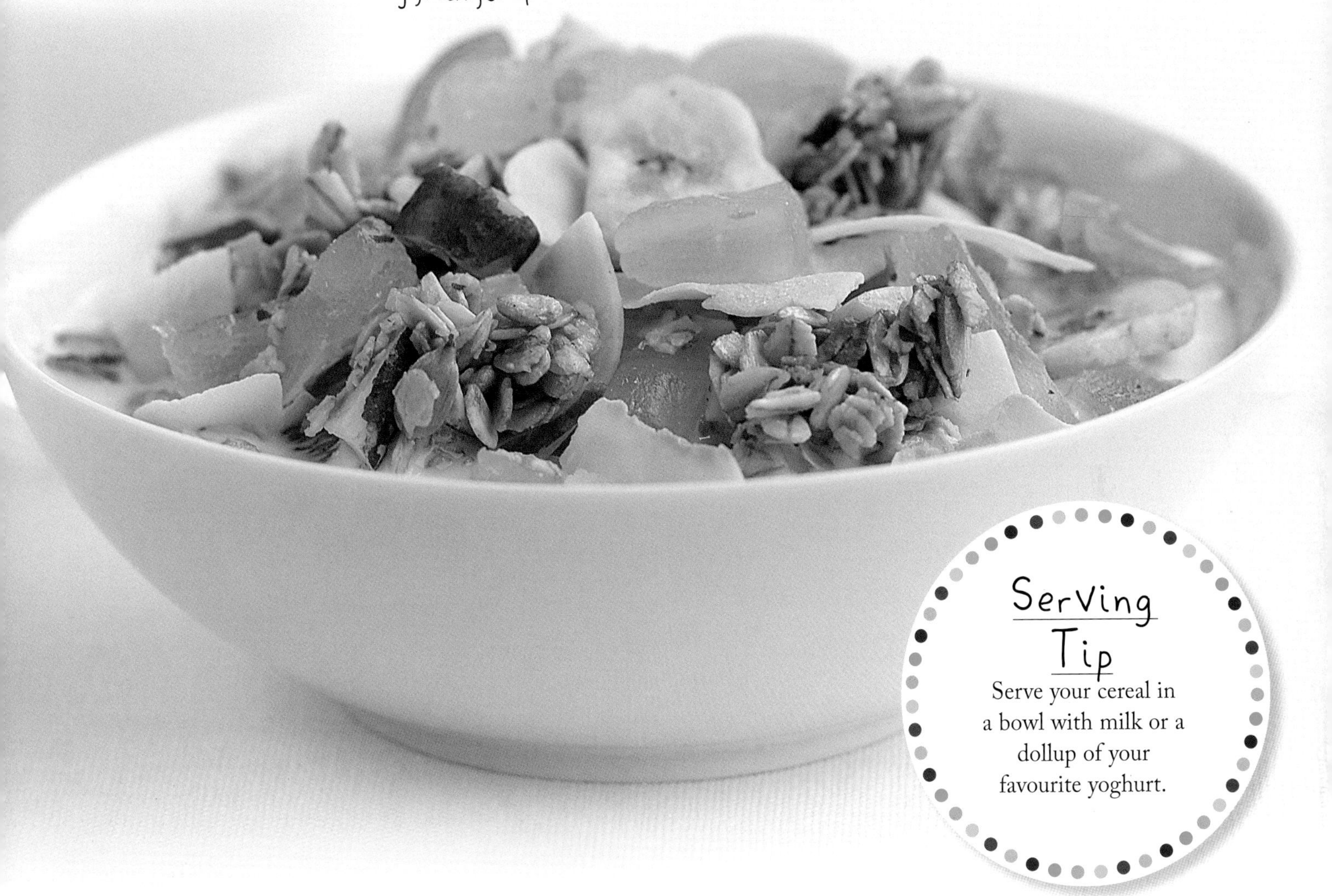

Serving Tip

Serve your cereal in a bowl with milk or a dollup of your favourite yoghurt.

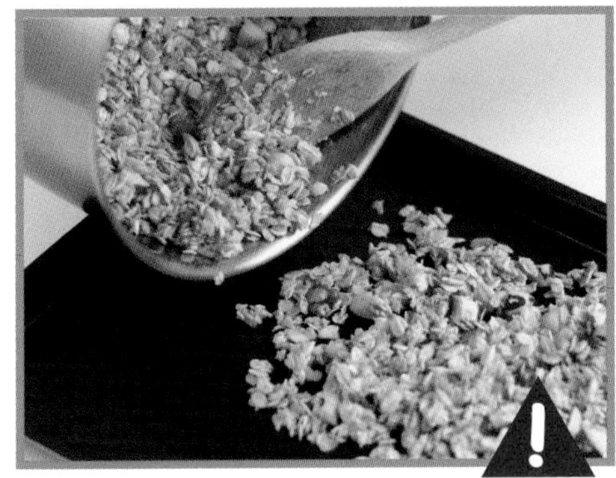

4 Tip the oat mixture onto a baking tray. Put it in the preheated oven for 10 minutes, or until the edges turn golden and the oats form clusters.

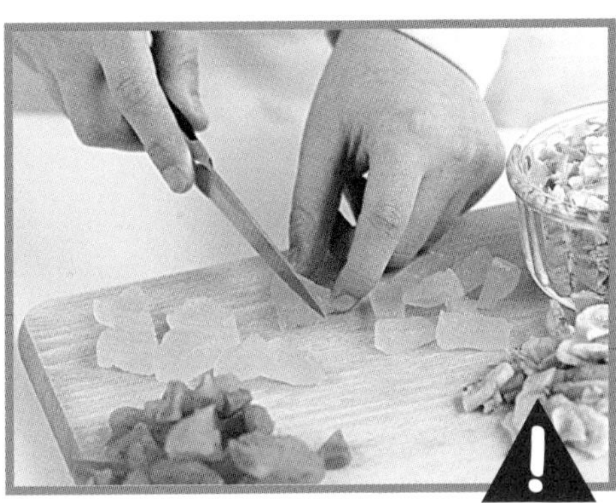

5 Cut the pineapple pieces in half, quarter the apricots, and break the banana chips into small pieces. Mix all the fruit and coconut together in a bowl.

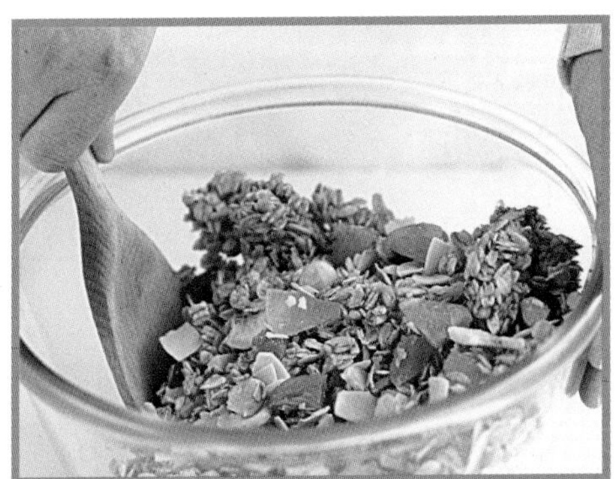

6 Spoon the oat clusters onto a plate and leave them to cool for a few minutes. Add the oat clusters to the bowl of fruit and coconut and mix them together.

• **Preparation** 10 mins • **Cooking** 6 mins • **Serves** 8

Mixed Fruit Puff

Shop-bought cereals can be full of unnecessary sugar but this healthier version relies on the natural sweetness of the dried fruit, which is also full of fibre and nutrients such as iron. Just add milk for a delicious and nutritious breakfast.

Tasty Twists

Any mixture of your favourite fruits and nuts can be used in this recipe. For a different texture, you could swap the puffed rice for oats to make muesli. Or try serving the cereal with a tasty topping of fresh fruit.

Ingredients

- 75g (3oz) whole hazelnuts
- 8 tbsp sunflower seeds
- 125g (4½ oz) dried apricots (cut into small pieces)
- 250g (9oz) sugar-free puffed rice cereal
- 125g (4½ oz) raisins
- 50g (2oz) flaked coconut

hazlenuts

rice cereal

dried apricots

Equipment

- frying pan
- wooden spoon
- small bowl
- freezer bag
- rolling pin
- kitchen scissors
- mixing bowl

rolling pin

frying pan

Did you know?

More than 10 billion pints of milk are sold every year in Great Britain and over 25% of that milk is consumed with tea.

1 Put the nuts in a frying pan and dry fry over a medium-low heat. Turn the nuts using a spatula and cook for 3 minutes or until they begin to turn golden.

2 Pour the nuts into a bowl and leave them to cool. Put the sunflower seeds in the frying pan and fry them for 2 minutes. They should be golden but not burnt.

3 Leave the sunflower seeds to cool. Pour the cooled nuts into a small plastic food bag. Fold over the open end and hold it closed with one hand.

Storing the cereal in an airtight container will keep it fresh for longer.

4 Using your other hand, bash the nuts with the rolling pin until they are broken into small pieces. Then cut the apricots into small pieces.

5 Put the puffed rice cereal into a large mixing bowl. Add the apricots, nuts, seeds, raisins, and coconut and gently mix together with your hands.

Food Facts

Nuts and seeds provide a nutritious combination of B vitamins, iron, vitamin E, zinc, plus omega-6 fats, which are important for brain function and energy levels. Sunflower seeds help to keep your immune systems strong as they provide zinc, magnesium, and selenium. Their vitamin E content helps to keep skin healthy.

sunflower seeds

• **Preparation** 10 mins • **Cooking** 5 mins • **Serves** 2

Strawberry Scrunch

Toasted oats and seeds add crunchiness to this layered breakfast, and provide important nutrients too. The yoghurt is a low-fat source of protein and calcium, while the strawberries and orange juice are rich in vitamin C. Honey adds sweetness, but you could use maple syrup instead.

Tasty Twists

Swap the strawberries for your favourite fruits such as bananas, nectarines, or peaches. Fruit purée also taste great!

Ingredients

- 150g (5½oz) strawberries (about 6–8)
- 4 tbsp fresh orange juice
- 50g (2oz) whole porridge oats
- 3 tbsp sunflower seeds
- 3 tbsp pumpkin seeds
- 2–3 tbsp clear runny honey
- 12 dsp thick natural bio yoghurt

pumpkin seeds

honey

strawberries

Equipment

- small sharp knife
- chopping board
- small bowl
- frying pan
- wooden spoon

chopping board

1 Cut the green stalks and leaves from the strawberries and then thickly slice the fruit. Put the strawberries in a bowl and add the orange juice. Set aside.

2 Put the oats in a frying pan and dry fry over a medium-low heat for 3 mins. Turn the oats occasionally with a wooden spoon to make sure they cook evenly.

3 Next add the sunflower and pumpkin seeds and dry fry for another 2 minutes or until light golden. Take care the pumpkin seeds may pop a little!

4 Take the pan off the heat. Stir in the honey – it will sizzle at first but keep stirring until the oats and seeds are coated. Allow to cool slightly.

5 Put a layer of the oats in the bottom of each glass. Add 2 heaped dessert spoonfuls of yoghurt and then some of the fruit. Add another layer of each.

Food Facts

Oats are a carbohydrate food. They are perfect for breakfast because the fibre in them is digested by the body slowly. This makes you feel full for longer and keeps your blood sugar levels steady. Oats are also a great source of vitamins E, B1, and B2.

oats

• **Preparation** 15 mins • **Cooking** 20 mins • **Serves** 4

Yoghurt Swirl with Dippers

Unlike shop-bought yoghurts, you won't find refined sugar or additives in this recipe. Instead these tasty yoghurts are low in fat and high in calcium, protein, and potassium and have a swirl of vitamin-rich dried fruit. Have fun dipping the toasted fruit bread fingers into your breakfast!

Taste Twists

Fresh fruit or fruit purées are also good mixed into yogurt. Try mango, strawberry, raspberry, or stewed appples.

Ingredients

- 100g (3½oz) dried dates or apricots (chopped)
- 250ml (9fl oz) water
- 3 tbsp fresh apple juice
- 500g (1lb 2oz) thick natural bio yoghurt
- 4-8 slices raisin bread

dried dates

dried apricots

Equipment

- medium saucepan with lid
- blender
- spoon
- 4 bowls

bowl

1 Put the dates or apricots and water in the saucepan. Bring to the boil and then reduce the heat to low. Cover, and cook the fruit for 15-20 mins, or until soft.

Fruit muffins or bagels could also be dipped!

Food Facts

Bio yoghurt contains beneficial bacteria that may help to boost your immune system and help fight off infection.

bio yoghurt

Did you know?

Yoghurt has been around since ancient times and the word itself originates from the Turkish language.

2 Leave the dates or apricots to cool for about 30 minutes and then stir in the apple juice. Spoon the mixture into a blender and whiz until smooth.

3 Divide the yoghurt between four bowls. Put 2 tablespoons of the fruit purée on top of each serving and then stir gently to make a swirled pattern.

4 Toast the raisin bread until it is light golden. Cut the toast into narrow strips and dip them into the yoghurt mixture. Delicious!

• **Preparation** 5 mins • **Cooking** 5–10 mins • **Serves** 2

Boiled Eggs

Eggs can be cooked in a variety of different ways and are an excellent source of protein. The simplest method is to boil them for a delicious and nutritious breakfast. The most important thing to remember when boiling eggs is timing because this makes the difference between a soft-boiled egg and a hard-boiled egg.

1 Half-fill a small saucepan with water and place it on the hob. Gently lower the eggs into the pan and bring the water to the boil.

Ingredients

eggs

- 2 eggs
- 2 slices of wholemeal bread
- spreadable butter or margarine

Equipment

- small saucepan
- slotted spoon
- toaster
- bowl of cold water
- 2 egg cups
- tea spoon

saucepan

2 Boil the eggs for 4 minutes. While the eggs are cooking, you can make the toast. Place the bread in the toaster and toast until golden brown.

3 Remove the eggs with a slotted spoon and briefly dip them in cold water. This will cool the eggs and prevent them from cooking any further.

4 Place each egg in an egg cup and tap the top with the back of a teaspoon. Carefully slice off the top with the spoon. Serve with strips of buttered toast.

Food Facts

Although the yolk of your soft-boiled egg will be runny, a properly cooked egg should always have a firm egg white. If the white of your egg is still runny, it hasn't been cooked for long enough!

Eggs

Helpful Hints

For hard-boiled eggs, boil the eggs for 6–7 minutes and make sure that they cool completely in step 3.

- **Preparation** 5 mins • **Cooking** 5 mins • **Serves** 1

Scrambled Eggs

Get cracking with this great breakfast idea! The secret of scrambled eggs is not to overcook them in step 4 otherwise they will become dry and rubbery.

Ingredients

- 2 eggs
- 1 tbsp milk
- salt and pepper
- a knob of unsalted butter
- 1 slice of bread (toasted)
- spreadable butter or margarine
- 1 dollop ofketchup

eggs

Equipment

- mixing bowl
- whisk
- medium saucepan
- wooden spoon

Serving Tip

Scrambled eggs taste great on lightly-buttered toast, with a dollop of ketchup!

1 To crack the eggs, tap each one in turn on the side of the bowl. Then gently pull the shell apart so that the insides drop into the bowl.

2 Add the milk to the bowl of eggs. Season with salt and black pepper and whisk the ingredients together until they are mixed in completely.

3 Over a low heat, gently melt the butter in the saucepan. Take extra care when doing this because if the pan gets too hot, the butter will spit.

4 Carefully pour the beaten egg mixture into the pan and stir constantly for 2–3 minutes. The egg will become a firm scramble but should look moist.

Egg Cups

Eggs are a great source of high quality protein – ideal for kick-starting your day. This recipe is perfect for a filling weekend brunch or even a light meal!

Helpful Hints

Timing and temperature are really important when cooking scrambled eggs. If they are cooked for too long over too high a heat, the eggs become dry and crumbly.

Did you know?

The breed of hen determines the colour of the egg shell. Those with white feathers and ear lobes lay white eggs and those with red feathers and ear lobes lay brown eggs.

Ingredients

- 4 crusty rolls
- 3 tomatoes (optional)
- 8 free-range eggs
- 5 tbsp milk
- salt and pepper
- 50g (2oz) unsalted butter

crusty rolls

tomatoes

Equipment

- sharp knife
- chopping board
- small mixing bowl
- whisk or fork
- medium saucepan

whisk

chopping board

1 Slice the top off the rolls and then use your fingers to scoop out the centre of each roll. (The insides can be used to make breadcrumbs.)

2 Cut the tomatoes in half and then scoop out the seeds with a teaspoon. Then slice the de-seeded tomatoes into small, bite-sized pieces.

3 Crack each egg into a small bowl by tapping them firmly against the side of the bowl, pushing your thumbs into the crack and pulling the shell apart.

4 Add the milk to the bowl. Whisk the eggs and milk together using a fork or small hand whisk. Season the mixture with a little salt and pepper.

Food Facts

Eggs are one of the most nutritious foods and make a valuable contribution to our diets. They contain B vitamins, iron, calcium, and zinc, as well as protein. However, four eggs per week is the maximum recommended intake as they are high in cholesterol. The eggs of many different types of birds can be eaten, but those of the female chicken (hen) are most widely available.

eggs

5 Put the butter into the saucepan and melt it over a medium to low heat. When the butter begins to bubble, add the tomatoes and cook for 1 minute.

6 Pour in the egg mixture. Stir gently to prevent the egg sticking to the pan. Continue for 3 minutes or until the eggs are firm. Remove from the heat.

7 Spoon a serving of scrambled egg and tomatoes into each roll. Balance the roll lids on top and serve. A glass of orange juice is the perfect accompaniment

• **Preparation** 10 mins • **Cooking** 15 mins • **Serves** 1

Breakfast Omelette

This omelette is a tasty variation of a traditional breakfast fry-up. It has all the right ingredients for a filling weekend brunch – eggs, bacon, tomato, mushrooms – and could even be served with a salad as a light or main meal.

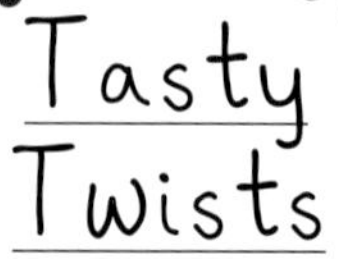

Tasty Twists

Experiment with different fillings, such as ham, onions, courgettes, peppers, or even plain cheese!

The omelette should be firm but still moist when it is cooked in step 6.

Ingredients

rashers of bacon

- 2 eggs
- 30g (1 oz) Cheddar cheese
- a pat of unsalted butter
- 2 tbsp milk
- salt and pepper
- 2 rashers of bacon
- 60g (2oz) mushrooms
- 1 tsp sunflower oil
- 1 tomato

Cheddar cheese

eggs

Equipment

wooden spoon

- whisk
- wooden spatula
- jug
- 2 plates
- grate
- kitchen paper
- wooden spoon
- sharp knife
- 2 chopping boards
- small non-stick frying pan or omelette pan

chopping board

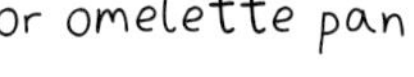

frying pan

whisk

Serving Tip

A dollop of ketchup or a serving of baked beans would taste great with this omelette.

1 Whisk the eggs and milk together in a jug. (This will make it easy to pour in step 5.) Grate the cheese and stir it in to the egg mixture. Season.

2 Cut the tomato into chunks and slice the mushrooms. On a separate board, remove the rind from the bacon and cut the meat into cubes.

3 Place the frying pan over a medium heat and fry the bacon for 3 minutes or until cooked completely. Tip the bacon onto a plate, lined with kitchen

4 Heat the oil and fry the mushrooms for 2 minutes. Add the tomato to the pan and cook for 1 minute. Put the tomato and mushrooms onto a plate.

5 Melt the butter in the pan. Pour in the egg so that it covers the base of the pan. Cook the egg on a medium heat until the edges begin to cook and set.

6 Using a spatula, push the cooked egg into the centre of the pan. The uncooked egg will run to the sides. Repeat until all the egg is cooked.

7 Shake the pan to release the omelette and spoon the filling over one half. Slide the omelette out onto a plate and gently flip the unfilled half over the top.

- **Preparation** 10 mins
- **Cooking** 20 mins
- **Serves** 4–6 mins

Breakfast Tortilla

A tortilla is a thick, flat omelette and is a popular dish in Spain. This is a twist on the classic combination of eggs, onion, and potatoes and makes a filling breakfast or perfect after-school tea.

Did you know?

"Tortilla" is the Spanish word for omelette. In Italy it is called "frittata". However, in Mexico, "tortilla" means a thin (unleavened) bread usually made from corn.

Ingredients

eggs

- 4 good quality sausages (or vegetarian alternative)
- 4 medium-sized potatoes (peeled, cooked and left to cool)
- 2 tbsp sunflower oil
- 8 cherry tomatoes (halved)
- 5 eggs (lightly beaten)
- salt and pepper

cherry tomatoes

potatoes

Equipment

- foil
- tongs
- chopping board
- medium frying pan
- spatula or wooden spoon
- jug
- whisk or fork
- small sharp knife

frying pan

spatula

1 Preheat the grill to medium-high. Line the grill pan with foil and grill the sausages all over for 10-15 mins, or until cooked through and golden brown.

2 While the sausages are cooling slightly, cut the cooked potatoes into bite-sized chunks. Then cut the cooled sausages into 2.5cm (1in) pieces.

Food Facts

The best sausages are called "lean" and contain much less fat and fewer additives than quality sausages. Turkey sausages usually have a lower fat content than those made from red meats such as pork or beef.

sausages

Vegetarian sausages, lean bacon, or cooked chicken would also taste great in this tortilla. Other vegetables such as mushrooms, peppers, or asparagus could also be added.

3 Heat the oil in a frying pan. Add the potatoes and fry them over a medium heat for 8 minutes or until golden. Add the tomatoes and cook for 2 mins.

4 Crack the eggs into a jug and then beat them together. Season the beaten eggs with salt and pepper. Add the sausages to the frying pan.

5 Add a little more oil to the frying pan if necessary. Pour the eggs into the pan and cook, without stirring, for 5 minutes until the base of the tortilla is set.

6 To cook the top of the tortilla, carefully place the pan under the grill and cook for another 3–5 minutes, or until the top is set.

7 Carefully remove the pan from the grill and leave to cool slightly before sliding the tortilla on to a serving plate. Cut into wedges and serve.

- **Preparation** 10 mins
- **Cooking** 20 mins
- **Serves** 8

Blueberry Pancakes

Making batter is a useful skill to learn and the small size makes these pancakes perfect for first-time flippers! Here's a handy tip – if you leave the batter to stand for half an hour before adding the fruit and cooking it, it has a much lighter texture.

Serving Tip

These pancakes taste great served with slices of banana and some maple syrup.

Ingredients

- 150g (5oz) plain flour
- 1 tsp baking powder
- 3 pinches of salt
- 1 egg
- 150 ml (1/4 pint) milk
- 30g (1oz) caster sugar
- 125 g (4oz) fresh blueberries
- 1 large banana, peeled and sliced (optional)
- maple syrup (optional)

blueberries

Equipment

- sieve
- metal spatula
- mixing bowl
- wooden spoon
- whisk
- measuring jug
- large frying pan
- serving spoon or ladle
- dessert spoon

1 Sieve the flour, baking powder, and salt into the mixing bowl. Stir in the sugar with a wooden spoon and leave to one side.

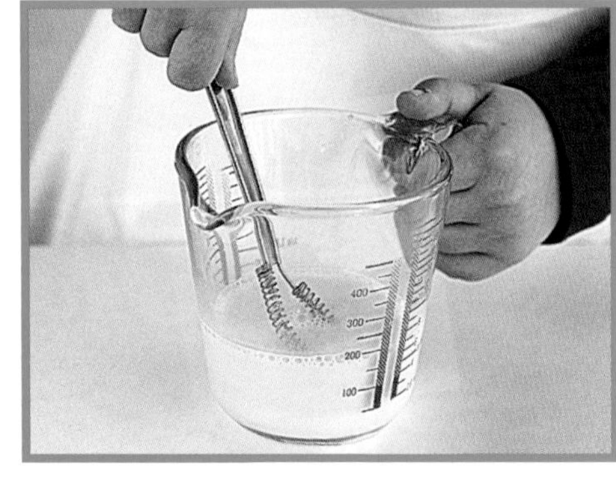

2 Crack the egg into a bowl, add it to the milk, and whisk them together. It is best to do this in a jug so the mixture can be poured easily in step 3.

3 Pour the milk and egg mixture into the flour and beat with a wooden spoon. Gently fold in the blueberries, taking care not to crush them.

Tasty Twists

The blueberries can be replaced with 1 large banana (chopped) in step 3. You can even try plain pancakes, served with lemon juice and sugar or maple syrup.

4 Over a medium heat, melt a quarter of the butter in a large frying pan. When the butter begins to bubble, you are ready to start cooking!

5 Ladle two spoonfuls of batter into the frying pan. Fry the pancakes for 2 minutes or until bubbles appear on top and the undersides turn golden.

6 Use a metal spatula to flip the cakes. Cook the other side for 2 minutes, or until the cakes are cooked through. Repeat with the rest of the batter.

• **Preparation** 10 mins+ 30 mins resting • **Cooking** 20 mins • **Makes** 12 pancakes

These American-style pancakes make a tasty and nutritious brunch when served with summer berries and a drizzle of maple syrup. Fruit sauce and yoghurt would also taste delicious.

Helpful Hints

It is important that the batter is free from lumps. If you do get lumps in your batter, press it through a sieve using the back of a spoon.

Ingredients

- 100g ($3\frac{1}{2}$oz) self-raising flour
- 40g ($1\frac{1}{2}$oz) self-raising wholemeal flour
- 2 tbsp caster sugar
- 1 egg
- 175ml (6fl oz) milk
- 2 bananas (peeled)
- butter (for frying)

wholemeal flour

Equipment

- sieve
- 2 mixing bowls
- wooden spoon
- jug
- whisk or fork
- large non-stick frying pan
- ladle
- spatula
- masher or fork

ladle

mixing bowl

1 Sift both types of flour into a mixing bowl, adding any bran left in the sieve. Stir in the sugar and make a well in the centre of the mixture.

2 Measure the milk in a jug and then crack the egg into the jug. Lightly beat the egg and milk together with a fork until they are mixed together.

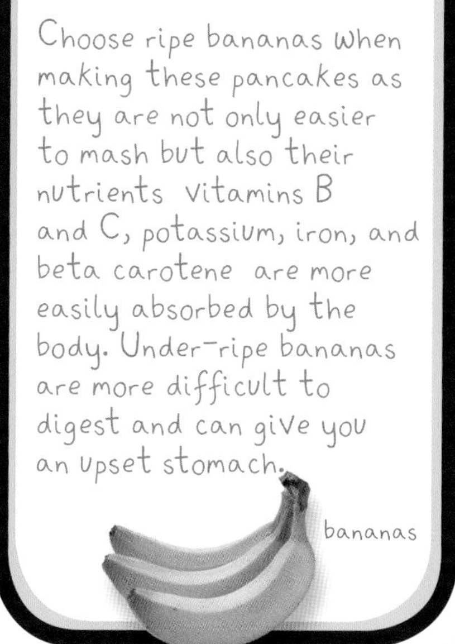

3 Pour the egg mixture into the well in the centre of the flour and sugar. Beat with a wooden spoon until you have a smooth, creamy batter.

4 Leave the batter to rest for at least 30 minutes – this will make the pancakes lighter. Mash the bananas in a bowl then stir them into the rested batter.

Did you know?

In France pancakes are known as "crêpes", in Russia they are called "blinis", and in Latin America they are called "panqueques".

5 Heat a small knob of butter in a frying pan. Add 3 small ladlefuls of batter to make 3 pancakes, each one about 8cm (3¼in) in diameter.

6 Cook for 2 mins, or until bubbles appear on the surface. Flip the pancakes over and cook for another 2 minutes until both sides are light golden.

7 Keep the cooked pancakes warm in a low oven while you cook the remaining pancakes, adding a little knob of butter between each batch.

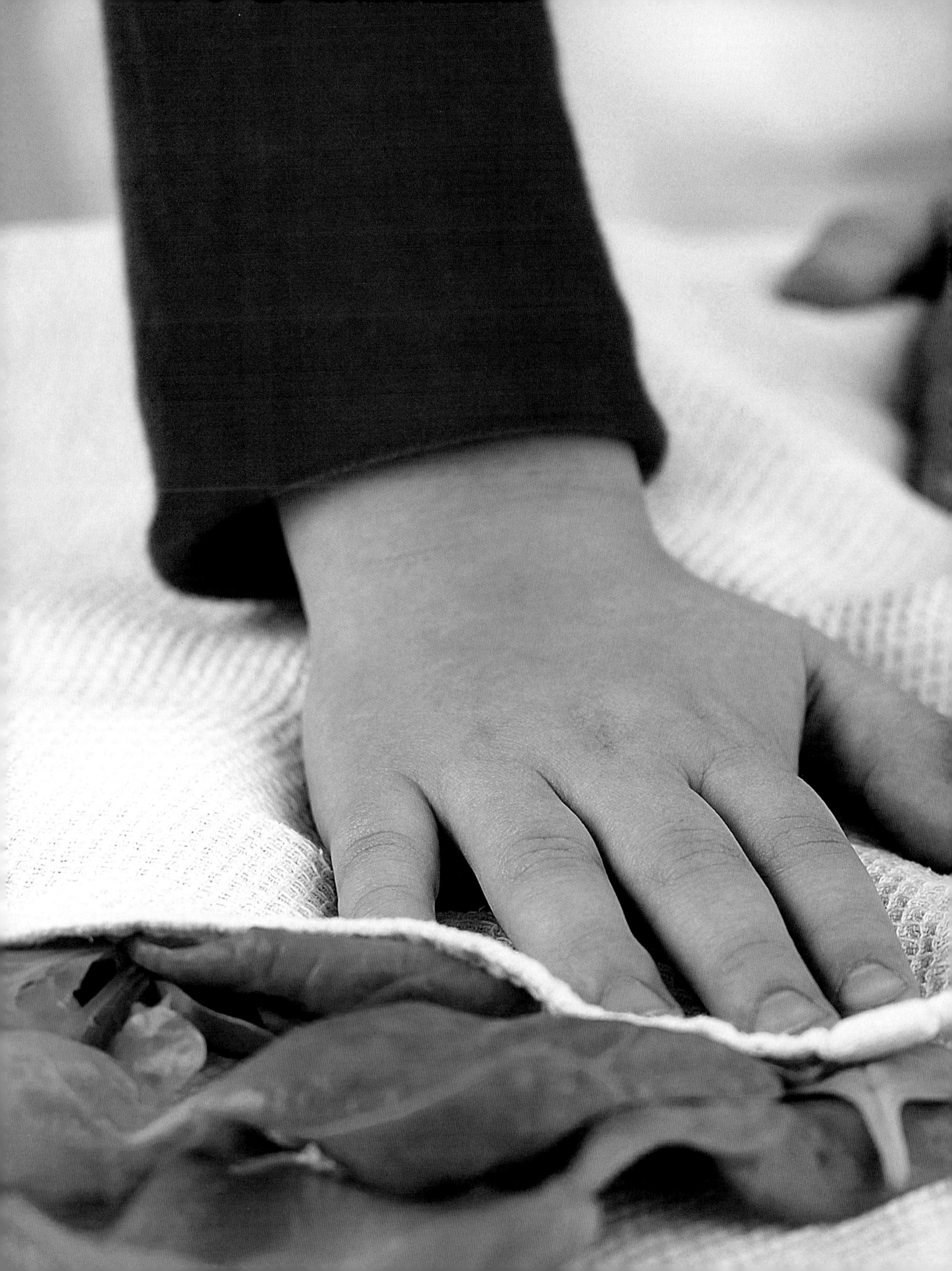

Light Meals

Light Meals

It is important to keep energy levels up throughout the day. Regular meals are essential, but topping them up with a couple of healthy snacks will help to give concentration and memory a boost. There are plenty of recipes for delicious and nutritious light meals and snacks to choose from in this section, but here are some more to try!

Veggie Burgers

Put 125g (4½oz) canned kidney beans (drained), 1 small onion (chopped), 1 carrot, 50g (2oz) wholemeal breadcrumbs, 1 tablespoon peanut butter (optional) and 1 egg into a food processor. Process to a coarse puree, season and chill the mixture for 1 hour. Form into 4 burgers and dust each one in flour. Brush with oil and grill for 5–6 minutes on each side.

Crudités

Most vegetables are better for you when they are raw. Try dipping strips of raw vegetables such as celery, peppers, carrots, or cucmber into houmous or guacamole.

Houmous

Blend 400g (14oz) canned chickpeas (drained), 2 garlic cloves (peeled), 2 tbsp light sesame seed paste (tahini), the juice of 1 lemon, and 4 tbsp olive oil, until smooth and creamy.

Toast Toppings

Mash ½ ripe avocado then spread it thickly on top of wholemeal toast. Houmous or peanut butter taste great on toast too!

Simply Souper!

Boost the nutritional content of shop-bought soups by adding canned beans, cooked lentils or extra vegetables.

Coleslaw

Add ½ finely shredded small white or red cabbage, 2 grated carrots, 1 grated apple, and 2 chopped spring onions to a bowl. Mix together 2 tbsp olive oil, 1 tbsp lemon juice, and 4 tbsp mayonnaise and stir into the cabbage mixture.

Burger Relish

Roughly chop 4 tomatoes, 1 large apple (peeled and cored), and 1 onion. Place them in a saucepan with 75ml (3fl oz) white wine vinegar and 50g (2oz) sugar. Bring to the boil, then reduce the heat, cover, and simmer for 15 minutes. Uncover the pan and cook for another 20 minutes, or until soft. Purée if you prefer a smooth relish.

Peanut Butter

Place 75g (3oz) shelled nuts, such as peanuts, cashews, or hazelnuts, in a dry frying pan. Toast them for 2–3 minutes over a medium-low heat, until light golden. (Stir frequently to prevent burning.) Put the nuts in a food processor and process until finely chopped. Pour in 3–4 tablespoons sunflower oil and process to a coarse paste. Store in an airtight jar.

Miso Soup

Miso is made from fermented soya beans and is very nutritious. For a more filling soup, add cooked egg noodles and thin slices of spring onion, carrot, and red pepper.

Jacket Potato

Preheat an oven to 200°C (400°F/ Gas 6). Scrub the potatoes and prick with a fork or insert a skewer through the middle. Bake for 1–1½ hours, until tender in the centre and the skin is crisp. Serve with a healthy filling such as tuna, sweetcorn, and peppers.

Preparation 15 mins • **Cooking** 20 mins • **Serves** 4

Green Salad with Dressing

Salad is delicious as a light meal or snack and can also be served as a nutritious accompaniment to a main meal.

1 Spoon all the dressing ingredients into a clean jar and put the lid on tightly. Shake the jar to mix the ingredients together.

Ingredients

salad leaves

- 200g (7oz) mixed salad leaves (e.g. lettuce, spinach, watercress)
- 1/2 large cucumber (diced)
- 12–18 cherry tomatoes (halved)

Dressing:

olive oil

- 3 tbsp olive oil
- 1 tbsp fresh lemon juice
- 1 tsp wholegrain mustard
- 1 tsp clear runny honey
- salt and pepper

Equipment

salt and pepper

- teaspoon
- jar with secure lid
- colander
- clean tea towel
- large mixing bowl

wholegrain mustard

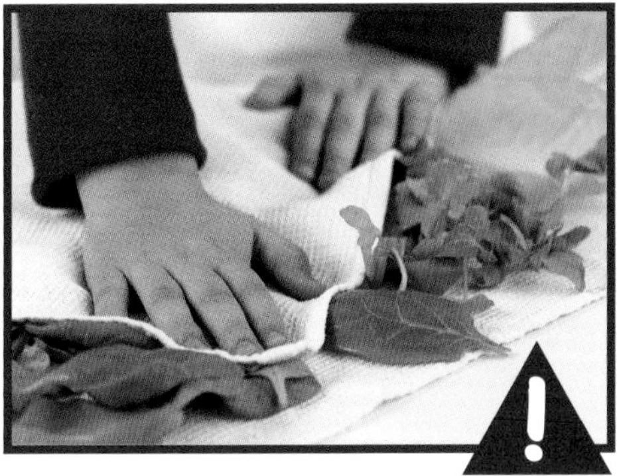

2 Rinse and drain the salad leaves using a colander. Tip them onto a clean tea towel and gently pat dry. Tear the leaves into smaller pieces.

3 Using your hands, carefully mix the salad leaves, cucumber, and tomatoes together in a large bowl. Transfer the mixed salad into individual bowls.

4 Shake the dressing again and drizzle some over each bowl of salad. Leave the jar of dressing on the side so that you can add more if you like.

Serving Tip

Always drizzle the dressing just before you eat the salad, so that it does not turn soggy!

Try adding other ingredients to your salad such as olives, onions, nuts, cheese, or croutons.

• **Preparation** 15 mins • **Cooking** 2 mins • **Serves** 4

Picnic Salad

This recipe is a simplified version of a traditional Greek salad. You could substitute the feta with any of your favourite cheeses such as Cheddar, mozzarella, or brie and add other ingredients, such as olives, peppers, spring onions, and lettuce.

Tasty Twists

Tinned beans such as chickpeas, cannellini, or borlotti beans are a great alternative to cheese. Tuna, salmon, or prawns would also taste delicious.

Ingredients

- 2 wholemeal pitta breads
- 1 small cucumber
- 12 small tomatoes (quartered)
- 1/2 red onion (thinly sliced)
- 150g (5 1/2oz) feta cheese (cut into chunks)

Dressing:

- 3 tbsp olive oil
- 1 tbsp lemon juice or white wine vinegar
- 1/2 tsp Dijon mustard

pitta breads

onion

tomatoes

cucumber

Equipment

- small sharp knife
- chopping board
- teaspoon
- empty clean jam jar
- mixing bowl

mixing bowl

sharp knife

1 Preheat the grill to medium. Cut along one side of each pitta to open it up. Toast the pitta bread on both sides until golden and crisp. Leave to cool.

2 Slice the cucumber in half lengthways and then scoop out the seeds using a teaspoon. Cut the lengths in half and then chop into bite-sized pieces.

3 Put the cucumber, tomatoes, and red onion into a salad bowl. Cut the cooled pitta bread into small pieces and add them to the bowl.

4 To make the dressing, put the olive oil, lemon juice and mustard in a clean jar. Put the lid on and shake until the ingredients are mixed together.

5 Pour the dressing over the salad. Mix the salad using clean hands until it is coated in the dressing. Finally, scatter over the feta cheese and then serve.

Food Facts

True feta cheese is only produced in Greece. Traditionally it was made from ewes' milk but nowadays it is often made with cows' or goats' milk. Like all cheeses, feta is an excellent source of calcium and protein. However, it is also high in fat so it should be eaten in moderation.

feta cheese

- **Preparation** 15 mins
- **Cooking** 20 mins
- **Serves** 4

Jewel Salad

Salad is delicious as a light meal or snack and can also be served as a nutritious accompaniment to a main meal.

Ingredients

cucumber

- 200g (7oz) couscous
- 300ml (1/2pt) hot vegetable stock
- 250g (9oz) cherry tomatoes
- 1/2 cucumber
- 1 medium sized pomegranate
- 30ml (2tbsp) olive oil
- grated zest and juice 1 lemon
- 1 small red onion (thinly sliced)
- 200g (7oz) feta cheese (crumbled)
- large bunch (about 6tbsp) freshly chopped mint

olive oil

Equipment

- 3 bowls
- measuring jug
- fork
- chopping board
- knife
- teaspoon
- wooden spoon

wooden spoon

bowl

1 Place the couscous in a large bowl and pour over the hot stock and leave for 5 minutes until all the liquid has been absorbed. Allow to cool completely.

2 Cut the cherry tomatoes in half. Halve the cucumber lengthways and scoop out the seeds with a teaspoon, then cut into pieces.

3 Cut the pomegranate in half, and hold one half over a bowl. Lightly tap the pomegranate with a wooden spoon, until the seeds fall into the bowl.

4 Stir the lemon juice, zest and olive oil into the couscous. Add the tomatoes, cucumber, red onion, feta cheese and mint, then stir in the pomegranate seeds.

Helpful Hints

You can buy pomegranate seeds from the supermarket if you are in a hurry!

You can find pomegranates in the shops from October to January.

Pasta Salad

Pasta is high in carbohydrates so it is a great source of energy. This recipe also has eggs and tuna for protein, while the beans and tomatoes provide essential vitamins and minerals. Tuna and other oily fish are really good for you and you should try and eat them twice a week.

Helpful Hints

Check out p.36–37 for more information on hard-boiling eggs. And see p.299 for more egg tips.

Ingredients

- 250g (8oz) dried penne pasta
- 1 pinch of salt
- 125g (4oz) green beans (tailed and halved)
- 1 small tin of tuna
- 2 spring onions (trimmed and sliced)
- 2 eggs
- 4 plum tomatoes (cut into wedges)
- salt and pepper
- 16 black olives, halved (optional)

green beans

eggs

penne pasta

For the dressing

- 5 tbsp olive oil
- 2 tbsp white wine vinegar
- 2 tsp wholegrain mustard

wholegrain mustard

Equipment

- large saucepan
- slotted spoon
- colander
- jar with lid
- sieve
- large mixing bowl
- plate
- metal mixing spoon
- small saucepan
- bowl of cold water
- chopping board
- sharp knife

1 Fill two-thirds of the large saucepan with water and bring it to the boil. Season with a pinch of salt, add the pasta, and boil for 12–14 minutes.

2 When the pasta has been cooking for about 6–7 minutes add the green beans to the pan. Finish cooking and drain the pasta and beans in a colander.

3 Refresh the pasta and beans with cold water. Drain the tuna, using a sieve and then use your fingers to break the tuna into small flakes.

Pasta cooking times vary, so make sure that you check the packet.

Tasty Twists

Other pasta shapes could be used for this recipe. You could also use sweetcorn instead of green beans and cooked chicken instead of tuna.

4 Hard-boil the eggs for 6–7 minutes and put them in cold water. Tap the cooled eggs to crack the shell. Peel the eggs and cut them into wedges.

5 Spoon the olive oil, white wine vinegar, and mustard into a jar. Screw the lid on tightly and shake vigorously to mix the dressing ingredients

6 Mix the pasta with half of the dressing. Fold in the tomatoes, beans, tuna, onions, olives, and remaining dressing. Season and serve with some wedges of egg.

• **Preparation** 10 mins • **Cooking** 15 mins • **Serves** 4

Chicken Pasta Salad

This mildly spiced pasta and chicken salad makes a perfect light lunch or is ideal for a school sandwich box.

Ingredients

lemon

- 125g (4oz) pasta bows
- 2 tsp sunflower oil
- 1 tbsp medium curry paste
- 3 spring onions (chopped)
- 1 ripe mango
- juice of 1/2 lemon
- 100ml (1/2 cup) low-fat yoghurt
- 100ml (1/2 cup) mayonnaise
- 350g (12oz) cooked chicken breast (diced)
- 2 tbsp freshly chopped coriander
- 150g (5oz) mixed red and green grapes (halved)

pasta bows

Equipment

- large saucepan
- small frying pan
- wooden spoon
- knife
- mixing bowl

frying pan

1 Bring a large pan of lightly salted water to the boil. Add the pasta and cook according to package instructions. Drain and rinse under cold running water.

2 Meanwhile, in a small frying pan heat the oil, add the curry paste and spring onions, and cook for 2 minutes. Leave to cool.

4 Cut away the two sides of mango, close to the stone. Cut the flesh into criss-cross patterns, press each half inside out, and carefully cut off the cubes.

5 Place the spice mixture in a bowl and stir in the lemon juice, yoghurt, mayonnaise, and coriander. Add the chicken, mango, and grapes.

The spicy and sweet flovours in this pasta salad are a tasty combination.

Tasty Twists

If you are a vegetarian, just leave out the chicken. Try adding tofu instead.

• **Preparation** 5 mins • **Cooking** 15 mins • **Serves** 4

Potato Salad

This simple potato salad substitutes traditional mayonnaise for a lighter creamy sauce, flavoured with chives.

Tasty Twists

If you like hot and spicy flavours, try adding 15ml (1 tbsp) of horseradish sauce.

Ingredients

low-fat yoghurt

- 500g (1¼lb) baby new potatoes
- 43ml (3 tbsp) reduced fat crème fraiche
- 43ml (3 tbsp) low-fat yoghurt
- 30ml (2 tbsp) freshly chopped chives

baby new potatoes

Equipment

mixing bowl

- knife
- cutting board
- saucepan
- 2 mixing bowls
- metal spoon

saucepan

1 Wash and cut any larger potatoes in half.

2 Cook in a pan of lightly salted boiling water for 12 to 15 minutes. Drain and allow to cool. Place in a bowl.

4 In a small bowl, mix together the crème fraîche, yoghurt, and fresh chives.

5 Gently stir the chive mixture into the potatoes. Season to taste. Keep refrigerated until ready to serve.

This is a healthier version of an old favourite. Perfect for picnics!

Helpful Hints

Make sure the potatoes are cool, or you will have a warm potato salad!

• **Preparation** 15 mins • **Cooking** 8–12 mins • **Serves** 4 – 6

Colourful Seafood Salad

Protein, carbohydrates, vitamins, minerals, healthy fats – this salad has it all! In the green corner, avocadoes contain more protein than any other fruit and are also rich in beta-carotene and vitamin E. While in the red corner, tomatoes are good for your immune system and an excellent source of vitamins A, C, and E.

Tasty Twists

If you don't like prawns or can't get hold of them, cooked chicken is a healthy alternative. Vegetarians could add cooked tofu or pine nuts instead.

Ingredients

avocadoes

- 150g (5½ oz) pasta shells
- 250g (9oz) cooked peeled prawns
- 12 small tomatoes (quartered)
- 1 large avocado
- lettuce leaves (cut into strips)

tomatoes

Dressing:

- 4 tbsp mayonnaise
- 2 tsp lemon juice
- 2 tbsp tomato ketchup
- 2 drops Tabasco sauce (optional)
- salt and pepper

pasta shells

Equipment

mixing bowl

- large saucepan
- wooden spoon
- small sharp knife
- chopping board
- mixing bowl
- small bowl
- teaspoon

1 Bring a large saucepan of water to the boil. Add the pasta and follow the cooking instructions on the packet. Drain well and leave to cool.

2 Carefully cut the avocado around its middle and gently prise it apart. Scoop out the stone with a teaspoon and then cut each half into quarters.

3 Peel off the skin and cut the avocado into chunks. Put the avocado into a bowl and spoon over half of the lemon juice to stop the fruit turning brown.

Did you know?

Avocadoes were first cultivated in South America. It was believed that a Mayan princess ate the very first avocado and that it held magical powers.

4 Put the tomatoes, avocado, and prawns into a bowl with the pasta and season. Divide the shredded lettuce leaves between the serving bowls.

5 Mix together all the ingredients for the dressing in a small bowl. Add the pasta salad to the serving bowls and then drizzle over the dressing.

Food Facts

Like all shellfish, prawns are packed full of healthy minerals and are bursting with flavour. Prawns help to boost the immune system since they contain important minerals called zinc and selenium.

prawns

• **Preparation** 15–20 mins • **Cooking** 35 mins • **Serves** 2–4

Tomato Soup

Soup is the perfect choice for a light meal or as a starter for a special dinner party. This recipe for thick and tasty tomato soup includes carrots, thyme, and garlic for extra flavour and is topped with cubes of toasted bread, called croutons.

Ingredients

chopped tomatoes

- 1 small onion
- 1 small carrot
- 400g (13oz) can chopped tomatoes
- 1tbsp of tomato purée
- 2tbsp of olive oil
- 1tsp of fresh thyme leaves (optional)
- black pepper
- 450ml (3/4pt) vegetable stock
- 1 garlic clove (crushed)
- 1 pinch of granulated sugar
- 1tbsp of plain flour
- 1 squeeze of lemon juice

For the croutons:

- 2 thick slices of bread
- 2tbsp of olive oil
- salt and pepper

Equipment

chopping board

- sharp knife
- peeler
- chopping board
- medium saucepan
- wooden spatula
- bread knife
- non-stick baking tray
- oven gloves
- ladle
- blender

1 Preheat the oven to 220°C/425°F. Peel and chop the onion and carrot. Heat the oil in the saucepan, over medium heat.

2 Add the onion and carrot and cook for about 5 minutes to soften, stirring occasionally. Stir in the garlic and flour and cook the mixture for 1 minute.

3 Add the tomatoes, paste, thyme, stock, sugar, and lemon juice to the pan and bring to a boil. Reduce the heat and simmer for 20–25 minutes.

If you like your soup less thick, add 600ml (1pt) stock in step 3.

4 Meanwhile, cut the bread into 2-cm cubes. Scatter the bread on the baking tray and drizzle over the olive oil. Season with salt and pepper.

5 Use your hands to coat the bread in the oil. Bake for 8–10 minutes, until crisp and golden. Shake the tray every few minutes for even cooking.

6 Carefully ladle the hot soup into the blender. Season the soup with pepper, and blend until smooth. Ladle the soup into bowls and serve.

• **Preparation** 15 mins • **Cooking** 30 mins • **Serves** 4–6

Corn Chowder

This recipe will really warm you up on a cold day! Chowder is a special kind of thick soup from New England in the USA. Although some chowders include fish, this simple recipe relies on nutritious potatoes, sweetcorn, and carrot.

Helpful Hints

If you prefer a chunky soup, leave out step 5. For a smooth soup, blend all the mixture in step 5 until it is creamy.

Ingredients

- 1 large onion
- 200g (9oz) fresh, frozen or tinned sweetcorn
- 1 large carrot
- 350g (12oz) potatoes
- 1 tbsp sunflower oil
- 1 bouquet garni (optional)
- 1 bay leaf
- 1.2 litres (2 pints) vegetable stock
- 300ml (10fl oz) milk
- salt and pepper

potatoes

onion

carrot

Equipment

- small sharp knife
- vegetable peeler
- chopping board
- large saucepan with lid
- wooden spoon
- blender

vegetable peeler

wooden spoon

1 Peel and roughly chop the onion. Scrub the carrot and then thinly slice them. Finally, peel the potatoes and then cut them into small pieces.

2 Heat the oil in a saucepan. Add the onion and sauté over a medium heat for 8 minutes or until soft and slightly golden. Stir the onion occasionally.

3 Next, add the corn, carrot, potatoes, bouquet garni and bay leaf to the onions. Cook for 2 minutes, stirring constantly. Add the stock and bring to the boil.

Season your soup to taste with the salt and pepper.

Tasty Twists

Chunks of smoked haddock would add a delicious smoky flavour to this soup. Add the fish in step 4 with the milk and simmer for 5 minutes or until cooked.

4 Reduce the heat to medium to low. Cover with a lid and cook for 15 minutes, stirring occasionally. Add the milk and cook for a further 5 minutes.

5 Scoop out some of the vegetables and blend the rest of the soup until smooth. Return the vegetables and blended soup to the pan and warm through.

Food Facts

Rich in complex carbohydrates, sweetcorn is also a good source of vitamins A, B, and C. If you use tinned sweetcorn in place of the fresh make sure you buy the type without added salt or sugar.

sweetcorn

• **Preparation** 15 mins • **Cooking** 30 mins • **Serves** 4

Italian Pasta Soup

This wholesome, tasty soup is based on a traditional Italian soup called minestrone. With the pasta, vegetables, and Parmesan topping it is a complete meal in a bowl!

Minestrone was originally eaten by poor Italians and was made with whatever ingredients were available.

Tasty Twists

Meat eaters could add some bacon to the soup, but make sure you cook it thoroughly in step 3. Tinned mixed beans, green beans, courgettes, or peppers would also taste great.

Ingredients

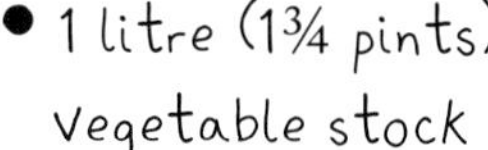

- 75g (3oz) pasta bows
- 1 large onion
- 2 sticks celery
- 1 large carrot (scrubbed)
- 2 potatoes
- 1 tbsp olive oil
- 1 bay leaf
- 1 tsp dried oregano
- 1 litre (1¾ pints) vegetable stock
- 400g (14oz) canned chopped tomatoes
- Parmesan cheese (grated)

potatoes

carrot

pasta bows

Equipment

- small sharp knife
- chopping board
- medium saucepan
- wooden spoon
- large saucepan with lid
- ladle

ladle

saucepan

1 Bring a medium-sized pan of water to the boil and add the pasta. Simmer until the pasta is just tender but not completely cooked. Drain well and set aside.

2 Chop the onion into small pieces. Peel the potatoes and cut them into bite-sized chunks. Slice the celery and carrot into bite-sized pieces.

Did you know?

Many people think that Venetian explorer Marco Polo introduced pasta to Italy from China in the 13th century. In fact, pasta has been eaten in Italy since as far back as Roman times!

Helpful Hints

When you drain the pasta in step 1, rinse it with cold water to prevent it sticking together and cooking further.

3 Heat the olive oil in a large saucepan. Add the onion and fry over a medium heat for 8 minutes or until it is softened and golden.

4 Next, add the celery, carrot, potatoes, oregano, and bay leaf then stir well. Pour in the stock and chopped tomatoes. Stir again and then bring to the boil.

5 When the soup is bubbling, reduce the heat to low. Half-cover the pan with a lid and simmer the soup for 15 minutes or until the potatoes are tender.

6 Remove the lid, add the pasta and stir well. Heat the pasta for 5 minutes. Ladle the soup into large bowls and sprinkle with Parmesan cheese.

Food Facts

Pasta is a carbohydrate food and it gives the body energy. Surprisingly it also provides a small amount of protein. It is best to use wholewheat pasta because it is higher in fibre, vitamins, and minerals than white pasta.

Wholewheat pasta

• **Preparation** 15 mins • **Cooking** 39 mins • **Serves** 4

Butternut Squash Soup

This substantial soup is made from roasted butternut squash, but you could try it with pumpkin instead if you prefer.

This wholesome, warming soup is perfect for a cold day.

Ingredients

- 1 kg ($2^1/_4$lb) butternut squash
- 15ml (1 tbsp) vegetable oil
- 1 onion (chopped)
- 600ml (20 fl oz) hot vegetable stock
- 30ml (2 tbsp) honey

vegetable oil

To serve

- French stick
- Gruyére or Swiss cheese
- freshly chopped parsley

onion

Equipment

baking tray

- knife
- 3 spoons
- cutting board
- vegetable peeler
- baking tray
- food processor
- saucepan

knife

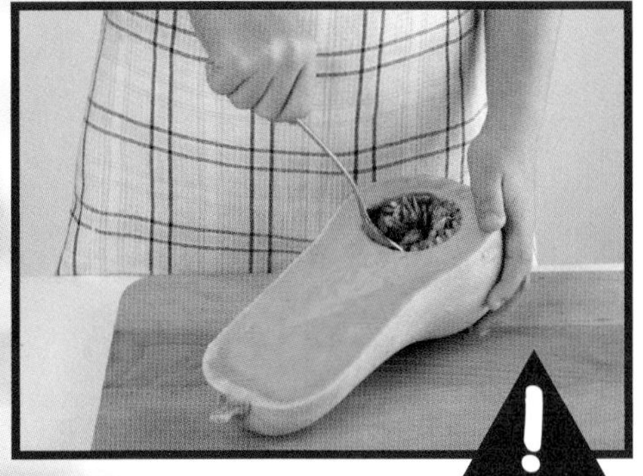

1 Preheat the oven to 200°C (400°F). Cut the butternut squash in half lengthwise, then, using a spoon, scoop out the seeds and pith.

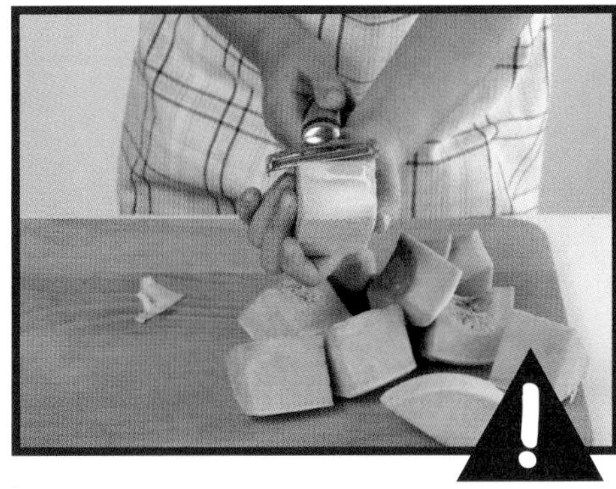

2 Cut into large chunks, then, using a peeler, remove the skin. Cut the chunks into 2.5cm (1in) cubes.

3 Place on a baking tray, seasin with salt and freshly ground black pepper, then drizzle over the oil. Roast for 20 minutes, then remove from the oven.

4 Add the onion and stir. Return to the oven and cook for a further 15 minutes.

5 Place the butternut squash and onion in a food processor with half of the stock and blend until smooth.

6 Place the purée in a saucepan with the remaining stock and honey. Simmer for 3 to 4 minutes. Serve with slices of toasted French stick, cheese, and parsley.

- **Preparation** 15 mins
- **Cooking** 1–1½ hours
- **Serves** 2

Baked Potato

Here's a top tip – if you like the skin of your jacket potato to be firm, roll the potato in a little olive oil after scrubbing it in step 1.

Ingredients

- 2 large baking potatoes

For the Filling:

- 2 tbsp sour cream
- butter (optional)
- 40g (3oz) broccoli (cut into tiny pieces)
- 125g (4oz) cheese (grated)
- pepper

potatoes

pepper

broccoli

Equipment

- fork
- chopping board
- sharp knife
- paper towels
- mixing bowl
- dessert spoon
- saucepan
- colander
- baking tray

chopping board

saucepan

Tasty Twists

Use your favourite fillings for this recipe – tuna and sweetcorn, baked beans and cheese, or just a little melted butter and a green salad.

1 Preheat the oven to 200°C (400°F/Gas 6). Scrub the potatoes in cold water, and pat them dry. Prick the potatoes all over with a fork.

2 Bake the potatoes for 1–1½ hours or until they are soft in the centre. Carefully remove the potatoes from the oven and cut a cross in the top of each.

3 While the potatoes are baking, boil the broccoli for 4 minutes. Drain the broccoli and mix it with the cheese and sour cream. Season with pepper.

4 Using kitchen paper to protect your hands, squeeze the bottom corners of each potato to open it up. Take care, the potatoes will still be very hot!

When the potato is cooked it will be soft in the middle. Use a knife or skewer to check this.

Serving Tip

Spread some butter on your potato and spoon over the filling. The cheese, butter, and sour cream will melt together and taste yummy!

• **Preparation** 40 mins • **Cooking** 5 mins • **Serves** 2

Bruschetta

Bruschetta is a tasty Italian starter or snack. It is traditionally made by piling ripe tomatoes onto toasted garlicky bread.

Ingredients

garlic

- 4 x 2.5cm ($\frac{1}{2}$in) slices Italian-style bread such as ciabatta
- 3 medium ripe tomatoes
- 1 tbsp olive oil
- 6 basil leaves
- 1 clove garlic (peeled)

tomatoes

Equipment

- knife
- cutting board
- metal spoon
- strainer
- bowl
- griddle pan

cutting board

1 Halve and deseed the tomatoes. Press the seeds through a strainer over a bowl, then discard the seeds. Dice the tomatoes and add to the bowl.

2 Add the olive oil, salt, and freshly ground black pepper. Leave to stand for 30 minutes. Roll up the basil leaves, chop finely, then add to the mixture.

3 Toast the bread on both sides, preferably in a griddle pan to create dark lines, or under a preheated grill.

4 Rub the hot bread with the clove of garlic. Place each piece of bread on a plate and heap with the tomato mixture.

Use the freshest ingredients to make these deliciously simple bruschetta.

• **Preparation** 10 mins • **Serves** 4

Club Sandwich

This club sandwich is made using ham, chicken, and cheese on toasted bread. However, you can use any combination of your favourite meats or cheeses.

This is a super deluxe sandwich perfect for a luxurious lunch!

Ingredients

iceberg lettuce

- 4 slices white bread
- 2 slices wholemeal bread
- 4 tbsp mayonnaise
- 1 tbsp lemon juice
- 100ml ($3\frac{1}{2}$ fl oz) milk
- 50g (2oz) shredded iceberg lettuce
- 2 slices ham
- 2 slices Swiss or Cheddar cheese
- 1 tomato (sliced)
- 50g (2oz) cooked chicken breast (shredded)

lemon

wholemeal bread

Equipment

- bread knife
- cutting board
- mixing bowl
- metal spoon
- toothpicks

mixing bowl

cutting board

1 Lightly toast the bread on both sides under a preheated moderate grill or in a toaster. Cut off the crusts.

2 In a small bowl mix together the mayonnaise and lemon juice. Season to taste. Stir in the shredded lettuce.

3 Spread 2 slices of the white toast with half of the lettuce and mayonnaise mixture.

4 Place a slice of ham, then a slice of cheese on top of each. Top with the wholemeal bread, spread with the remaining lettuce and mayonnaise.

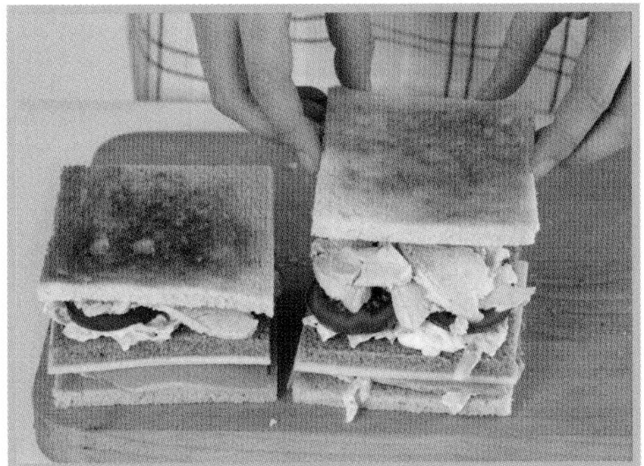

5 Add some slices of tomato and the chicken. Top with the remaining white toast.

6 Cut each sandwich into 4 triangles and secure each with a toothpick.

• **Preparation** 20 mins • **Marinating** 1 hour • **Cooking** 16 mins • **Serves** 4

Pitta Pockets

Tofu is a very versatile and nutritious ingredient. It naturally has a mild flavour but when marinated it takes on the flavour of the marinade. The sauce used in this recipe gives the tofu a delicious barbecue taste as well an appetising golden glow.

Did you know?

Tofu is also known as bean curd. Soya beans are cooked, puréed, and drained to produce a milky liquid. The liquid is mixed with a coagulant to form a custard or cheese-like substance.

Ingredients

tofu

pitta breads

- 250g (9oz) firm tofu
- a little olive oil
- 3 Cos lettuce leaves (shredded)
- 2 spring onions, peeled and cut into long strips
- a handful of alfalfa sprouts (optional)
- 4 wholemeal pitta bread (warmed in a toaster or warm oven)

For the marinade

- 2 tbsp sweet chilli sauce
- 2 tbsp tomato ketchup
- 2 tbsp soy sauce
- 1/2 tsp ground cumin

Equipment

- small sharp knife
- chopping board
- kitchen towel
- dessertspoon
- shallow dish
- griddle pan
- spatula or tongs

tongs

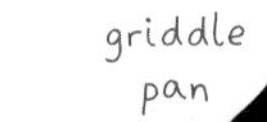
griddle pan

1 In a shallow dish, mix together all the ingredients for the marinade. Pat the tofu dry with a kitchen towel and then cut it into 8 long slices.

2 Put the tofu into the dish with the marinade. Spoon the marinade over the tofu until it is well coated. Leave the tofu to marinate for at least 1 hour.

3 Brush the griddle pan with a generous amount of olive oil and then put it on the heat. Carefully put 4 of the tofu slices into the hot pan.

Tasty Twists

Strips of chicken, pork, turkey, or beef or even a medley of vegetables such as pepper, courgette, and onion make a great alternative to the tofu.

Food Facts

Alfalfa is a seed with a long, slender shoot and a clover-like leaf that is usually bought as a sprouted plant. It is one of the few plants foods that is a complete protein and it is also an excellent source of vitamins B and C.

alfalfa

4 Cook the tofu for 4 minutes on each side, or until golden. As you cook, spoon over more of the marinade. Griddle the rest of the tofu in the same way.

5 Carefully slice along the edge of the pitta bread. Divide the lettuce, spring onions, and alfalfa sprouts between the pitta bread and then add 2 pieces of tofu.

• **Preparation** up to 1 hour • **Cooking** up to 1 hour • **Serves** 6–8

Dips and Dippers

These recipes are great as snacks but they can also be served with some other recipes. For example, potato wedges taste great with burgers and guacamole goes well with chicken wraps.

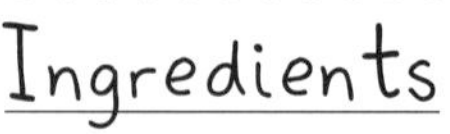

Ingredients

baking potatoes

Potato Wedges:

- 4 small baking potatoes
- 1 tsp ground paprika
- 2 tbsp olive oil
- salt and pepper

ground paprika

Guacamole:

- 3 ripe avocados
- 1/2 red onion (finely diced)
- 1 garlic clove (crushed)
- juice of 1 lime
- salt and pepper
- 2 tomatoes (deseeded and diced)
- 3 tbsp chopped fresh coriander
- 3–4 dashes Tabasco sauce

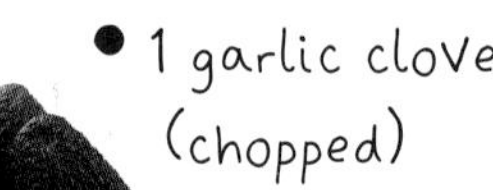
avocados

Houmous:

- 400g (13oz) can chick peas
- 1/2 tsp ground cumin
- 1 garlic clove (chopped)
- 3 tbsp olive oil
- 2 tbsp tahini paste
- 1 tsp baking powder
- juice of 1/2 lemon

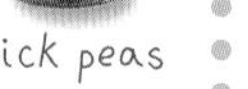
chick peas

olive oil

Tortilla Chips:

- 4 flour tortillas
- salt and pepper
- 30g (1oz) unsalted butter

tortillas

Equipment

mixing bowl

- kitchen scissors
- 2 non-stick baking trays
- oven gloves
- pastry brush
- sharp knife
- chopping board
- roasting tin
- food processor
- dessert spoon
- mixing bowl

sharp knife

Helpful Hints

Season the houmous with salt and pepper and sprinkle with a little paprika for decoration!

1 Preheat the oven to 180°C (350°F/Gas 4). Cut the tortillas into quarters and then cut them in half, to make 32 triangles. Lay them on baking trays.

2 Brush each piece with melted butter and season. Bake for 10–12 minutes or until crisp and golden. Allow the tortillas to cool before eating.

3 Preheat the oven to 220°C (425°F/Gas 7). Scrub each potato, pat dry, and cut them in half lengthways. Cut each half into three equal wedges.

4 Mix the oil, paprika, salt, and pepper together in a roasting tin. Coat the wedges in the mixture and bake for 40–45 minutes. Shake the pan occasionally.

5 Drain and then rinse the chick peas. Tip them into the food processor, add the remaining houmous ingredients, and blend until smooth.

6 Cut the avocados in half, working around the stone. Scoop out the stone and then the avocado flesh. Finely chop the flesh and put it into a bowl.

7 Put the onion, garlic, lime juice, tomato, pepper sauce, and coriander into the mixing bowl. Season and then mix all the ingredients together. Serve.

- **Preparation** 20–25 mins
- **Cooking** 10–15 mins
- **Serves** 4

Pesto Toasts

This recipe uses griddling. A griddle pan has a ridged design which gives the toasted bread a stripy pattern. Griddling is also a low-fat way of cooking meat or fish as the ridges help excess fat to drain away.

Helpful Hints

For a super-quick bite, miss out the grilling part in step 6. Pesto toasts don't need to be cooked to taste great!

Ingredients

For the Pesto:

- 1 garlic clove
- 30g (1oz) fresh Parmesan cheese
- 1 tbsp pine nuts
- 60g (2oz) fresh basil leaves
- 2 tbsp olive oil
- black pepper

parmesan cheese

garlic

peanuts

For the Toast:

- fresh crusty bread
- 1 pepper (roasted, skinned, and deseeded)
- 1 tbsp olive oil
- 1 small ball mozzarella (drained)

crusty bread

roasted pepper

Equipment

- sharp knife
- chopping board
- food processor
- pastry brush
- griddle pan or toaster
- tongs
- table knife
- oven gloves
- grill rack and foil-lined tray

tongs

oven gloves

1 Roughly chop the garlic and Parmesan cheese and put them in the food processor. Add the pine nuts and check that the lid is securely on the processor.

2 Blend the garlic, Parmesan, and pine nuts until they look like fine breadcrumbs. Add the basil and oil and blend again to make a smooth mixture. Season.

3 Cut 4 slices of bread, about 2.5 cm (1in) thick and brush both sides with the olive oil. Place the griddle pan over a medium-high heat.

You can buy roasted peppers in supermarkets or roast them yourself (see p.297).

Tasty Twists

The remaining pesto will stay fresh for up to a week, if you keep it in an airtight container in the fridge. Try stirring it into some pasta for a deliciously simple main meal.

4 Griddle the bread for 2–3 minutes on each side or until toasted. Don't worry, if you don't have a griddle – grill or toast the bread instead.

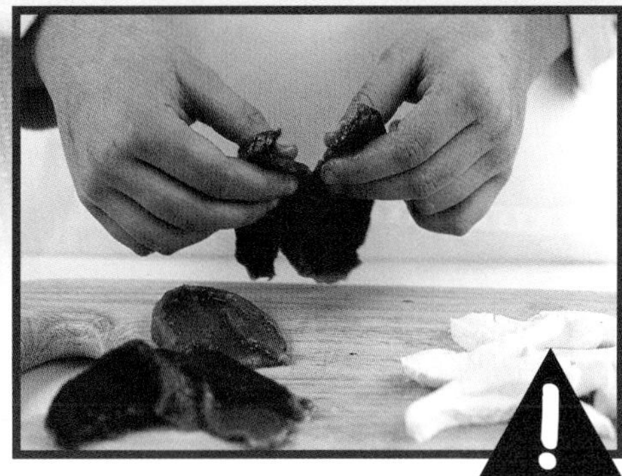

5 Slice the ball of mozzarella into 4 equal slices. Tear the pepper and mozzarella into smaller pieces. Preheat the grill to a medium heat.

6 Spread each toast with a layer of pesto and add some pepper and mozzarella. Grill for 3 minutes or until the cheese has melted. Season and then serve.

• **Preparation** 30–35 mins • **Cooking** 5–10 mins • **Serves** 4

Falafel with Tzatziki

Falafel are spicy chick pea patties and they originally came from the Middle East. Chick peas are part of a food group called pulses which are a good source of protein, vitamins, and minerals and are also high in fibre.

Tasty Twists

Try other tinned pulses, such as kidney beans, butter beans, cannellini beans beans, or black eye beans.

Ingredients

fresh parsley

- 400g (13oz) tin chick peas (drained)
- 1tbsp chopped fresh parsley
- 1/2 small onion (chopped)
- 1tsp of ground coriander
- 2tbsp of plain flour and extra for shaping
- 1tsp of ground cumin

tinned chick peas

sunflower oil

- 1 garlic clove (chopped)
- salt and pepper
- 200ml (7fl oz) sunflower oil

For the tzatziki:

- 1tsp of fresh lemon juice
- 1/2 cucumber
- 1 garlic clove (crushed)
- 1tbsp of chopped fresh mint (optional)
- 200g (7oz) Greek or natural yoghurt

ground coriander

Equipment

- food processor
- medium frying pan
- slotted metal spatula
- plate
- dessert spoon
- kitchen paper
- grater
- chopping board
- tea towel or cloth
- small bowl
- mixing bowl

chopping board

frying pan

1 Put the chick peas, onion, garlic, cumin, coriander, flour, parsley, and seasoning into the processor and blend them together until smooth.

2 Lightly flour the work surface and tip out the mixture. Divide it into 12 equal portions and shape each portion into a flat, round patty.

3 Pour the oil into the frying pan and heat it over a medium-high heat. Shallow fry the falafel for 2–3 minutes on each side, or until golden and crisp.

Helpful Hints

The falafel and tzatziki taste great by themselves or served with pitta bread!

To de-seed a cucumber slice it in half lengthways and scoop out the seeds with a teaspoon.

4 Take the cooked falafel out of the frying pan with a slotted metal spatula. Place them on a plate lined with kitchen paper to drain the excess oil.

5 De-seed and then grate the cucumber. Wrap it in a clean tea towel or cloth and firmly squeeze out any excess moisture, over a small bowl.

6 Mix together the grated cucumber, yoghurt, lemon juice, mint, and garlic. Season with salt and pepper and serve the tzatziki with the falafel.

- **Preparation** 35–45 mins
- **Cooking** 20 mins
- **Makes** 8 pasties

Cheese and Potato Pasties

Puff pastry is really difficult to make at home so even some of the best chefs buy it ready-made! It is really versatile and can be used for sweet or savoury pies and pasties.

Helpful Hints

Try other fillings such as spinach, mushroom, or bacon, but make sure that you cook them in steps 1 and 2. You could even try a sweet filling, such as the apple and cherry pie mixture from p.236–237.

Ingredients

flour

- 250g (8oz) potatoes (peeled and diced)
- 1 pinch of salt
- 1 onion (peeled and diced)
- 2 x 375g (12oz) ready-rolled puff pastry sheets
- 1tbsp of olive oil
- 1 egg (for glazing)
- 250g (8oz) Cheddar cheese (grated)
- salt and pepper
- flour (for rolling)

potatoes

puff-pastry sheets

egg

Equipment

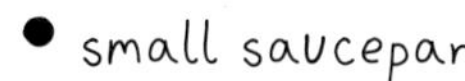
baking tray

- small saucepan
- slotted spoon
- frying pan or sauté pan
- wooden spoon
- saucer or small plate (approx 12cm/5in in diameter)
- knife
- pastry brush
- mixing bowl
- oven gloves
- metal mixing spoon
- fork
- non-stick baking tray

Food Facts

Brushing the pasties with beaten egg gives the pastry a golden glaze when it is cooked. You could also use milk for this.

1 Preheat the oven to 220°C (425°F/Gas 7). Half-fill a pan with water and bring to the boil. Add the potato and a pinch of salt and bring back to the boil.

2 Par-boil the potato for 5–7 minutes and then drain it. Heat the oil and gently fry the onion for 2 minutes, to soften. Leave the onion and potato to cool.

Helpful Hints

Allow the pasties to cool for at least 5 minutes before you eat them because they will be really hot!

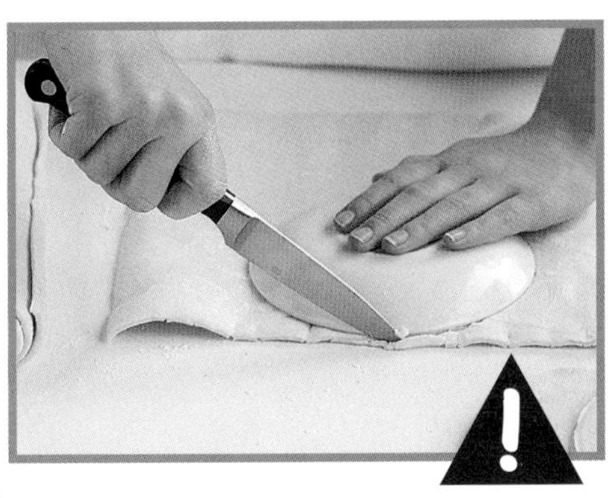

3 Unroll the pastry sheets onto a lightly floured surface. Using an upside-down saucer or small plate as a template, cut out 8 circles of pastry.

4 Put the cooled potato and onion into a bowl and add the cheese. Mix them all together with a metal spoon and season with salt and pepper.

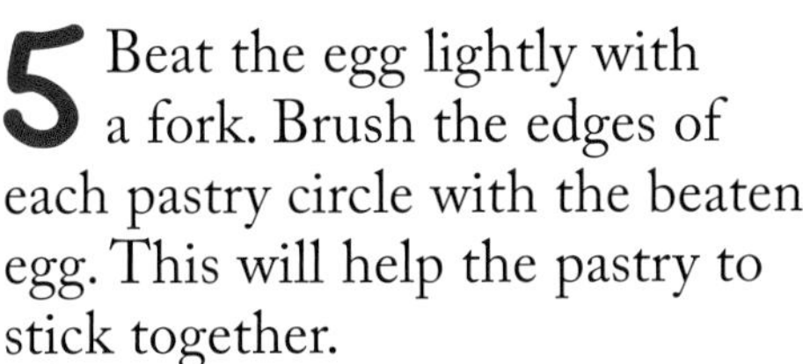

5 Beat the egg lightly with a fork. Brush the edges of each pastry circle with the beaten egg. This will help the pastry to stick together.

6 Place some of the cheese and potato mixture in the centre of each pastry circle. Bring the edges together to enclose the filling and form a semi-circle.

7 Gently crimp the edges by pinching the pastry in opposite directions. Glaze the pasties with beaten egg and bake for 20 minutes or until golden.

• **Preparation** 10 mins • **Cooking** 4 mins • **Serves** 2–4

Tuna Quesadillas and Carrot Salad

Quesadillas are simple to prepare and taste great with a variety of interesting fillings. Best of all, they are delicious hot or cold.

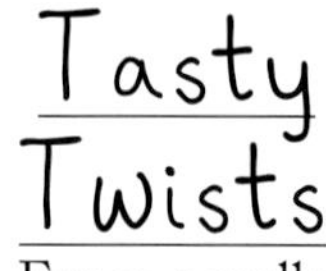

Tasty Twists

For an equally colourful vegetarian alternative, try pesto, sliced tomato, and mozzarella.

Ingredients

- 2 soft flour tortillas
- 60g (2½ oz) canned tuna in spring water (drained)
- 40g (1½ oz) mature Cheddar (grated)
- 2 spring onions (peeled and sliced)
- ½ small orange pepper (deseeded and cut into small pieces)
- a little olive oil

Cheddar cheese

Carrot Salad

- 1 large carrot
- 2 tbsp raisins
- 1 tbsp pine nuts
- 1 tbsp olive oil
- 2 tsp lemon juice

spring onions

orange pepper

Equipment

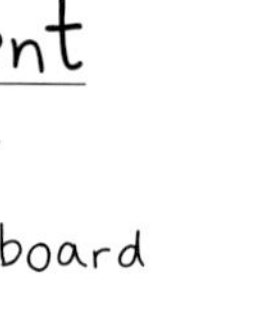

- spoon
- chopping board
- frying pan
- spatula
- 2 dinner plates
- small sharp knife
- fork
- grater
- 2 mixing bowls

chopping board

frying pan

1 Lay out one of the tortillas on a board or a clean and dry work surface. Leave a 2cm (¾in) border around the edge and spoon the tuna over the top.

2 Sprinkle the Cheddar cheese over the tuna and then add the spring onions and orange pepper. Place the second tortilla on top and press down firmly.

Food Facts

Tuna is an oily fish so it contains healthy omega-3 fats which are good for the brain, eyes, and skin. Tuna also provides vitamins B, D, and E.

tuna

3 Brush a large frying pan with olive oil. Cook the quesadilla for 2 minutes over a medium heat. Press down with a spatula to make sure the cheese melts.

4 Now you need to turn the tortilla over. Carefully slide it onto a large plate. Put another plate on top and gently turn the plates over.

5 Carefully put the quesadilla back in the pan and cook the other side for 2 minutes. Remove the cooked quesadilla from the pan and cut it into wedges.

Did you know?

Carrots were first grown in Afghanistan in the 7th century. At that time they were red, black, yellow, white, or purple – not

1 Carefully grate the carrot and then put it into a bowl mixing bowl. Add the raisins and pine nuts to the bowl and mix everything together.

2 To make the dressing, mix together the olive oil and lemon juice using a fork. Pour the mixture over the carrot salad and stir to coat the salad evenly.

• **Preparation** 20 mins • **Cooking** 25 mins • **Makes** 12 pancakes

Griddle Cakes

These American-style savoury pancakes are perfect for a light but filling meal or as a tasty weekend brunch.

Helpful Hints

Keep the bacon and cooked pancakes warm in the oven while you cook the rest of the griddle cakes. They are delicious served with guacomole.

Did you know?

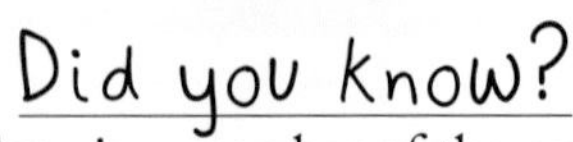

Corn is a member of the grass family so it isn't really a vegetable, it's a grain. The average ear of sweetcorn has 800 kernels, arranged in 16 rows.

Ingredients

wholemeal flour

- 110g (4oz) plain flour, white, or wholemeal
- 1 tsp bicarbonate of soda
- 1 tsp baking powder
- 1 free-range egg
- 100ml (3½ fl oz) milk
- 75g (3oz) sweetcorn (frozen or tinned)
- 284ml carton buttermilk
- 1 tsp sunflower oil
- 8 lean bacon rashers
- salt and pepper

sweetcorn

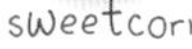

bacon

Equipment

whisk

- small jug
- fork or whisk
- sieve
- large mixing bowl
- wooden spoon
- tin foil
- large frying pan
- ladle
- spatula

frying pan

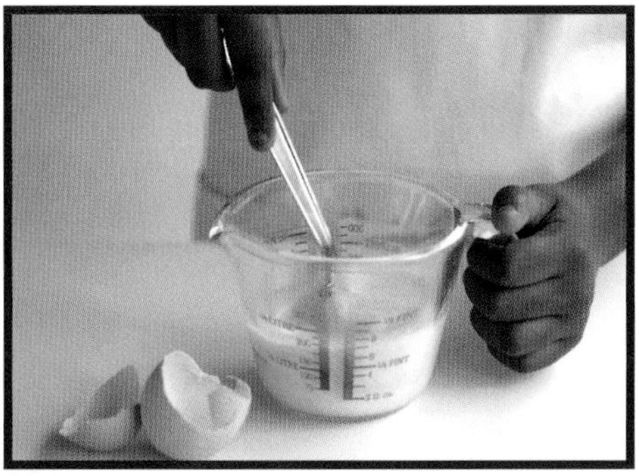

1 Pour the milk into a jug and then carefully crack the egg straight into the jug. Mix the milk and egg together with a fork or small whisk.

2 Sift the flour, bicarbonate of soda, baking powder and a pinch of salt into a large mixing bowl. Make a well in the centre of the bowl.

3 Pour the milk and egg mixture into the well into the centre of the flour mixture. Then carefully add the buttermilk and sweetcorn.

4 Gently beat the mixture until the ingredients are combined. Cover the mixture with a plate and leave to stand while you cook the bacon.

5 Line the grill rack with foil and preheat the grill to medium. Put the bacon under the grill and cook for 2–3 minutes on each side, or until crisp.

6 Heat the oil in the pan and then ladle in the batter to make griddle cakes about 10cm (4in) in diameter. Make sure there is space between the cakes.

7 Cook for 2–3 minutes, until golden underneath. Flip and then cook the other side. Make 12 cakes in this way, adding the rest of the oil when necessary.

Food Facts

Like all dairy foods, milk is an excellent source of calcium and phosphorus, both of which are essential for healthy teeth and bones. Interestingly, there's exactly the same amount of calcium in skimmed milk as there is in whole milk. Zinc and B vitamins are also provided by milk along with antibodies which help boost the immune system and the digestive system.

milk

● **Preparation** 20 mins ● **Cooking** 25 mins ● **Serves** 4

Pizzettas

Traditionally, a pizza base is made using yeast which helps it to rise. These yeast-free pizzettasare made with a base that does not need time-consuming kneading or rising but still taste light and crisp.

Tasty Twists

You can add any of your favourite toppings in step 7 before sprinkling the Cheddar. Mushrooms, peppers, onions, rocket, tuna, prawns, ham, olives, pepperoni, cooked chicken all taste great!

Ingredients

- 275g (9½ oz) white or wholemeal self-raising flour (plus extra for dusting)
- ½ tsp salt
- 125–150ml (4–5fl oz) semi-skimmed milk
- 4 tbsp olive oil

wholemeal flour

mozzarella

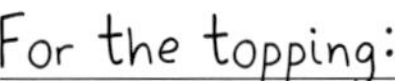

For the topping:

- 1 quantity Tomato Dipping Sauce (see pages 126–127)
- 1 x 150g (5½ oz) ball mozzarella (drained)
- 50g (2oz) mature Cheddar (grated)

Equipment

- sieve
- large mixing bowl
- wooden spoon
- rolling pin
- 2 large baking sheets
- spoon

sieve

mixing bowl

rolling pin

1 Preheat the oven to 200°C (400°F/Gas 6). Sift the flour and salt into a mixing bowl and then make a well in the centre of the mixture.

2 Pour the milk and oil into the well. Mix with a wooden spoon until the flour and liquids start to come together and form a soft dough.

Did you know?

More than 5 billion pizzas are sold worldwide each year. According to a recent poll, children aged between 3 and 11 prefer pizza to all other foods for lunch and dinner.

3 Lightly dust a work top and your hands with flour. Tip the dough out of the bowl and knead it for about 1 minute to form a smooth ball.

4 Dust 2 baking sheets with flour. Divide the dough into 4 smaller balls. Using a rolling pin, roll each piece into a 15cm (6in) circle.

Food Facts

Cheese provides valuable amounts of protein and calcium. However, cheese, especially hard cheese like Cheddar is high in saturated fat so try to eat in moderate amounts. Choose a mature cheese as its strong flavour means that you need less.

Cheddar cheese

5 Carefully, place 2 dough bases on each baking sheet. Top each base with 1–2 tablespoons of the Tomato Dipping Sauce.

6 Using the back of a spoon, spread the tomato in an even layer almost to the edge of the pizza base. Cut the mozzarella ball into 8-12 slices.

7 Add the mozzarella and any other toppings. Top with the Cheddar cheese. Bake the pizzas for 10 mins or until the base has risen and the top is golden.

• **Preparation** 20 mins • **Chilling** 30 mins • **Cooking** 16 mins • **Makes** 6 burgers

Homemade Burgers

This tasty, low-fat turkey burger is a healthy winner when partnered with a high-fibre bun. It's sure to get gobbled up in no time!

Tasty Twists

Vegetarians could use the veggie burgers recipe on p. 52, and meat eaters could try pork, beef, or lamb mince as a tasty alternative burger mix.

Ingredients

- 1 small onion
- 1 apple
- 450g (1lb) lean turkey, chicken, beef, pork, or lamb mince
- 1 small egg
- plain flour
- salt and pepper

To serve

- seeded burger buns (preferably wholemeal)
- lettuce leaves
- sliced tomatoes
- relish (see p. 53)

Equipment

- grater
- mixing bowl
- wooden spoon
- small bowl
- fork or whisk
- cling film
- large plate
- tin foil
- tongs

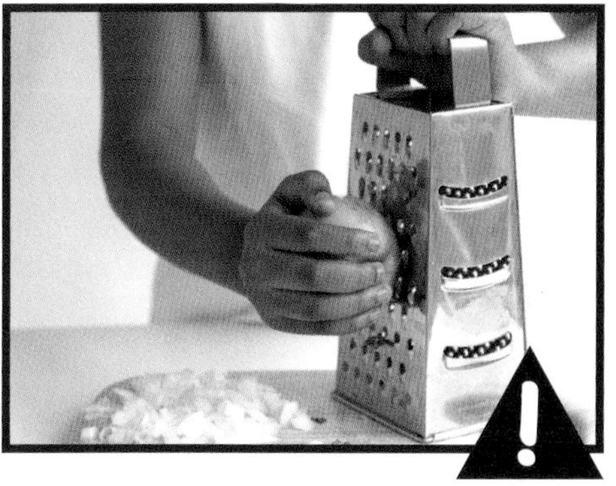

1 Peel and then finely chop the onion. Leaving the skin on, grate the apple coarsely. When you can see the core and pips – it's done!

2 Put the onion and apple into a mixing bowl and add the mince. Stir or use your hands to break up the mince and mix it with the onion and apple.

3 Crack an egg into a separate bowl and lightly beat the yolk and white together, using a fork or whisk. This will help bind the burger mixture together.

4 Pour the beaten egg into the mince, onion, and apple mixture. Season, then using clean hands mix it all together – this part is messy but a lot of fun!

5 Lightly cover a plate and your hands with flour. Take a handful of the mixture and shape into a round, flat burger. Put it onto the floured plate.

6 Do the same with the rest of the mixture and then lightly dust all 6 burgers with flour. Cover with cling film and chill for at least 30 minutes.

Food Facts

Turkey is a versatile meat that contains an array of valuable nutrients. including iron, zinc and selenium. It is a good source of B vitamins, which are essential for the body's processing of foods. Turkey is also high in protein and low in fat, making it one of the healthiest meats of all.

turkey mince

7 Preheat the grill to medium. Place the burgers onto a foil-covered grill rack and cook them for 8 minutes on each side, or until cooked through.

Baked Eggs

You will love these baked eggs, cooked in a rich tomato and pepper sauce. Serve with warmed tortillas or crusty bread for a light lunch or breakfast.

Ingredients

tortillas

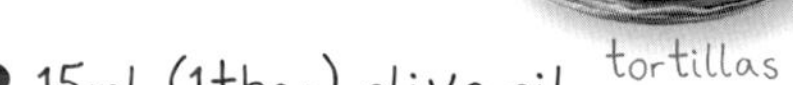

- 15ml (1tbsp) olive oil
- 1 small onion, chopped
- 1 clove garlic, crushed
- 1 mild green chilli, deseeded and finely chopped (optional)
- 1 small green pepper, deseeded and cut into thin strips
- 1 small red pepper, deseeded and cut into thin strips
- 400g (14oz) can chopped tomatoes
- 30ml (2tbsp) tomato ketchup
- 4 eggs
- a little paprika

eggs

garlic

paprika

Equipment

- medium saucepan
- wooden spoon
- 2 double, 4 individual or one large ovenproof dish
- spatula

saucepan

1 Preheat the oven to 180ºC, 350ºF, gas mark 4. Heat the oil in a medium pan and add the onion, garlic, chilli and peppers. Cook for 10 to 15 minutes.

2 Stir in the tomatoes and ketchup and season with salt and black pepper. Bring to the boil, then simmer for 5 minutes until thickened.

3 Spoon the mixture into some ovenproof dishes. Make 4 dips and break an egg into each. Place in the oven and bake for 12 to 14 minutes, until just set.

- **Preparation** 15 mins
- **Cooking** 12 mins
- **Serves** 2–4

Baked Eggs and Ham

These pies are so simple to make and taste delicious. Traditional pastry is high in fat so this recipe uses ham as a base instead. Serve with ripe, juicy tomatoes or crunchy salad. They're perfect for brunch too.

Tasty Twists

For a vegetarian alternative, use 4 large field or portobello mushrooms instead of ham. Wash the mushrooms and place them on a large, lightly greased baking tin. Then follow steps 3 and 4.

Ingredients

- a little vegetable oil
- 4 slices lean ham
- 4 free-range eggs

eggs

Equipment

- pastry brush
- muffin tin
- kitchen scissors
- small bowl
- oven gloves
- palette knife

oven gloves

1 Preheat the oven to 200°C (400°F/Gas 6). Lightly brush four holes of a large muffin tin with a little vegetable oil. This prevents the ham from sticking.

Did you know?

Pies have been around since ancient times. It is believed that the first ever pie recipe was published by the Romans and it was for rye-crusted goats cheese and honey pie.

Food Facts

boiled egg

Eggs can be cooked in many different ways. In this recipe the eggs are baked in the oven until set but they can also be fried, boiled, scrambled, or poached. To tell if an egg is fresh, place it in a bowl of water – if it sinks and lays flat it is fresh.

2 Arrange a slice of ham in each hole. Carefully trim the the slices to make them even, but make sure that the ham is still slightly above the edge of the tin.

3 One by one, crack an egg into a small bowl and pour it into each ham-lined hollow. Bake in the oven for 10–12 minutes, or until the egg has set.

4 Using oven gloves, remove the tray from the oven and leave it to cool for a few minutes. Then carefully lift out the pies with a palette knife.

- **Preparation** 20 mins
- **Cooking** 20 mins
- **Makes** 4 long rolls

Sushi Rolls

Impress your friends with these sophisticated sushi rolls. Once you have mastered the rolling technique in steps 5–7, they are quite simple. This recipe makes 4 long rolls with a carrot or cucumber filling which you can then cut up into delicious bite-sized pieces.

Serve the sushi with a side dish of soy sauce, for dipping.

Ingredients

seaweed (nori) sheets

carrot

- 250g (8oz) sushi rice (rinsed)
- 1tbsp of caster sugar
- 325ml (11fl oz) water
- 4 seaweed (nori) sheets
- 1/2 tsp of table salt
- 2tbsp of rice wine vinegar

sushi rice (rinsed)

For the filling:

- 1/2 small cucumber (halved lengthways)
- 1/2 carrot (peeled and halved lengthways)

cucumber

For dipping:

- soy sauce

soy sauce

Equipment

wooden spoon

- medium saucepan with lid
- serving spoon
- wooden spoon
- small saucepan
- shallow dish (approx. 15 x 20cm/6 x 8in)
- cling film
- chopping board
- teaspoon
- plate
- sharp knife
- bamboo sushi mat or squares of cling film

saucepan

Helpful Hints

Put the rolls onto a plate, cover with cling film, and chill for at least 1 hour. When the rolls are ready, rinse a sharp knife under cold water and slice them into 5 or 6 pieces.

Tasty Twists

Experiment with alternative sushi fillings such as tuna, salmon, crabmeat, cheese, avocado, or peppers.

1 Add the rice and water to the pan and cover with a lid. Bring to the boil and then reduce the heat. Simmer for 10 minutes. Remove the pan from the heat.

2 Leave the covered rice to stand for 10 minutes or until the liquid has been absorbed. Meanwhile, warm the vinegar, sugar, and salt until dissolved.

3 Line a shallow dish with cling film. Stir the sweetened vinegar mixture into the rice then carefully pack it into the dish. Leave to cool.

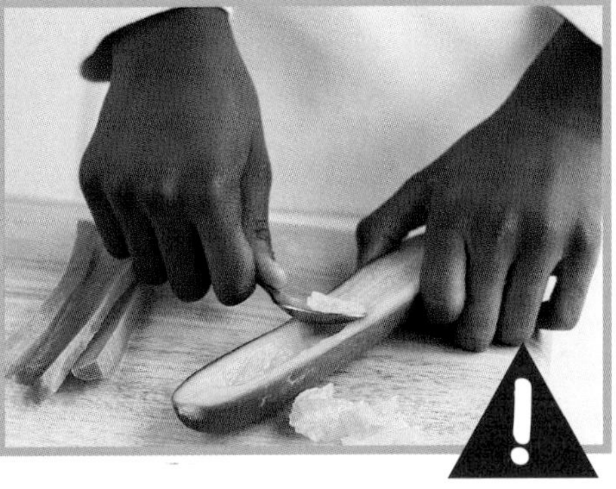

4 De-seed the cucumber, using a teaspoon and then slice it into 4 equal strips. If you are using a carrot instead, cut it into 4 long strips.

5 Place a nori sheet, shiny side down, onto a bamboo mat. Dip your hands in water and pat a quarter of the rice over two-thirds of the nori sheet.

6 Lay a piece of cucumber or carrot widthways along the centre of the rice. Holding the mat, roll the nori over and over, to the edge of the rice.

7 Tuck the rolled edge of the nori firmly under the filling. Dampen the remaining nori and roll it up. Using the mat, pull the sushi roll tightly to seal.

• **Preparation** 15 mins • **Cooking** 15–20 mins • **Serves** 2

Cheese Melt with Poached Egg

Adding a poached egg makes this recipe a tasty variation of cheese on toast. You can use any type of bread or cheese.

Ingredients

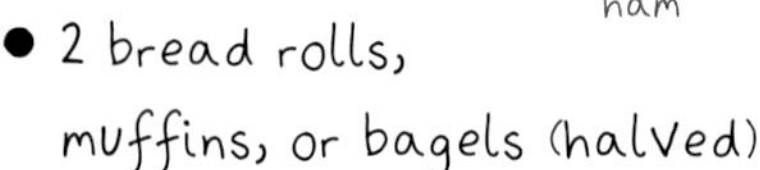
ham

- 2 bread rolls, muffins, or bagels (halved)
- 2 slices of ham (halved)
- 2–3 dashes of Worcestershire sauce (optional)
- salt and pepper
- 1 egg (beaten)
- 150g (5oz) cheese (grated)
- 2 eggs

muffins

eggs

Equipment

oven gloves

- mixing bowl
- foil-lined grill tray and rack
- 2 teaspoons
- oven gloves
- medium saucepan
- jug
- slotted spoon

bowl

1 Preheat the grill to a medium heat. Mix the grated cheese, Worcestershire sauce, beaten egg, and seasoning together in a mixing bowl.

Tasty Twists

Leave out the egg or ham, if you prefer a plain cheese melt.

2 Toast the rolls on both sides. Place a piece of ham on each half and top with the cheese mix. Grill for 3 minutes, or until melted and golden.

3 Meanwhile, crack an egg into a jug and gently tip it into a pan half-full of simmering water. Simmer for 3 minutes or until the egg white is cooked.

4 Remove the poached egg with a slotted spoon and serve on top of two cheese melts. Repeat step 3 with the second egg, season, and serve.

Helpful Hints

Line the grill tray with foil and place the rack on top. This makes the grill easy to wash up because any drips or spills will land on the foil, which can be thrown away.

Cheese melts taste great with a green salad.

• **Preparation** 15 mins • **Cooking** 15 mins • **Makes** 12

Veggie Spring Rolls

These crispy spring rolls filled with vegetables make an easy and delicious snack. Serve with sweet chilli dipping sauce or soy sauce if you prefer.

Ingredients

- 100g (3½oz) beansprouts
- 50g (2oz) cabbage, shredded
- 1 carrot, cut into thin strips
- ½ red pepper, deseeded and thinly sliced
- 6 spring onions, thinly sliced
- 1 clove garlic, crushed
- 2.5cm (1in) piece root ginger, peeled and grated
- 15ml (1tbsp) dark soy sauce
- 6 sheets filo pastry
- 25g (1oz) melted butter

ginger

Equipment

knife

- mixing bowl
- wooden spoon
- chopping board
- knife
- small bowl
- pastry brush
- baking tray

1 Preheat the oven to 190ºC, 375ºF, gas mark 5. In a large bowl, mix together all the ingredients, except the filo pastry and butter.

2 Place the sheets of pastry on top of each other and cut in half.

3 Place 1 sheet of the pastry on a board and brush the edges with a little of the melted butter. Place some of the filling on the bottom edge.

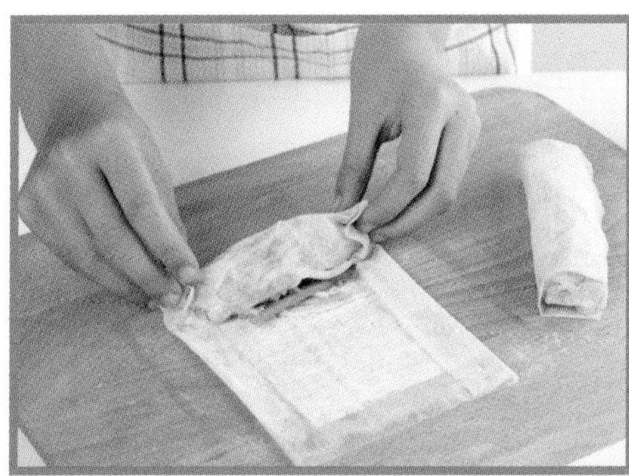

4 Roll up, folding the ends over. Repeat with remaining pastry and filling.

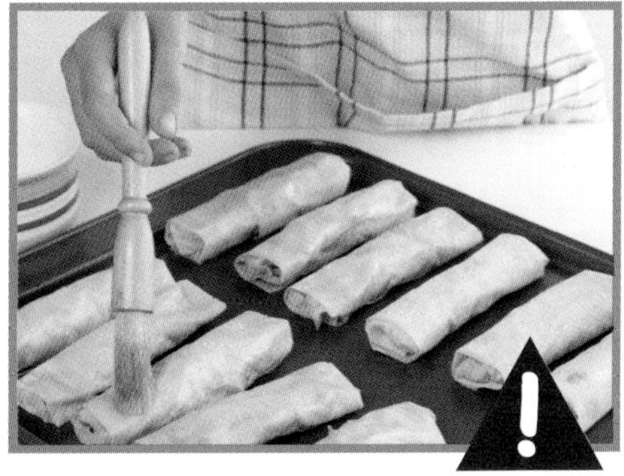

5 Place on a baking tray and brush with butter. Bake for 12 to 15 minutes until golden. Serve with sweet chilli dipping sauce.

Tasty Twists

You could try using sweetcorn, peas, or mushrooms if you prefer these fillings.

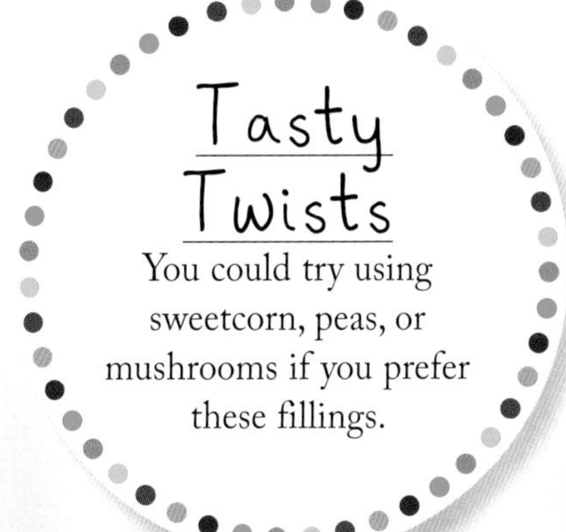

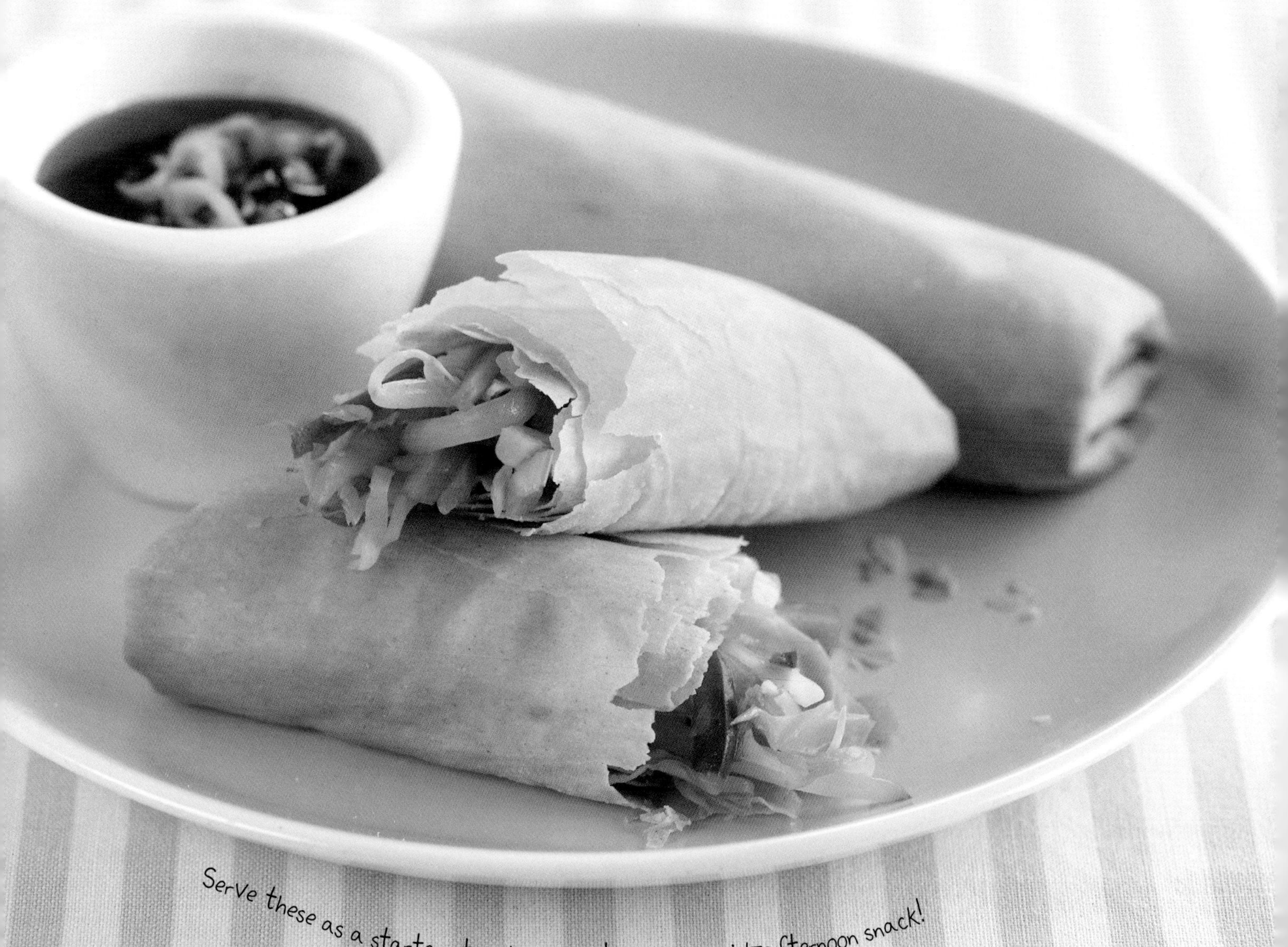

Serve these as a starter at a dinner party, or as a mid-afternoon snack!

Main Meals

Main Meals

Easy Pizza

Make shop-bought pizza healthier by adding your favourite toppings. Sweetcorn, mushrooms, olives, peppers, or spinach, add essential vitamins and minerals while ham, egg, tuna, or prawns are good sources of protein.

Pasta Salad

Salads can be much more than a side dish. Cook 125g (4½oz) pasta as per the packet instructions and then stir in 4 tbsp pesto. Cut a 150g (5½oz) ball of mozzarella into bite-sized pieces and stir into the pasta. Add a handful of basil leaves and 12 halved cherry tomatoes. Finish off with a sprinkling of pine nuts.

Balance is the key to a healthy main meal, so imagine that your plate is divided into three parts. A carbohydrate food such as pasta, potatoes, or rice should form the main part of your meal; there should also be a protein food such as meat, fish, poultry, eggs, nuts, or pulses and finally, some vegetables. Eat at least 2 hours before going to bed to give your body time to digest your food properly. You'll find lots of great recipe ideas in this section, but here are some simple ideas to tempt your tastebuds.

Sausage and Veg Roast

Preheat the oven to 200°C (400°F/Gas 6). Place chunks of butternut squash, potato, wedges of onion, and some sausages in a roasting tin with 1 tbsp olive oil. Roast in the oven for 20 minutes. Remove from the oven, turn the vegetables and sausage so they brown evenly then add some cherry tomatoes. Return to the oven for another 10–15 minutes.

Steamed Veg

Steamed vegetables are cooked over water, not in water as they are when boiled. This preserves many of the vitamins, especially the water-soluble ones.

Couscous

Couscous is a tasty alternative to rice or pasta. Put 225g (8oz) couscous into a bowl and pour in enough boiling water or stock to cover the couscous. Stir the couscous with a fork and leave to stand for 5–10 minutes, or until the liquid has been absorbed. Fluff up the couscous with a fork before serving.

Baked Beans

For a homemade baked beans, combine 200g/7oz haricot beans (drained and rinsed), 150ml (5fl oz) passata, 1 tsp Dijon mustard and 1 tbsp each of olive oil, Worcestershire sauce, maple syrup, and tomato purée in a saucepan. Bring to the boil then reduce the heat. Half-cover the pan and simmer for 15–20 minutes until the sauce has thickened, stirring occasionally.

Nuts and Seeds

Sprinkle a handful of nuts and seeds over salads, stir-fries, noodles, or rice. Just a handful can boost levels of vitamins B and E, iron, zinc and omega-6 essential fats. Walnuts and pumpkin seeds also contain omega-3 fats.

Stir Fry

Stir-frying is a healthy and quick way of cooking. Cut the ingredients into similar size pieces so they cook equally and use a small amount of oil. Carrots, peppers, mangetout, courgettes, mushrooms, onions, and beansprouts taste great stir-fried.

Mashed Potato

For tasty and colourful mash, try adding carrots, celeriac, squash, swede, or sweet potato. Use equal amounts of potato and the vegetable of your choice and cook in boiling water for 15–20 minutes, or until tender. Drain, then return to the pan and mash. Add milk and a little butter to make a creamy mash.

• **Preparation** 5 mins • **Cooking** 15 mins • **Serves** 4

Tuna Pasta

Tuna is a good source of low-fat protein and a very common addition to pasta in Italy. Although tinned tuna is slightly lower in omega-3 fat than fresh, it still provides valuable, brain-boosting nutrients. Best of all, this simple dish takes only minutes to make.

Tasty Twists

Serve with a green vegetable. Steamed broccoli is a great choice – the vitamin C in the tomato sauce will help your body absorb the iron in the broccoli. To give the sauce a protein boost, add some canned beans, such as chickpeas.

Ingredients

- 275g (9½ oz) pasta bows
- 2 tbsp olive oil
- 2 large cloves garlic (crushed)
- 1 tsp dried oregano (optional)
- 2 tsp tomato purée
- 800g (1lb 5oz) canned chopped tomatoes
- ½ tsp sugar (optional)
- 200g (7oz) tinned tuna in olive oil (drained and broken up into chunks)
- salt and pepper

garlic

pasta bows

Equipment

- small sharp knife
- chopping board
- medium saucepan with lid
- large saucepan
- wooden spoon
- colander
- tablespoon

colander

saucepan

1 Bring a large saucepan of water to the boil. Add the pasta and cook according to the packet instructions, until the pasta is tender but not too soft.

2 Meanwhile, heat the oil in a saucepan over a medium heat. Fry the garlic for 1 minute. Stir in the oregano, the chopped tomatoes, and tomato purée.

3 Bring the sauce to the boil and reduce the heat. Half cover the pan and simmer for 15 minutes or until the sauce has reduced by a third and thickened.

You only need to add sugar in step 4 if the tomatoes taste a little sharp.

4 Stir the tuna into the sauce. Half-cover the pan and heat through for 2 mins, stirring occasionally. Add some sugar to the sauce if necessary and season.

5 Drain the pasta but save 2 tablespoons of the water. Return the pasta to the saucepan. Add the water and stir in the sauce until the pasta is coated.

Food Facts

Tomatoes get their red colour from lycopene. It is one of the few nutrients that is more easily absorbed by the body when it is heated or in a concentrated form, such as in a purée or sauce. Great for strengthening our immune systems and fighting colds, lycopene is an important antioxidant.

• **Preparation** 15 mins • **Cooking** 25mins • **Serves** 4

Mixed Bean Burrito

A burrito is a delicious Mexican dish consisting of rolled up flour tortilla filled with meat or vegetables.

Guacamole is the perfect accompaniment.

Ingredients

- 1 tbsp olive oil
- 1 large onion, chopped
- 400g (14oz) tin mixed beans (drained and rinsed)
- 1 tsp dried oregano
- 400g (14oz) tin chopped tomatoes
- 1 tbsp tomato purée
- 1 tsp ground cumin
- few drops Tabasco (optional)
- salt and pepper

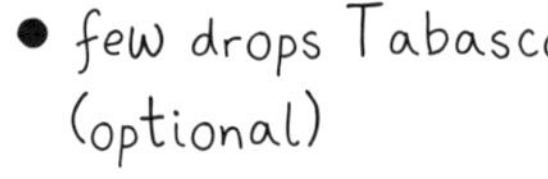

Cheddar cheese

To serve:

- 4 soft flour tortillas
- 50g (2oz) mature Cheddar cheese, grated
- shop-bought guacamole (optional)

onion

tortillas

Equipment

chopping board

- small sharp knife
- chopping board
- medium saucepan with lid
- large spoon
- spatula or wooden spoon

saucepan

1 Heat the oil in a medium-sized saucepan. Add the onion and cook, stirring occasionally, for 8 minutes until the onion is softened and slightly golden.

2 Add the oregano, chopped tomatoes, tomato purée, and cumin to the saucepan. Tip the beans into the pan, stir and bring to the boil.

Tasty Twists

For a meaty filling, swap the beans for 400g (14oz) minced beef. Follow step 1 and then fry the mince for 5 minutes in step 2. Continue with steps 3 to 6.

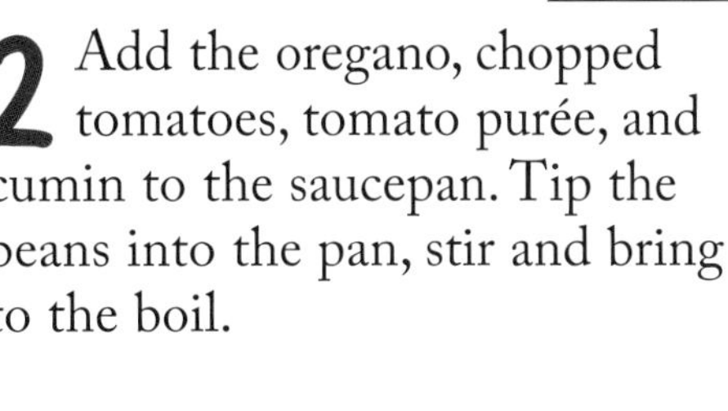

Food Facts

Beans are also known as pulses. They are an excellent combination of carbohydrates and protein and what's more they are low in fat. Beans also count as a portion in the five-a-day fruit and veg guidelines.

mixed beans

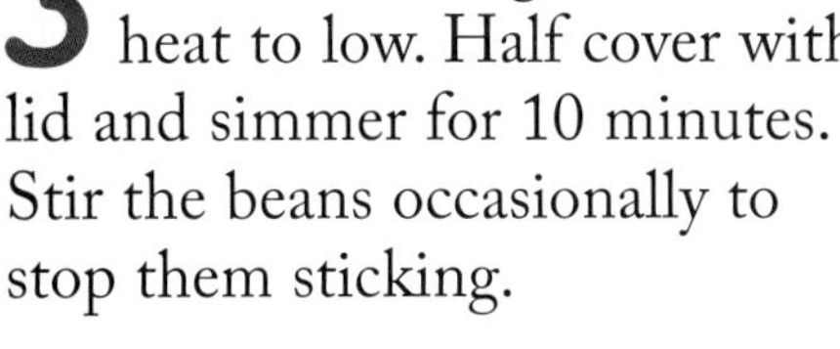

3 When bubbling, reduce the heat to low. Half cover with a lid and simmer for 10 minutes. Stir the beans occasionally to stop them sticking.

4 Taste the beans and add salt and pepper along with a few drops of Tabasco if you like. Cook for another 5 minutes, stirring occasionally.

Did you know?

The word burrito means "little donkey" in Spanish. It is thought that the dish gets its name because a rolled up tortilla resembles the ear of a donkey!

5 Warm the tortilla in a microwave. Place each one on a plate and top with the bean stew. Sprinkle with Cheddar and top with a dollop of guacamole.

6 Fold in one end of the tortilla and then carefully fold over one side. Gently roll the tortilla over to make a tight and secure burrito.

- **Preparation** 2–4 mins
- **Marinading** 1 hour
- **Cooking** 30 mins
- **Serves** 2–4

Chicken Drumsticks

The yoghurt marinade gives the chicken drumsticks a lightly spiced flavour but also keeps them tender and tasty. All you need is a simple green salad and warm naan bread to serve.

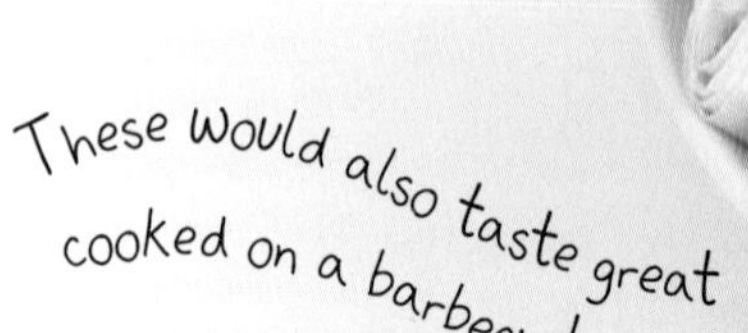

These would also taste great cooked on a barbecue!

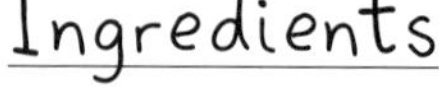

Ingredients

- 4 skinless chicken drumsticks

Marinade

- juice of 1/2 lemon
- 100ml (3 1/2 fl oz) thick natural yoghurt
- 2 tbsp tandoori spice blend
- 1 tbsp sunflower oil

To serve:

- mango chutney (optional)
- 4 small naan bread
- lettuce

lettuce

Equipment

- kitchen paper
- spoon
- large, shallow dish
- bowl
- cling film
- baking tray
- pastry brush
- tongs
- oven gloves

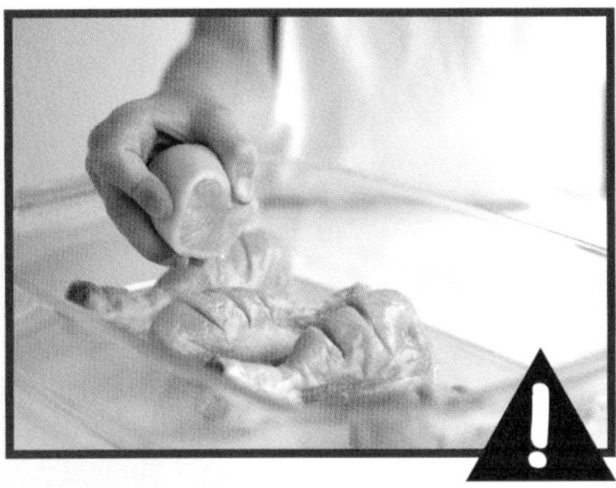

1 Pat the chicken with kitchen paper. Make three deep cuts in each drumstick and place them in a large, shallow dish. Squeeze the lemon juice over the drumsticks.

2 Put the yoghurt and tandoori spices in a bowl then mix together. Spoon the yoghurt marinade over the chicken until it is completely covered.

Tasty Twists

If you prefer meat without bones, choose chicken breasts instead of drumsticks. Follow steps 1–4 in the recipe and then cook the breasts for 20–25 minutes or until cooked through.

Did you know?

Spices are the seeds, fruit, pod, bark, and buds of plants. They were once so prized that wars were fought over them, and they have even been used as currency.

3 Cover the drumsticks with cling film and chill them for at least 1 hour. After 50 minutes, preheat the oven to 200°C (400°F/Gas 6).

4 Brush the oil over the bottom of a baking tray. Place the chicken darumsticks on the baking tray and cook them in the oven for 15 minutes.

5 After 15 minutes, turn the chicken over and spoon over any remaining marinade. Cook the drumsticks for a further 15 minutes or until cooked through.

6 Check that the chicken is cooked through. (There should be no trace of pinkness.) Try serving with mango chutney, warm naan bread, and lettuce.

Food Facts

Chicken is a great source of protein. It contains selenium, a nutrient that helps to fight infections. It is also low in fat, particularly if the skin is removed.

- **Preparation** 15 mins
- **Marinating** 1 hour
- **Cooking** 25–30 mins
- **Serves** 4

Barbecue Chicken

Marinating is a simple but effective way of adding extra flavour to meat, fish, and vegetables. Soaking these chicken pieces in a marinade for at least an hour before you cook them gives them a delicious barbecue taste. On a warm summer's day, they could be cooked on an outdoor barbecue.

Helpful Hints

Chicken breasts or thighs also taste great cooked this way but always check that the meat is completely cooked.

Ingredients

tomato ketchup

sunflower oil

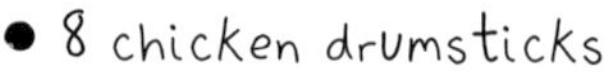

- 8 chicken drumsticks
- 2tbsp of tomato ketchup
- 2tbsp of soy sauce
- 2tbsp of fresh orange juice
- 1tbsp of sunflower oil
- 3tbsp of clear runny honey
- 1 garlic clove (crushed)
- 1tsp of mustard

chicken drumsticks

Equipment

chopping board

- small mixing bowl
- whisk
- kitchen paper
- sharp knife
- chopping board
- cling film
- oven gloves
- foil-lined grill tray
- tongs
- dessert spoon
- large dish (approx. 5cm/2in deep)

1 Put all the ingredients except the chicken drumsticks in a bowl and whisk them together. Pour the mixture into a large, shallow dish.

2 Pat the chicken pieces with paper towels. Make 3 deep cuts in each drumstick. This is known as scoring and helps the meat to soak up the marinade.

3 Put the chicken in the dish and roll each piece until it is coated with sauce. Cover with cling film and leave to marinate in the fridge for 1 hout.

Wrap the cooled chicken in a napkin and eat with your fingers!

Helpful Hints

You must always wash your hands thoroughly after touching raw meat to avoid spreading any germs.

Serving Tip

The chicken will need to stand for 2–3 minutes before you are ready to serve it.

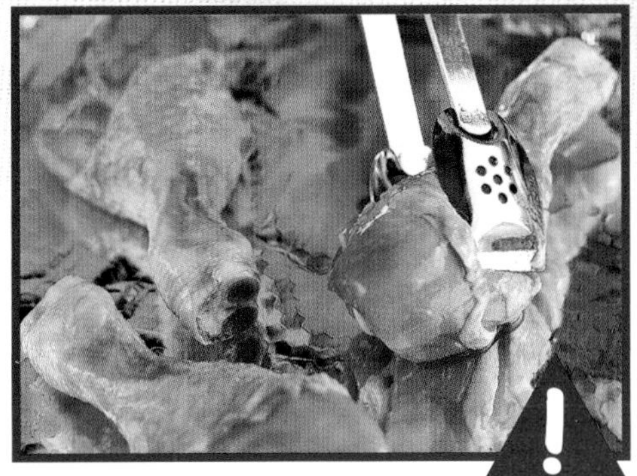

4 Preheat the grill to medium heat. Lay the coated chicken (uncut side up) on a foil-lined grill pan. Put the marinade to one side.

5 Grill the chicken pieces for 7–8 minutes. Using tongs, turn the chicken over and grill the other side for a further 7–8 minutes.

6 Turn the chicken again. Spoon on half the sauce. Grill for 5 minutes, turn, and spoon on the rest of the sauce. Grill for a final 5 minutes.

• **Preparation** 15 mins • **Cooking** 14 mins • **Serves** 4

Pesto Pasta

Pasta is the ultimate quick, simple, and nutritious meal. Try stirring in a spoonful of homemade pesto for an equally quick and mouthwateringly tasty sauce.

Tasty Twists

Peas, green beans, carrots, or cauliflower could be used instead of the broccoli. Meat eaters could add some cooked chicken or bacon.

You could swirl a spoonful of pesto in soup, stir it into bread dough, or spread it over toast.

Ingredients

spaghetti salt pepper

- 250g (9oz) spaghetti
- 15–20 small florets broccoli

pine nuts

Pesto:

- 2 large cloves garlic (roughly chopped)
- 3 tbsp pine nuts

garlic

- 4 tbsp fresh finely grated Parmesan cheese (plus extra for serving)
- 60g ($2^1/_2$ oz) fresh basil leaves
- 75ml (3fl oz) olive oil
- salt and pepper

basil leaves

Equipment

- small sharp knife
- chopping board
- food processor
- jar with a lid
- large saucepan
- wooden spoon
- colander
- pasta spoon

colander

chopping board

1 Put the garlic and pine nuts in a food processor and blend until coarsely chopped. Next, add the Parmesan and basil and blend again until a coarse purée.

2 Pour the olive oil into the food processor and blend to make a smooth mixture. Season to taste. Transfer the pesto to a jar with a lid.

Did you know?

Pesto is an Italian sauce from the city of Genoa. It dates back to Roman times. The word "pesto" comes from an Italian word meaning "to crush".

3 Fill a large saucepan three-quarters full of water. Add 1 teaspoon of salt and bring the water to the boil. Lower the pasta into the pan.

4 Cook the pasta according to the instructions on the packet. About 4 minutes before the pasta is cooked, add the broccoli and simmer.

5 Drain the pasta and broccoli but reserve 2 tablespoons of the cooking water. Return the pasta and broccoli to the pan with the cooking water.

Broccoli is a super-veg thanks to its impressive range of nutrients, from B vitamins and iron to zinc and potassium. Broccoli belongs to the same family as cabbage, cauliflower, kale, and brussel sprouts.

broccoli

6 Add enough pesto to coat the pasta and broccoli (you may have a some leftover). Stir and divide the pasta between four shallow bowls.

Preparation 15 mins • Marinating 30 mins • Cooking 25 mins • Serves 4

Griddled Chicken and Potato Salad

This healthy dish is really easy to make, but bursting with colour and flavour.

Helpful Hints

To check that the chicken is thoroughly cooked, insert a skewer or the tip of a knife into the thickest part – there should be no sign of any pink. If the chicken is not completely done, cook it for another minute or two.

The chicken could also be served with a green salad or on a bed of rice.

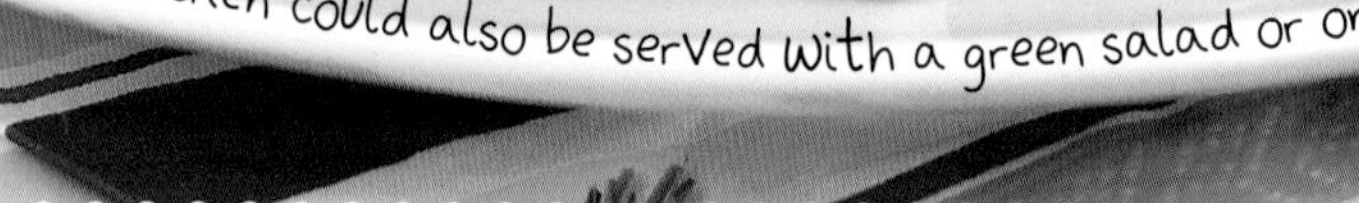

Ingredients

spring onions

- 4 skinless chicken breasts (each 150g/5½oz)

Marinade:

- 2 tsp paprika
- 3 tbsp olive oil

Potato salad:

- 400g (14oz) baby new potatoes (cut in half if necessary)
- 2 spring onions (finely chopped)
- 8 cherry tomatoes (halved)
- 3 tbsp chopped fresh mint
- 2 tbsp extra-virgin olive oil
- 1 tbsp lemon juice

cherry tomatoes

Equipment

tongs

- large, shallow dish
- tablespoon
- cling film
- griddle
- tongs
- small sharp knife
- chopping board
- medium saucepan
- salad bowl

sharp knife

1 Mix the paprika and the olive oil in a large, shallow dish. Add the chicken and spoon over the marinade. Cover with cling film and chill for 30 minutes.

Food Facts

A griddle is similar to a frying pan but it is usually square and has a ridged base. The design makes griddling a healthier way of cooking because most of the fat collects in the ridges of the pan, rather than in the food. Meat, fish, and vegetables can all be cooked on a griddle. As well as being a healthy way to cook, griddling also gives food a delicious, slightly barbecued flavour.

griddle

2 Heat a griddle pan until it is very hot. Reduce the heat to medium and place 2 chicken breasts in the pan. Griddle for 6 minutes on one side.

3 Carefully turn the chicken over using tongs. Spoon over a little of the marinade and then cook for another 6 minutes, or until cooked through.

4 Cook the remaining chicken breasts in the same way, making sure there is no trace of pink in the middle. Serve with the potato salad.

1 Put the potatoes in a medium saucepan and cover with water. Bring to the boil and cook the potatoes for 10 minutes or until they are tender.

2 Drain the potatoes and leave them to cool in a bowl. Finely chop the spring onions and halve the tomatoes. Put them in the bowl. Add the mint.

3 Mix the extra-virgin olive oil and lemon juice together, using a fork. Then pour the dressing over the salad and stir well to mix it in.

• **Preparation** 15 mins • **Cooking** 20 mins • **Serves** 4–6

Lamb Kebabs and Tomato Dip

Soak the wooden skewers in water for 30 minutes to prevent them burning.

These kebabs contain just the right amount of spice to give them plenty of flavour without being too hot and spicy.

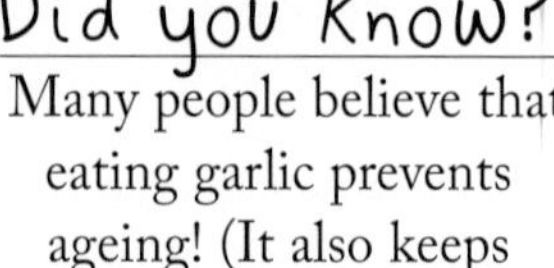

Did you know?

Many people believe that eating garlic prevents ageing! (It also keeps vampires away, of course!)

Ingredients

lean minced lamb

- 450g (1lb) lean minced lamb
- 1 small onion (finely chopped or processed)
- 2 cloves garlic (crushed)
- 1/2 tsp ground cinnamon
- 2 tsp ground cumin
- 1 tsp ground coriander
- olive oil (for brushing)
- salt and pepper

Tomato Dipping Sauce

- 2 tbsp olive oil
- 2 cloves garlic (crushed)
- 300ml (10fl oz) passata (sieved tinned tomatoes)
- 1 tbsp sun-dried tomato purée (or tomato purée)
- 1/2 tsp sugar

olive oil

Equipment

tongs

- medium saucepan
- large mixing bowl
- wooden spoon
- baking tray
- 12 wooden or metal skewers
- tongs

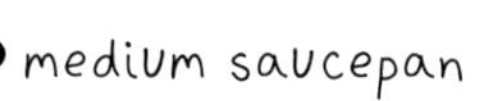

wooden skewer

wooden spoon

1 Pour the olive oil into a pan and heat gently. Fry the garlic for 1 minute, stirring constantly. Add the passata, tomato purée, and sugar and bring to the boil.

2 Reduce the heat, partially cover the pan and simmer for 15 minutes. Stir the sauce occasionally to prevent it sticking to the bottom of the pan.

Tasty Twists

For an Italian flavour, replace the cinnamon, cumin, and coriander with 2 tsp dried oregano and 2 tbsp finely chopped sun-dried tomatoes. Alternatively, 1 tbsp mild curry powder will give an Indian flavour.

1 Put the lamb mince in a mixing bowl and break it up using a fork. Add the chopped onion, garlic, cinnamon, cumin, and coriander to the bowl.

2 Season with salt and pepper and then stir the ingredients until they are all combined. Preheat the grill to medium and lightly oil a baking tray.

3 Divide the lamb mixture into 12 pieces. Shape each one into a sausage and then thread them onto the skewers. Press or roll to lengthen the kebabs.

4 Place the lamb kebabs onto the baking tray. Grill them for about 10 minutes. Turn them over halfway through, until golden all over and cooked through.

Food Facts

Every country in the world includes onions in its cooking and along with garlic, it has become an essential flavouring in a wide variety of dishes. For centuries, onions and garlic have also been used in all kinds of traditional remedies. Both are antibacterial and antiviral, helping to fight colds and relieve asthma and hayfever.

Preparation 45 mins • **Cooking** 9 mins • **Serves** 4

Cream Cheese Burgers

These burgers have a surprise cream cheese, herb, and garlic filling. Serve in bread rolls with salad or with potato wedges.

These unusual burgers are delicious and much tastier than shop-bought ones.

Ingredients

onion

- 675g (1½lb) lean minced beef
- 1 small onion (finely chopped)
- 60ml (4tbsp) freshly chopped parsley

Cream cheese filling

- 75g (3oz) soft cream cheese
- 1 clove garlic, crushed (optional)
- 30ml (2tbsp) freshly chopped chives
- little oil for brushing

garlic

Equipment

- large bowl
- wooden spoon
- small bowl
- pastry brush
- flipper

wooden spoon

1 In a large bowl, mix together all the ingredients for the burgers, with a little salt and freshly ground black pepper.

2 Divide into 8 equal portions and flatten into rounds.

3 In a small bowl, mix together the cream cheese, garlic, and chives. Place a quarter of the mixture onto 4 of the burger rounds.

4 Place the other 4 burgers rounds on top and pinch together the edges. Mould into 4 burgers. Chill for 30 minutes.

5 Brush the burgers with a little oil and grill for 8 to 9 minutes each side, until thoroughly cooked through. Serve in bread rolls with salad.

- **Preparation** 15 mins • **Cooking** 17 mins • **Serves** 4

Salmon Parcels

Salmon is full of brain-boosting, healthy oils that help with concentration and memory. If you are not usually a fan of fish, this tasty recipe is sure to win you over!

Did you know?

Japan consumes the highest amount of salmon per person, and has the lowest level of heart disease in the world.

Vegetarians could use a selection of vegetables such as carrot, red pepper, mangetout, broccoli, spring onions, or courgettes.

Ingredients

carrot

- 2 tbsp sesame seeds
- 4 slices fresh ginger (peeled and cut into thin strips)
- 2 tbsp soy sauce
- 4 tbsp orange juice
- 4 thick salmon fillets (about 150g/5½oz each)
- 1 carrot (cut into thin strips)
- 1 red pepper (deseeded and cut into thin strips)
- 3 spring onions (cut into thin strips)
- salt and black pepper
- 250g (9oz) noodles

fresh ginger

noodles

Equipment

sharp knife

- small sharp knife
- chopping board
- frying pan
- baking tray
- baking paper

1 Preheat the oven to 200°C (400°F/Gas 6). Toast the sesame seeds in a dry frying pan until golden. Remove from the pan and set aside.

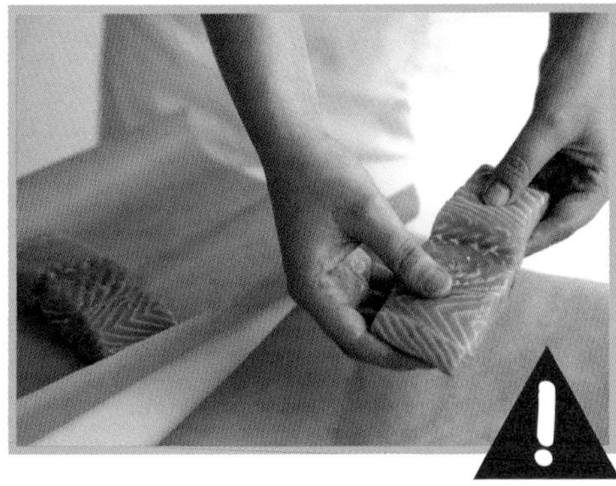

2 Cut the baking parchment into 4 pieces, at least twice the size of the salmon fillets. Place each piece of salmon on a piece of baking parchment.

3 Arrange a mixture of the carrot, red pepper, spring onion, and ginger strips on top of each salmon fillet. Drizzle over the soy sauce and orange juice.

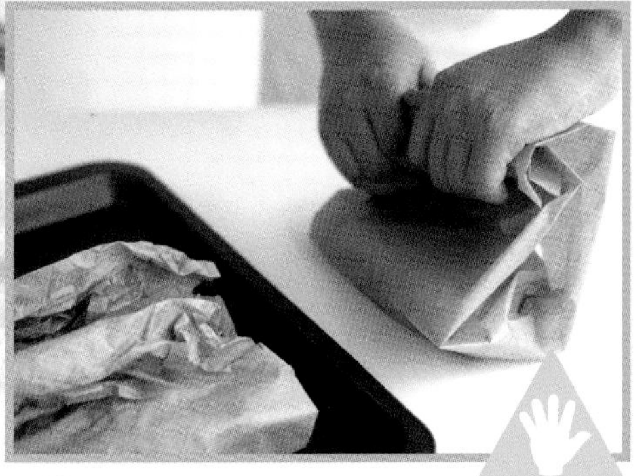

4 Season with salt and pepper. Carefully fold in the top and bottom of each parcel and then gather up the sides. Gently fold to make 4 loose parcels.

5 Put the parcels on a baking tray and bake for 15 minutes. Add the noodles to a pan of boiling water and cook, following the instructions on the packet.

Tasty Twists

Chicken breasts would also taste delicious cooked in this way. Follow the recipe but bake the chicken slightly longer than the salmon – about 20–25 minutes, or until cooked through.

6 Remove the fish from the oven and leave to cool slightly before opening the parcels. Serve with the noodles and a sprinkling of sesame seeds.

Food Facts

Salmon is an excellent source of polyunsaturated fatty acids, known as omega-3. These are the healthier kind of fats and have been shown to help reduce heart disease and are good for the brain, skin, eyes, and nerves too.

salmon

Preparation 20 mins • **Cooking** 30 mins • **Serves** 4

Roasted Vegetable Pasta

Roasting vegetables is a great way to make them sweet and melt-in-your mouth tasty, without losing their goodness.

Tasty Twists

Butternut squash, aubergines, leeks, or carrots would also taste great. Meat eaters could add ham or tinned tuna in step 2 or chicken, bacon, or sausage that has been browned first.

Ingredients

- 1 aubergine
- 1 large courgette
- 1 large red onion
- 6 cloves garlic (whole)
- 1 large red pepper (deseeded)
- 3 tbsp olive oil
- 12 cherry tomatoes
- 300g ($10^1/_2$oz) pasta spirals or tubes
- 4 tbsp low-fat crème fraiche
- 75g (3oz) mature Cheddar cheese (grated)
- 1 tbsp wholegrain mustard
- salt and pepper

Equipment

- small sharp knife
- chopping board
- roasting tin
- large saucepan
- wooden spoon
- small mixing bowl
- teaspoon

1 Preheat the oven to 200°C (400°F/Gas 6). Slice the aubergine, courgette, and red pepper into bite-sized chunks. Cut the onion into 8 wedges.

2 Put the aubergine, courgette, onion, garlic, and red pepper in a roasting tin. Drizzle the oil over the vegetables and turn them so they are coated in it.

Food Facts

Red peppers are bursting with vitamin C so are great for healthy skin, teeth, and bones. Red peppers have an extra benefit – they contain higher amounts of beta carotene, which is good for fighting viruses.

red peppers

3 Roast for 15 minutes and then remove the tin from the oven. Add the tomatoes and coat them in the oil. Roast for 10 mins or until the vegetables are tender.

4 Meanwhile, bring a large saucepan of water to the boil. Add the pasta and cook according to the packet, until it is tender but not too soft.

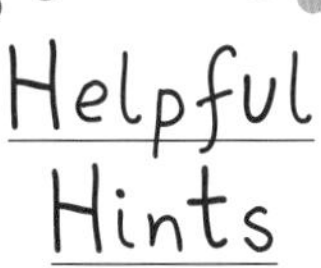

Helpful Hints

There are lots of different pasta shapes to choose from. Opt for one that can "hold" the sauce like penne, rigatoni, or farfalle, rather than long pasta such as spaghetti or tagliatelle.

5 Remove the garlic cloves from the roasting tin. Drain the pasta and add it to the vegetables in the tin. Now peel and finely chop the garlic.

6 Mix the garlic with the crème fraîche and mustard. Add the crème fraîche mixture to the pasta and vegetables and sprinkle with the Cheddar.

7 Season and stir to mix it all together. Put the tin back in the oven for 5 mins or until the cheese has melted and everything is warmed through.

• **Preparation** 20 mins • **Marinating** at least 1 hour • **Cooking** 1 hour • **Serves** 4

Sticky Ribs with Baked Potato

The ribs can be marinated overnight for maximum flavour.

Give pork spare ribs a delicious sticky sweetness with this simple barbeque sauce – they're best eaten with your fingers!

Ingredients

pork spare ribs

- 1kg (2lb 4oz) pork spare ribs
- 4 medium baking potatoes, scrubbed
- 4 tbsp sour cream (optional)
- 2 tbsp chopped chives (optional)

pepper sauce

Marinade:

- 2 tbsp honey
- 1 tbsp balsamic vinegar
- 4 tbsp tomato ketchup
- 2 tbsp soft brown sugar
- 1 tbsp Dijon mustard
- 1 tbsp olive oil
- 3 drops pepper sauce (optional)

Equipment

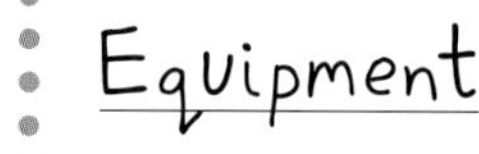

baking tray

- jug
- fork
- extra-wide foil
- baking tray
- oven gloves
- knife

extra-wide foil

1 Put the marinade ingredients in a jug and mix them together. Place the ribs on a large piece of double-thickness foil. Pour the marinade over the ribs.

2 Make sure that the ribs are well coated. Scrunch the foil loosely around the ribs and twist to seal. Leave to marinate in the fridge for at least 1 hour.

3 Preheat the oven to 200°C (400°F/Gas 6). Scrub the potatoes and prick them all over with a fork. Bake the potatoes for 1 hour or until soft in the centre.

4 Remove the foil parcel with the ribs from the fridge and carefully place it onto a baking tray. Cook them in the oven with the potatoes for 30 minutes.

5 Carefully open up the foil parcel. Cook the ribs in the open parcel for a further 30 minutes, or until they are completely cooked.

Tasty Twists

This delicious marinade could be used to coat chicken, turkey, fish, vegetables, and tofu. You could also try barbecuing instead of roasting.

6 Cut the potatoes in half and open them up. (Take care – they will be hot!) Top each potato with some sour cream and chives. Serve with the ribs.

Food Facts

Baking is a great way to cook potatoes. Not only is it a very simple method of cooking, but there is no need to add any fat. Potatoes are a popular starchy carbohydrate food and provide your body with energy as well as immunity-boosting vitamins B and C, plus iron and potassium. The skin contains the highest concentration of fibre, which helps your digestive system work efficiently.

potatoes

Preparation 20 mins • **Cooking** 50 mins • **Serves** 4

Jambalaya

This is a colourful Creole or Cajun rice dish from Louisiana in the USA. It is easy to make because all the ingredients are cooked in the same pot. The recipe can be adapted for vegetarians by replacing the chicken and ham with extra vegetables, meat-free sausages, or tofu.

Tasty Twists

Prawns, pork, beans, or vegetables, such as peas and courgettes, would also be tasty in this rice dish.

Ingredients

- 2 tbsp olive oil
- 3 skinless chicken breasts,
- 1 large onion (chopped)
- 200g (7oz) smoked ham
- 2 large cloves garlic (chopped)
- 1 red pepper (deseeded and cut into bite-sized pieces)
- 1 tsp paprika
- 1 green chilli, deseeded and finely chopped (optional)
- 1 tsp dried thyme
- 700ml ($1^1/_4$ pints) warm chicken or vegetable stock
- 3 tbsp tinned chopped tomatoes
- 250g (9oz) brown rice
- 50g (2oz) peas
- salt and pepper

pepper

peas

Equipment

- sieve
- small sharp knife
- chopping board
- large saucepan with lid
- wooden spoon

chopping board

saucepan

1 Put the rice in a sieve and rinse it under cold water until the water runs clear. Washing the rice before cooking stops the grains of rice sticking together.

2 Chop the onion into small pieces and set aside. Then carefully cut the chicken and ham into bite-sized pieces. Heat the oil in the large saucepan.

3 Fry the chicken and onion for 8 mins over a medium heat until the chicken is golden all over. Stir frequently to prevent sticking to the bottom of the pan.

Add the peas 2 minutes before the rice is cooked in step 5 for extra colour and goodness!

Did you know?

One seed of rice yields more than 3,000 grains. It is the highest yielding cereal grain and can grow in many kinds of environments.

4 Add the ham, garlic, red pepper, and chilli, and cook for 2 mins. Add the paprika, thyme, rice, stock, and tomatoes. Stir and bring to the boil.

5 Reduce the heat to low, cover the pan and simmer for 35 mins or until the rice is cooked and the stock is absorbed. Season the rice and stir before serving.

Food Facts

Rice is a staple food all over the world and its cultivation dates back to 5,000 BCE. It is an excellent source of energy. Brown rice is healthier than white rice because it contains fibre and richer amounts of vitamins and minerals. White rice has the husk, bran, and germ removed, which significantly reduces its nutritional value.

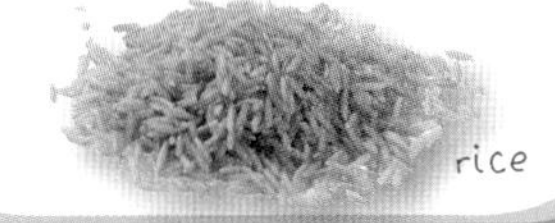
rice

• **Preparation** 20 mins • **Marinating** 1 hour • **Cooking** 20 mins • **Serves** 4

Colourful Kebabs

These are great fun to make and, of course, to eat! They would also make a perfect vegetarian dish for a summer barbecue.

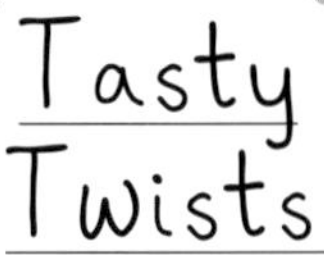

Tasty Twists

Cubes of chicken, beef, pork, lamb, or fish like salmon or tuna would all work in this recipe. Mushrooms, aubergine, and spring onion could also be added to the red pepper, red onion, and courgette.

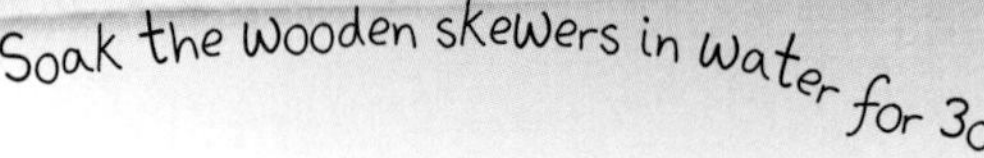

Soak the wooden skewers in water for 30 minutes to prevent them burning.

Ingredients

- 250g (9oz) firm tofu
- 2 small courgettes(each cut into 8)
- 2 medium red onions (peeled and each cut into 8 wedges)
- 1 medium red pepper (deseeded and cut into 16 chunks)
- 250g (9oz) egg noodles
- 1 tbsp toasted sesame seeds (optional)

noodles

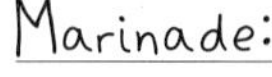

Marinade:

- 2 tbsp olive oil
- 1 tbsp soy sauce
- 3 tbsp black bean sauce
- 1 tbsp clear runny honey
- 2 cloves garlic, crushed
- salt and pepper

red onion

red pepper

Equipment

tongs

- large shallow dish
- sharp knife
- kitchen towel
- chopping board
- spoon
- 8 wooden or metal skewers
- pastry brush
- saucepan
- tongs and colander
- large dish

colander

1 Pat the tofu dry with some kitchen paper and then cut it into 16 cubes. Put the cubes into the dish with the courgettes, onions, and red pepper.

Tasty Twists

Swap the oriental marinade for a Mediterranean one. Mix together 4 tablespoons olive oil, 2 tablespoons balsamic vinegar, 2 crushed cloves garlic, and 1 tablespoon clear runny honey.

2 Mix the ingredients for the marinade in a large dish. Use a spoon to coat the tofu and vegetables in the marinade. Put in the fridge for at least 1 hour.

3 Preheat the grill to medium-high. Thread a piece of red pepper, tofu, red onion, and courgette onto a skewer. Repeat and then make 7 more kebabs.

Food Facts

Tofu is one of the few plant foods that is a complete protein. This means it contains a healthy balance of amino acids that are essential for repairing and maintaining your body. It is also low in fat and a good source of iron, calcium, magnesium, and vitamins B1, B2, and B3. Firm tofu can be fried, stir-fried, deep-fried, sautéed, or grilled. Because tofu itself is fairly bland, it is best marinated or used in recipes with strongly flavoured ingredients.

tofu

4 Place the kebabs on the grill and brush them with the marinade. Grill for 15–20 mins, turning halfway through and brushing with more marinade.

5 While the kebabs are cooking, bring a pan of water to the boil, add the noodles, and cook as instructed on the packet. Drain the noodles in a colander.

6 Serve two kebabs per person. Arrange some noodles on a plate and place the kebabs on top. Sprinkle the sesame seeds over the noodles.

- **Preparation** 20 mins
- **Cooking** 45 mins
- **Serves** 4

Sausage Hotpot

Fruit gives this savoury casserole a natural sweetness and an extra vitamin boost. Enjoy this winter warmer with fluffy mash and steamed green vegetables.

Tasty Twists

Turkey, pork, beef, or vegetarian sausages would all work in this recipe. The sausages are browned in step 2 and then slowly cooked through in the oven.

Ingredients

stock

- 2 eating apples
- 2 tbsp olive oil
- 6–8 sausages (turkey, pork, beef, or vegetarian)
- 1 onion (chopped)
- 1 carrot (diced)
- 2 cloves garlic (finely chopped)
- 1 tsp mixed herbs
- 1 tbsp tomato purée
- salt and pepper
- 110g (4oz) lean back bacon, cut into bite-sized pieces (optional)
- 400g (14oz) tinned borlotti or pinto beans (drained and rinsed)
- 400ml (14fl oz) chicken or vegetable stock
- 4 tbsp tinned chopped tomatoes

sausages

Equipment

chopping board

- vegetable peeler
- small sharp knife
- chopping board
- large ovenproof pan with lid (or large saucepan and large casserole dish with lid)
- oven gloves
- wooden spoon
- jug
- tongs

saucepan

1 Carefully remove the skin of the apples using a vegetable peeler. Quarter them and remove the core. Cut the apples into bite-sized pieces.

2 Preheat the oven to 200°C (400°F/Gas 6). Heat the oil in a large saucepan or ovenproof pan and cook the sausages for 5 minutes, or until browned all over.

Food Facts

There could be something in the saying that "An apple a day keeps the doctor away!" Apples are an excellent source of energy, antioxidants – especially vitamin C – and they help to clear toxins from the body.

apples

3 Remove the sausages from the pan and set aside. Put the onion and carrot into the pan and fry over a medium heat for 5 minutes, stirring frequently.

4 Next, add the garlic, bacon, and herbs, stir well, and cook for 6 minutes. (Transfer to a large casserole dish if you aren't using an ovenproof pan.)

Did you know?

Sausages were called "bangers" during the Second World War because they contained so much water they exploded when fried! Every day, 5 million Britons will eat sausages.

5 Add the beans, tomatoes, tomato purée, apples, and sausages and stir. Pour in the stock and bring to the boil. Add the beans and stir well.

6 Cover with a lid and place in the preheated oven. Cook for 25 minutes. The sauce should reduce and thicken and the apples will become tender.

7 Take care when removing the casserole dish from the oven as the hotpot will be very hot. Season with salt and pepper. Serve with mash and vegetables.

● **Preparation** 30 mins ● **Cooking** 30 mins ● **Serves** 4

Fish Sticks and Sweet Potato Wedges

Try this healthier version of traditional fish fingers and chips – it is easy to make and absolutely delicious!

Did you know?

Fish and chips shops first made an appearance in the UK at the end of the 19th century. Fish and chips quickly became Britain's most popular and famous fast food, and has remained so ever since.

Ingredients

- 400g (14oz) hoki fillets or other firm white fish (patted dry)
- 100g (3½oz) fine cornmeal or polenta
- 2 tsp Cajun spice mix or
- paprika (optional)
- 1 free-range egg (beaten)
- salt and pepper
- 2 tbsp olive oil

polenta

Sweet potato wedges

- 2 large sweet potatoes (scrubbed)

fish fillets

Equipment

- small sharp knife
- chopping board
- kitchen towel
- roasting tin
- plate
- baking tray
- tongs

chopping board

baking tray

1 Preheat the oven to 200°C (400°F/Gas 6). Cut the sweet potatoes in half and then cut each half into smaller wedges. Pat the wedges dry with kitchen roll.

2 Put half of the oil into a roasting tin and add the potato wedges. Coat them in the oil and bake for 30 minutes, turning halfway through cooking.

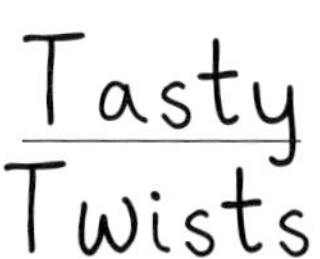

Tasty Twists

You could also use ordinary baking potatoes instead of the sweet potatoes to make these crisp potato wedges. Just follow the recipe in exactly the same way.

3 Meanwhile, cut the hoki into 1cm (½in strips). Mix the cornmeal or polenta and the spices together on a plate. Season with salt and pepper.

4 One at a time, dip each fish strip into the beaten egg and then roll it in the cornmeal mixture until evenly coated. Repeat with all the fish sticks.

5 Add the remaining oil to a baking tray and then the fish strips. When the wedges have been cooking for 25 minutes, put the fish strips in the oven.

6 Bake the fish strips for about 8 minutes, turning halfway through. They should be golden and cooked through. Serve with the potato wedges and peas.

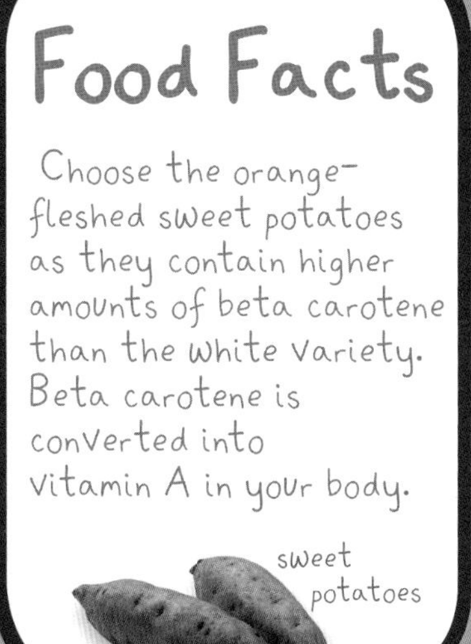

Food Facts

Choose the orange-fleshed sweet potatoes as they contain higher amounts of beta carotene than the white variety. Beta carotene is converted into vitamin A in your body.

• **Preparation** 20 mins • **Marinating** 1 hour • **Cooking** 10 mins • **Serves** 4

Rainbow Beef

Did you know?

Mangetout means "eat everything" in French, and they are so called because you eat the whole vegetable, including the pod. Mangetout are also called snow peas.

Stir-frying is a quick and easy way to make a colourful and nutritious meal. You could also serve this stir-fry with rice instead of noodles.

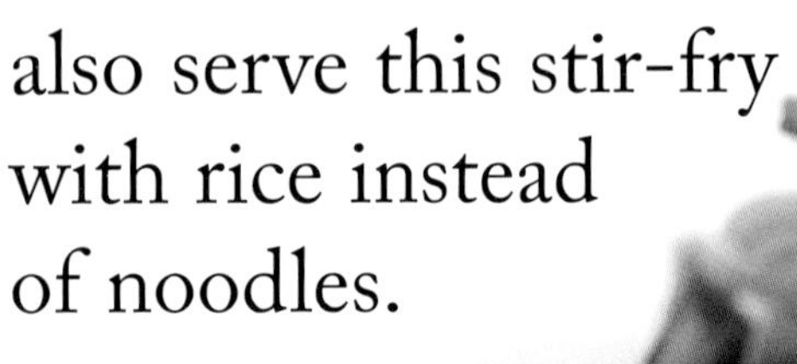

Ingredients

baby corn

- 300g (10½oz) lean beef (cut into thin strips)
- 1 tbsp sunflower oil
- 250g (9oz) medium egg noodles
- 1 red pepper (deseeded and cut into thin strips)
- 6 baby corn (halved)
- 75g (3oz) mangetout

mangetout

- 3 spring onions (sliced on the diagonal)
- 2 cloves garlic (chopped)
- 2 tsp grated fresh ginger
- 4 tbsp fresh orange juice

Marinade:

- 6 tbsp hoisin sauce
- 2 tbsp soy sauce
- 1 tbsp runny clear honey
- 1 tsp sesame oil

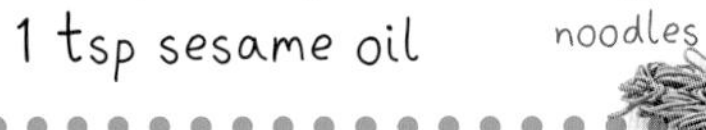

noodles

Equipment

tongs

- small sharp knife
- chopping board
- spoon
- shallow dish
- wok or large frying pan
- spatula or wooden spoon
- tongs
- medium saucepan
- colander

colander

1 Put the marinade ingredients in a shallow dish. Mix them together and then add the beef strips. Coat them in the marinade, cover and set aside for 1 hour.

2 Heat the sunflower oil in a wok or frying pan. Remove the beef from the marinade using tongs and carefully put it into the wok or frying pan.

3 Stirring continuously, fry the beef on a high heat for 1½ minutes or until browned all over. Remove the beef using the tongs and set aside.

4 Bring a saucepan of water to the boil. Add the noodles to the water, stir to separate them and then cook according to the packet instructions until tender.

Tasty Twists

Strips of pork and chicken are a good alternative to the beef, or you could try prawns or tofu. For the best flavour, it's important to marinate them first.

5 Add a little more oil to the wok if it looks dry. Add the red pepper, baby corn, mangetout, and spring onions. Stir-fry for 2 minutes.

6 Add the garlic, ginger, beef, and the leftover marinade and stir-fry for 1 minute. Pour in the orange juice, and cook, stirring, for another minute.

7 Drain the noodles in a colander and divide them between 4 shallow bowls. Spoon the vegetable and beef stir-fry over the noodles and serve.

• **Preparation** 15–20 mins • **Cooking** 15 mins • **Serves** 2

Noodle Soup

This is a healthy, filling, and complete meal in a bowl. Best of all, it only uses one saucepan so there is less to wash up afterwards!

Ingredients

lime

- 2 spring onions (trimmed and sliced diagonally)
- 2tsp of vegetable oil
- juice of 1/2 lime
- 1 thin slice of fresh ginger, peeled (optional)
- 600ml (1pt) fish stock (made with 1/3 of stock cube)
- 1tsp of soy sauce
- 60g (2oz) baby corn (halved)
- 75g (2 1/2oz) fine egg noodles
- 60g (2oz) sugar snap peas
- 1 drop of sesame oil
- 125g (4oz) ready-to-cook raw prawns (shelled)
- 2tsp of chopped fresh coriander (optional)

raw praws

baby corn

Equipment

- medium saucepan
- wooden spoon
- measuring jug

saucepan

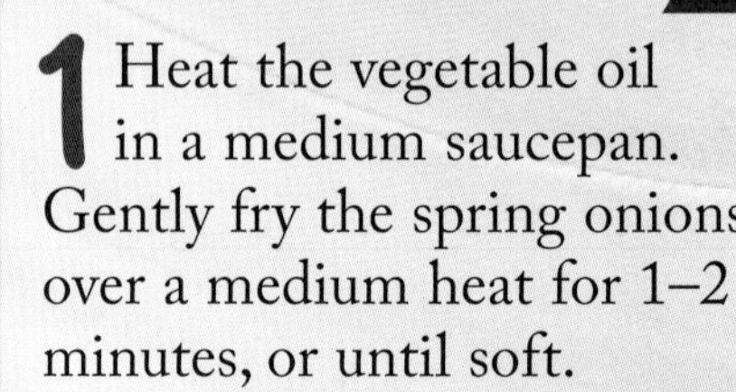

1 Heat the vegetable oil in a medium saucepan. Gently fry the spring onions over a medium heat for 1–2 minutes, or until soft.

2 Stir the ginger, stock, lime juice, and soy sauce into the spring onion and bring to the boil. Lower the heat and then simmer for 2–3 minutes.

3 Remove the ginger. Add the noodles and corn and bring to the boil. After 1½ minutes, add the sugar snap peas and cook for a further 1½ minutes.

4 Lower the heat to bring the soup back to a simmer. Stir in the prawns and cook them for 2–3 minutes, or until pink. Stir in the sesame oil and coriander.

Raw prawns are grey or white in colour, but they turn pink when they are cooked!

Food Facts

Do not overcook the prawns because it makes the texture rubbery! And if you are using frozen prawns, make sure that you defrost them completely before cooking them.

prawns

• **Preparation** 15–20 mins • **Cooking** 10-15 mins • **Makes** 8

Chicken Wraps

The combination of red and yellow peppers and green mange tout make these wraps look really colourful and the simple flavouring gives the chicken a refreshing zingy taste.

Don't overcook the vegetables they taste better slightly crunchy!

Tasty Twists

Vegetarians could use tofu instead of chicken or double the amount of vegetables.

ginger

lime

Ingredients

- 4 skinless and boneless chicken breasts (each cut into 6 strips)
- 1 small yellow pepper
- 1 small red pepper
- 125g (4oz) mange tout
- 8 flour tortillas
- juice of 1/2 lime
- 2.5cm (1in) fresh ginger, peeled and grated (optional)
- 2tbsp of clear runny honey
- 1 pinch of salt
- 1tbsp of sunflower oil
- 3-4 dashes of pepper sauce (optional)

sunflower oil

chicken breasts

Equipment

- 2 chopping boards
- vegetable knife
- sharp knife
- medium bowl
- small whisk
- wooden spatula
- large frying pan
- tongs
- ovenproof plate
- kitchen foil
- oven gloves

bowl

Tasty Twists

Chicken wraps taste great served with a dollop of guacamole and sour cream on the side.

1 Preheat the oven to 200°C (400°F/Gas 6). De-seed both peppers and slice them into 12 equal strips.

2 Mix the oil, honey, ginger, pepper sauce, and salt together in a bowl. Stir in the chicken strips until they are completely coated with the flavouring.

3 Heat the frying pan for 2 minutes. Add the coated chicken and fry it for 4–5 minutes. The chicken will turn golden and then caramelize.

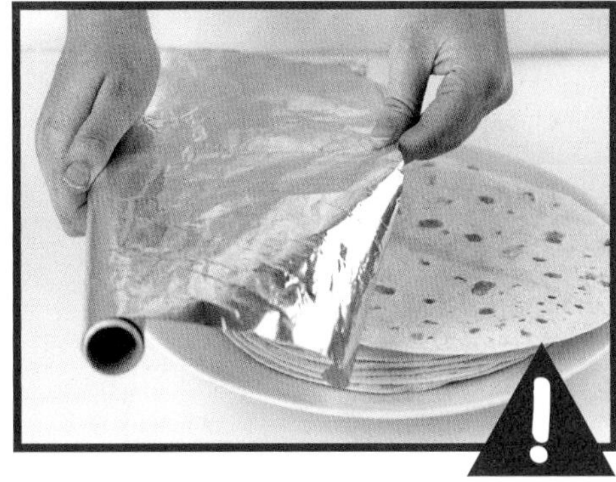

4 Place the tortillas on the ovenproof plate and cover with foil. Put them in the preheated oven for 6–7 minutes, or until they are warmed through.

Serving Tip

In step 5 the chicken and vegetables will continue to cook in the hot frying pan, so serve immediately or transfer them to a serving dish.

5 Add the peppers, mange tout, and lime juice to the chicken. Cook for 4–5 minutes on a medium–high heat. Stir occasionally to prevent sticking.

6 Lay some of the filling along the top of each tortilla, leaving the other end and sides empty. If you over-fill your tortilla, you will not be able to wrap it.

7 To wrap, fold the empty end inwards and overlap the sides. The filling should be securely wrapped but peeping out appetisingly from the open end!

- **Preparation** 20 mins • **Cooking** 25–30 mins • **Serves** 4–6

Pepperoni Pasta

This delicious recipe provides a wide range of nutrients, from carbohydrates in the pasta to protein in the sausage, and vitamins in the tomatoes and peppers.

Tasty Twists

Any type of cooked or cured sausage would taste delicious in this recipe and if you don't have sun-dried tomato paste, tomato purée will be fine.

Ingredients

salt and pepper

- 2 garlic cloves
- 1 red onion
- 1tsp of dried oregano
- 2 red peppers (roasted, peeled, and de-seeded)
- 125g (4oz) pepperoni
- 200ml (7fl oz) vegetable stock
- 4 dashes of pepper sauce (optional)

chopped tomato

spaghetti

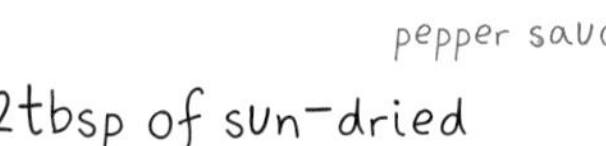
pepper sauce

- 2tbsp of sun-dried tomato paste
- 400g (13oz) tin chopped tomatoes
- 1tsp of Worcestershire sauce (optional)
- 1tbsp of caster sugar
- salt and pepper
- 75g (2 1/2oz) per person spaghetti
- 1tbsp of olive oil
- 10 fresh basil leaves (torn)

basil leaves

Equipment

- chopping board
- sharp knife
- garlic crusher
- 2 large saucepans
- wooden spoon
- slotted metal spoon
- colander
- pasta spoon

wooden spoon

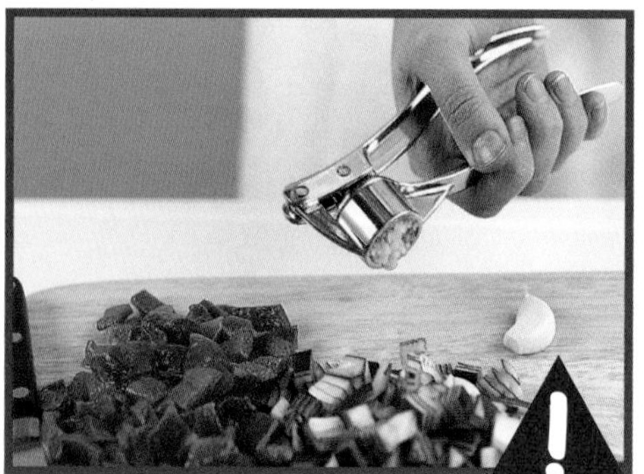

1 Dice the red onion and roasted peppers. Peel and crush the garlic cloves.

2 Cut the pepperoni into diagonal slices, about 1.5cm (¾in) thick. Add the oil to the saucepan and heat it over a medium heat.

3 Sauté the onion for 2–3 minutes. Add the garlic and oregano and cook for 1–2 minutes. Add the pepperoni and cook for a further 2 minutes.

A sprinkling of freshly grated Parmesan cheese adds extra flavour.

Serving Tip

Use the pasta spoon to transfer the spaghetti into pasta bowls. Season the sauce and serve it on top of the spaghetti.

4 Add the tomatoes, tomato paste, peppers, sugar, stock, Worcestershire and pepper sauces. Bring to the boil and then simmer for 20 minutes.

5 Half-fill a large saucepan with water and bring it to the boil. Add a pinch of salt then lower the spaghetti into the pan, using a slotted spoon.

6 Boil the pasta for 10–12 minutes (check the exact timings on the pack). Drain the pasta and then stir the fresh basil into the tomato sauce.

• **Preparation** 35–40 mins • **Cooking** 15–20 mins • **Serves** 2–4

Chicken Curry

Curry originally came from Asia, and this recipe is influenced by the fragrant curries of Thailand.

Ingredients

spring onions

mushrooms

olive oil

broccoli

wooden spoon

For the paste:

- 6 spring onions (trimmed and roughly chopped)
- 1 garlic clove
- 5cm (2in) piece fresh root ginger
- 20g (3/4oz) fresh coriander
- 20g (3/4oz) fresh coriander
- 1tsp of coriander seeds, crushed (optional)
- 2tsp of lemon zest
- 1tsp of lime zest
- 1tbsp of soft dark brown sugar
- 2tbsp of olive oil
- 2–3 drops of pepper sauce

For the curry:

- 200ml (7fl oz) coconut milk
- 2 skinless and boneless chicken breasts (cubed)
- 60g (2oz) per person long grain rice
- 200ml (7fl oz) chicken stock
- 125g (4oz) mushrooms (sliced)
- 225g (7½oz) broccoli (cut into florets)

Equipment

- chopping board
- sharp knife
- food processor
- wok or large saucepan
- wooden spoon
- medium saucepan with lid
- measuring jug

1 Peel and chop the ginger. Roughly chop the garlic and fresh coriander. Put all the paste ingredients into a processor and blend until smooth.

2 Place a wok or saucepan over a medium heat. Pour in half of the coconut milk and stir in half of the paste. Cook for 1 minute, stirring constantly.

3 Add the chicken and cook it for 3–4 minutes. Rinse the rice with cold water and tip it into a saucepan. Add double the amount of water to the rice.

For extra zing, you could add green or red chillies instead of the pepper sauce in step 1.

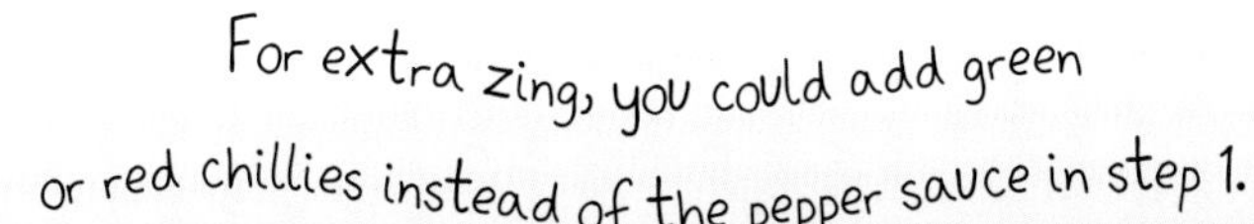

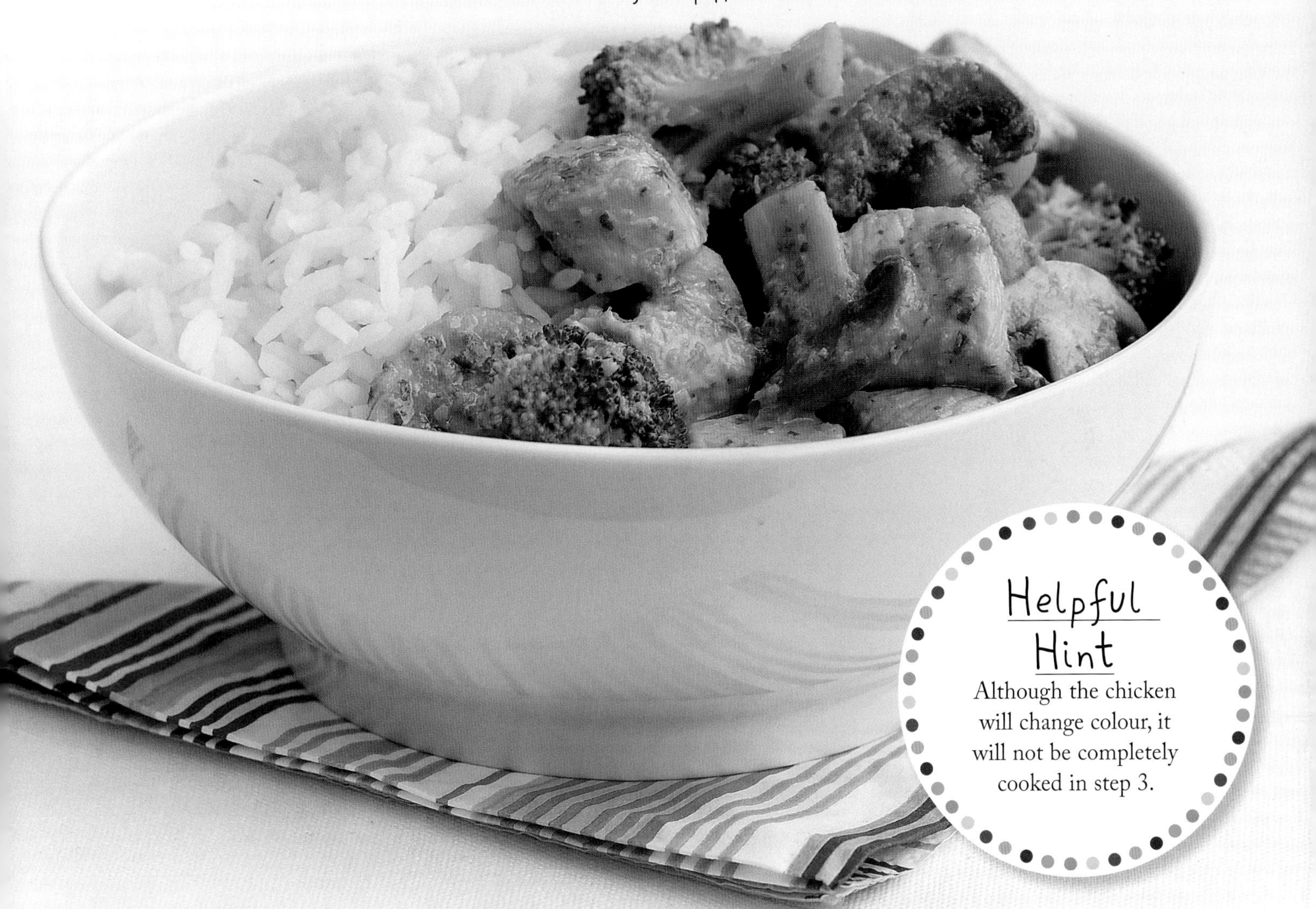

Helpful Hint

Although the chicken will change colour, it will not be completely cooked in step 3.

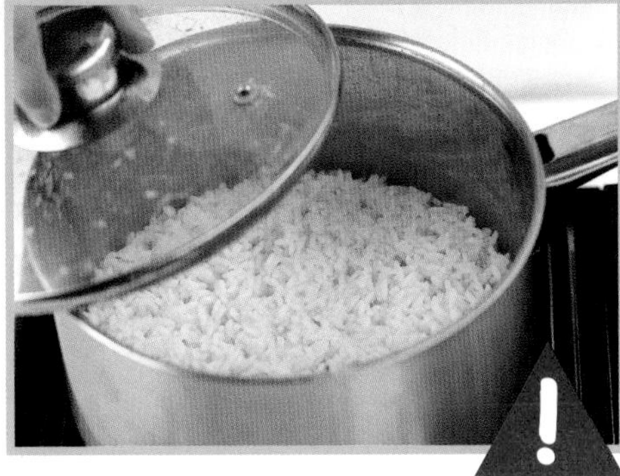

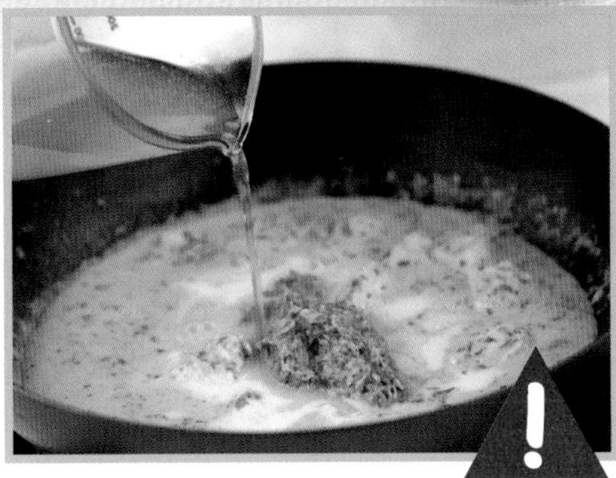

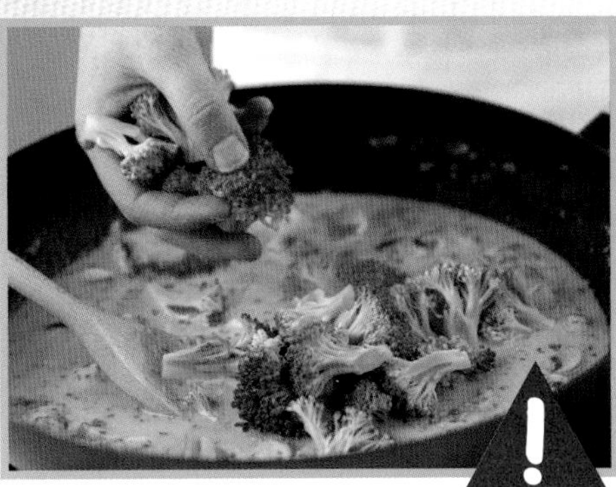

4 Cover the rice and bring it to the boil. Simmer until all the water is absorbed. If the rice is not quite cooked, add water and cook for a few more minutes.

5 While the rice is cooking, add the remaining coconut milk and paste to the wok. Add the stock, stir, and boil for 1 minute. Reduce the heat to a simmer.

6 Add the mushrooms and simmer for 1 minute. Then add the broccoli and simmer for a further 4–5 minutes. Serve with the cooked rice.

- **Preparation** 20 mins
- **Cooking** 15–20 mins
- **Serves** 2–4

Stir-fry With Noodles

Stir-frying is a quick way to cook – the ingredients are stirred continually over a high heat for a short amount of time so the vegetables remain crunchy. This recipe is made with tofu, a great alternative to meat that is high in protein and calcium.

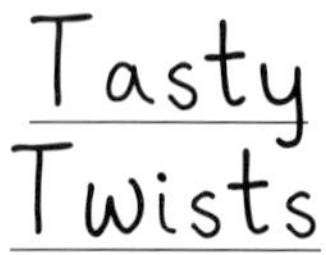

Tasty Twists

Chicken or prawns could be used instead of tofu but make sure you cook them thoroughly in step 4.

Ingredients

- 250g (8oz) firm tofu
- 2 spring onions (trimmed)
- 1 red pepper (de-seeded)
- 1 carrot (peeled)
- 2tsp of sunflower oil
- 60g (2oz) baby corn
- 75g (2½oz) per person dried medium egg noodles
- 60g (2oz) unsalted cashew nuts (optional)
- 60g (2oz) sugar snap peas

red pepper

Stir-fry sauce:

- 1tsp of clear runny honey
- 1tbsp of fresh orange juice
- 1tsp of sesame oil
- 1tbsp of soy sauce
- 2tbsp of sunflower oil

honey

sugar snap peas

egg noodles

Equipment

- medium saucepan with lid
- kitchen paper
- chopping board
- sharp knife
- jug
- whisk
- wok or large frying pan
- wooden spatula
- plate
- tongs
- colander
- pasta spoon

Helpful Hint

Cooking vegetables for only a short time means that they retain most of their nutrients, which can sometimes be lost through over-cooking.

1 Half-fill a medium saucepan with water, cover, and bring to the boil. Drain the tofu and pat it dry with kitchen paper. Cut the tofu into cubes.

2 Diagonally slice the spring onions. Cut the carrot in half and then into long sticks. Slice the pepper into strips and cut the corn in half.

3 To make the stir-fry sauce, whisk the honey, orange juice, sesame oil, sunflower oil, and soy sauce together in a small jug until they are fully mixed in.

4 Heat half of the oil and fry the tofu over a high heat for 7 minutes, or until golden. Take it out of the wok and place it on a plate lined with kitchen paper.

5 Lower the noodles into the boiling water. Bring the pan back to the boil and cook the noodles for 4 minutes or as instructed on the packet.

6 Use the remaining oil to stir-fry the spring onions, carrot, and pepper for 2–3 minutes. Add the corn, nuts, peas, and sauce. Stir-fry for 2 minutes.

7 Add the cooked tofu and stir-fry for a further 2 minutes. Drain the noodles and serve the stir-fried vegetables and tofu over the noodles.

• **Preparation** 20–30 mins • **Cooking** 1 hour • **Makes** 4 pies

Mashed Potato Pies

This recipe is a tasty variation on a traditional cottage pie. It is a filling and nutritious main meal and can easily be made with beef, pork, lamb, or vegetarian mince. If you don't have four small dishes, you can use one large dish instead.

Always use oven gloves to handle hot dishes.

potatoes

rosemary

Ingredients

- 1tbsp of olive oil
- 1 carrot
- 1 onion
- 2tsp of chopped rosemary leaves (optional)
- 500g (1lb) lean minced beef
- 1 garlic clove
- 1tbsp of tomato purée
- 150ml (1/4pt) beef stock
- 125g (4oz) mushrooms (quartered)
- 2tsp of Worcestershire sauce (optional)
- salt and pepper
- 400g (13oz) can chopped tomatoes

For the topping:

- 550g (1lb 2oz) potatoes
- 1 pinch of salt
- 2tbsp of milk
- 30g (1oz) unsalted butter
- 75g (2 1/2oz) cheese (grated)

cheese

minced beef

olive oil

tomato purèe

Equipment

- chopping board
- peeler
- oven gloves
- sharp knife
- garlic crusher
- 2 large saucepans
- wooden spoon
- colander
- masher
- four ovenproof dishes
- large baking tray
- slotted spoon
- teaspoon
- dessert spoon

knife

Serving Tip

Allow the pies to cool for a few minutes before eating them. They taste great served with vegetables, such as broccoli or peas.

Tasty Twists

These pies can also be made using vegetarian mince and vegetable stock for a meat-free alternative.

1 Preheat the oven to 200°C (400°F/Gas 6). Peel and dice the onion and carrot. Crush the garlic. (See p.296 for expert cutting and crushing tips.)

2 Heat the oil and fry the beef for 4 minutes or until browned, stirring constantly. Add the onion, carrot, rosemary, and garlic and fry for 3–5 minutes.

3 Add the mushrooms, stock, tomato purée, Worcestershire sauce, and tomatoes. Bring to the boil and then reduce to a simmer for 20 minutes. Season.

4 Half-fill a pan with water and bring it to the boil. Peel and chop the potatoes and add them to the pan, with the salt. Boil for 12–15 minutes, or until soft.

5 Drain the potatoes in a colander and then tip them back into the saucepan. Mash the potatoes with the milk, butter, and half of the cheese.

6 Place the dishes on a baking tray and divide the meat filling equally between them, using a slotted spoon. Top each with a quarter of the mashed potato.

7 Sprinkle the remaining cheese on top of the mashed potato and bake the pies for 25–30 minutes, or until they are golden and bubbling.

• **Preparation** 35–40 mins • **Cooking** 14–16 mins • **Chilling** 30 mins • **Makes** 18 meatballs

Meatballs With Salsa

Give classic meatballs a sweet and sour twist with this tasty recipe. Grilling is healthier than frying, and using skewers makes it much safer and easier to cook the meatballs evenly. When using skewers, you must soak them in water for at least 1 hour so that they don't splinter or burn during cooking.

Chilling the meatballs before cooking stops them from falling apart.

lime

Ingredients

- 2 medium slices of bread
- 1tbsp of soy sauce
- 1/2 small red onion (roughly chopped)
- 1 garlic clove (chopped)
- zest of 1 lime
- 1 egg yolk
- 1tbsp of tomato ketchup
- 500g (1lb) minced pork

For the Salsa:

- 1tsp of fresh lime juice
- 1–2 drops of pepper sauce (optional)
- 2–3 pinches of caster sugar
- 1 small tin pineapple pieces (drained)
- 12 cherry tomatoes (quartered)
- 3 spring onions (trimmed and finely chopped)
- salt and pepper
- 1tsp of olive oil

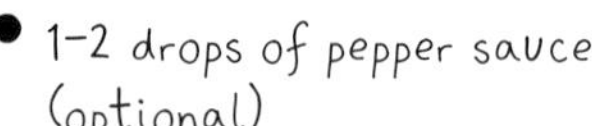

minced pork

chopped spring onions

red onion

Equipment

- bread knife
- chopping board
- food processor
- 2 large mixing bowls
- wooden spoon
- plate
- cling film
- dessert spoon
- 6 wooden skewers
- oven gloves
- grill rack and foil-lined tray
- fork
- bowl

knife

1 Cut the crusts off and tear the bread into chunks. Put the bread into the food processor and blend it until it becomes fine breadcrumbs.

2 Tip the breadcrumbs into a bowl. Put the onion and garlic into the food processor and finely blend them. Add them to the bowl of breadcrumbs.

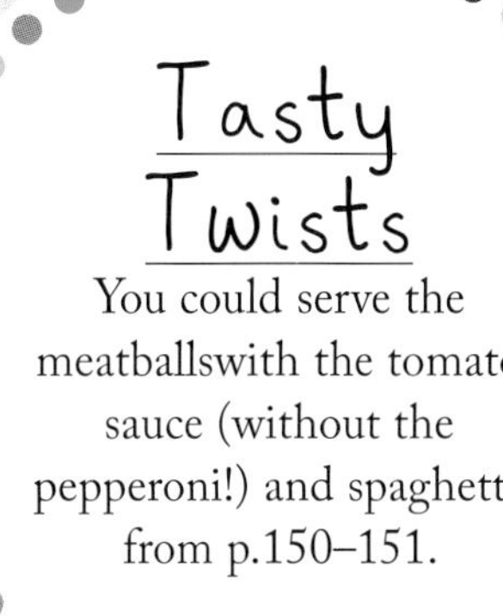

Tasty Twists

You could serve the meatballswith the tomato sauce (without the pepperoni!) and spaghetti from p.150–151.

3 Add the meat, lime zest, tomato ketchup, soy sauce, and egg yolk to the bowl. Using a wooden spoon or your fingers, mix until fully combined.

4 Using your hands, shape the meat mixture into 18 equal balls. Place the meatballs on a plate, cover with cling film, and chill them for 30 minutes.

5 Put the pineapple into a mixing bowl and stir in the spring onions, tomatoes, lime juice, pepper sauce, sugar, and olive oil. Season and set aside.

6 Preheat the grill to a medium heat. Carefully place 3 meatballs on each skewer. Grill them for 14–16 minutes, turning them every 3–4 minutes.

7 When the meatballs are cooked completely, use a fork to slide them carefully off the skewers. Serve the meatballs with some salsa on the side.

- **Preparation** 45–50 mins
- **Cooking** 1 hour 15 mins
- **Serves** 6–8

Roasted Vegetable Lasagne

For this recipe, it is important to use the type of dried lasagne that does not need pre-cooking. Check the packet to make you sure that you buy the right kind! Fresh lasagne would also be fine but you would have to reduce the cooking time.

Ingredients

aubergine

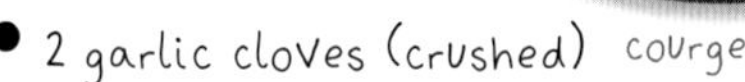
courgettes

- 2 large red onions
- 2 large carrots (peeled)
- 2 large courgettes
- 2 red peppers (de-seeded)
- 1 medium aubergine
- 2tsp of chopped fresh rosemary
- 1 tbsp of tomato purée
- 2 yellow peppers (de-seeded)
- 400g (13oz) can chopped tomatoes
- 9 dried lasagne sheets
- salt and pepper

lasagne sheets

- 2 garlic cloves (crushed)
- 4tbsp of olive oil

For the sauce:

- 500ml (17fl oz) warm milk
- 60g (2oz) unsalted butter
- 30g (1oz) plain flour
- salt and pepper
- 125g (4oz) Parmesan cheese (grated)

Parmesan cheese

yellow peppers

tomato pureé

Equipment

- chopping board
- sharp knife
- roasting tin
- oven gloves
- large saucepan
- wooden spoon
- small saucepan
- whisk
- serving spoon
- lasagne dish (approx 25 x 18cm and 5cm deep or 10 x 7in and 2in deep)

knife

Tasty Twists

For an alternative filling, try the meat mixture from the mashed potato pies on p. 156–157.

Helpful Hint

If your sauce goes lumpy in step 4, don't worry! Sieve out the lumps, before you add the cheese.

1 Preheat the oven to 220°C (425°F/Gas 7). Cut the onions into wedges and then chop the carrots, courgettes, aubergine, and peppers into chunks.

2 In the roasting tin, mix the oil, rosemary, and garlic with the vegetables and season. Roast for 35 minutes, shaking the tin occasionally.

3 Gently warm the tomatoes and tomato purée through in a large saucepan. Take the pan off the heat and carefully stir in the roasted vegetables.

4 Over a low heat, melt the butter in a small pan. Stir in the flour for 1 minute and whisk in the milk. Stir until thickened. Add half the cheese and season.

5 Lower the oven to 190°C (375°F/Gas 5). Spoon a third of the vegetables into the base of the lasagne dish and top with 3 lasagne sheets.

6 Add another third of the vegetables and pour over half the sauce. Top with another layer of lasagne sheets and add the remaining vegetables.

7 Finally add the 3 remaining lasagne sheets and sauce. Sprinkle the cheese over the top and bake for 35 minutes or until golden and bubbling.

Tuna Fishcakes

Like all oily fish, tuna contains vitamins and minerals that are good for the brain, skin, and eyes. This recipe involves shallow frying, like the falafel in p.88–89. This gives the fishcakes a crispy, golden coating but it is important to drain them on kitchen paper in step 6 to remove the excess oil.

Ingredients

salad leaves

- 250g (8oz) potatoes (peeled and chopped)
- 1 pinch of salt
- 350g (11½oz) tinned tuna (drained weight)
- 2tsp of Dijon mustard
- 1 spring onion (trimmed and finely chopped)
- salt and pepper
- 2tsp of chopped fresh parsley
- 90g (3oz) plain flour
- 150g (5oz) breadcrumbs (approx 7 slices, without crusts)
- 2 eggs
- 200ml (7fl oz) vegetable oil

lemon

To serve:

- salad leaves
- lemon or lime wedges

tuna

Equipment

- medium saucepan
- colander
- masher
- mixing bowl
- fork
- large plate
- cling film
- dish
- 2 medium plates
- medium sauté or frying pan
- slotted metal spatula
- kitchen paper

frying pan

1 Half-fill the saucepan with water. Add the potato and a pinch of salt. Bring the water to the boil and cook for 12–15 minutes or until soft.

2 Thoroughly drain the potatoes and put them back into the pan. Mash and leave them to one side until they are cool enough to handle in step 4.

3 Break the tuna into small pieces in a bowl. Stir in the mashed potato, mustard, spring onion, and parsley until they are fully mixed in. Season.

Serving Tip

Fry the fishcakes in batches of 2 or 4 and keep the cooked ones warm in the oven. Serve with salad and lemon or lime wedges.

Use tuna in spring water or brine rather than oil, because it is lower in fat.

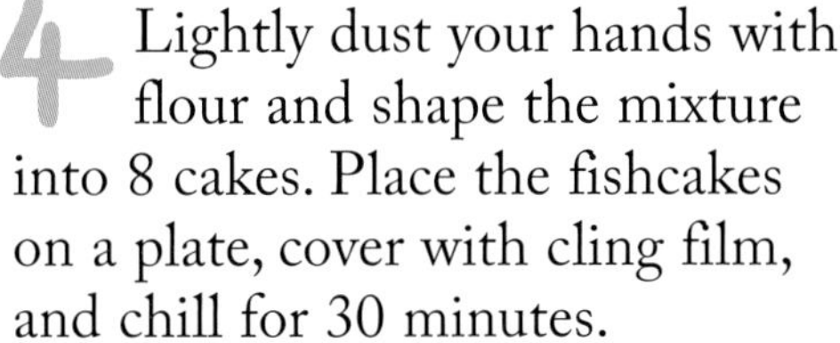

4 Lightly dust your hands with flour and shape the mixture into 8 cakes. Place the fishcakes on a plate, cover with cling film, and chill for 30 minutes.

5 Beat the eggs together in a dish and put the breadcrumbs and flour on separate plates. Coat each fishcake in flour, egg, and then breadcrumbs.

6 Heat the oil over a medium heat. Shallow fry the cakes for 2 minutes on each side, or until golden. Drain them on a plate lined with kitchen paper.

Preparation 20–25 mins • **Standing** 30 mins • **Cooking** 30–35 mins • **Makes** 12

Sausage Popovers

The secret to good popovers is to make sure that the oil is very hot in step 3 before you add the sausages and then the batter in step 4. Leaving the batter to stand for half an hour before cooking also helps to give the popovers a lighter texture.

Ingredients

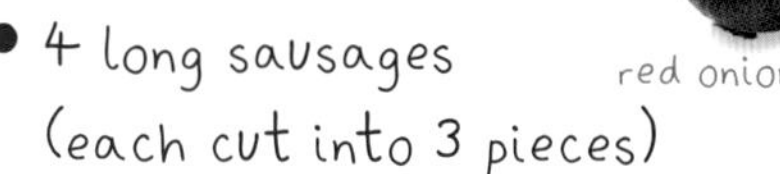

- 1 pinch of salt
- 3 eggs
- 250ml (8fl oz) milk
- 4tbsp of vegetable oil
- 1tsp of snipped fresh chives (optional)
- 150g (5oz) plain flour
- 1tbsp of wholegrain mustard (optional)
- 4 long sausages (each cut into 3 pieces)

Onion gravy:

- 1tbsp of vegetable oil
- 1tsp of dark brown soft sugar
- 1tsp of balsamic vinegar (optional)
- 1 small red onion (thinly sliced)
- 15g (1/2oz) unsalted butter
- 300ml (1/2pt) beef stock
- 1tbsp of plain flour

Equipment

- sieve
- mixing bowl
- ramekin
- whisk
- oven gloves
- non-stick 12-hole muffin tray
- tongs
- ladle
- small plate
- small saucepan
- wooden spoon

mixing bowl

Tasty Twists

For a plain popover, leave out the chives, mustard, and sausage. Heat the oil in the tray, as in step 3, and cook the batter for 18-20 minutes.

Serving Tip

Pour the onion gravy over the popovers and serve with vegetables, such as peas. Sieve the gravy if you prefer a smoother sauce.

1 Preheat the oven to 220°C (425°F/Gas 7). Sieve the flour and salt into a bowl and make a hole in the centre. Crack the eggs and add them, one by one.

2 Using a whisk, beat the milk into the eggs and flour until you have a smooth batter, with no lumps. Stir in the chives and mustard (optional).

3 Add 1tsp of oil to each muffin hole and heat the tray in the oven for 3 minutes. Take the hot tray out of the oven and add some sausage to each hole.

4 Put the tray back into the oven for 4 minutes. Remove the tray and half-fill each hole with batter. Put it back in the oven and cook for 18–20 minutes.

5 Meanwhile, heat the oil in the saucepan and stir in the onion, sugar, and vinegar. Gently cook the onion for 10 minutes until soft and browned.

6 Spoon the onion out of the pan onto a plate and melt the butter in the same pan. Add the flour and stir for 30 seconds, or until browned.

7 Add the stock and bring it to the boil. Boil for 1 minute, and then add the onion. Lower the heat and then simmer for 10 minutes, or until thickened.

- **Preparation** 20–30 mins
- **Cooking** 1h 20 mins
- **Serves** 4

Roast Chicken

Everyone loves an old-fashioned roast dinner! With this easy-to-follow recipe, you can produce a meal to be proud of. Make sure you read the recipe carefully and check that the chicken is cooked properly in steps 5 and 6.

Serving Tip

Serve your roast chicken with mashed potato and your favourite vegetables, such as peas and carrots. It also tastes great with a splash of gravy.

Ingredients

- 1.5kg (3lb) whole chicken
- 75g (2½oz) unsalted butter (softened)
- salt and pepper
- 1 lemon + 1 tsp of zest
- 1tbsp of fresh thyme leaves + 2 extra sprigs

To serve:

- mashed potato
- 175g (6oz) peas
- 2 carrots

carrots

peas

thyme

chicken

Equipment

- chopping board
- kitchen paper
- small mixing bowl
- 2 dessert spoons
- sharp knife
- string
- roasting tin
- oven gloves
- rack
- tray
- carving knife

chopping board

1 Preheat the oven to 200°C (400°F/Gas 6). Rinse inside the chicken with cold water. Place it on a board and pat it dry, inside and out, with kitchen paper.

2 To make the stuffing, mix the softened butter with the thyme leaves, lemon zest, salt, and pepper in a bowl until it forms a smooth mixture.

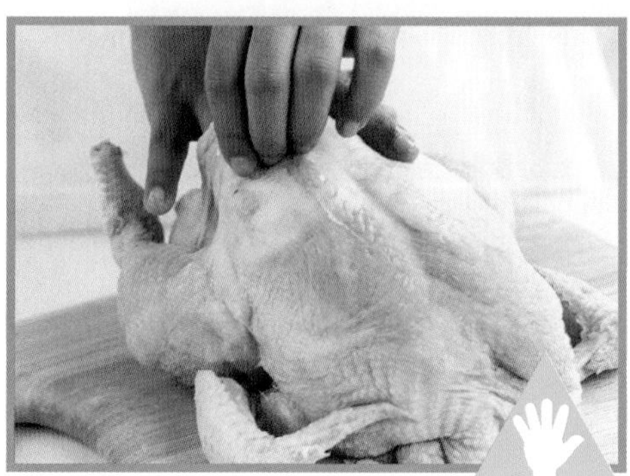

3 Lift the skin at the top of the breastbone and slide your hand in to form pockets on either side. Stuff half of the flavoured butter into each pocket.

Helpful Hint

Tying the chicken's legs together in step 4 helps the chicken to keep its shape during cooking. You should also tuck the wing tips underneath.

4 Cut the lemon in half. Place one half inside the chicken, with the thyme sprigs. Tie the legs together with string and put the chicken into a roasting tin.

5 Season the chicken and roast it for 1 hour 20 minutes, or until golden brown. Baste the meat after 30 minutes and then every 15 minutes after that.

6 Carefully transfer the cooked chicken to a rack (over a tray to catch any drips) and leave to rest for 10–15 minutes before carving and serving.

• **Preparation** 15 mins • **Cooking** 70 mins • **Makes** 16

Cheesy Potato Skins

Crispy bacon and melted cheese make these potato skins a firm favourite. If you and your friends don't like bacon, substitute it with tuna or chicken or leave it out completely.

Ingredients

cheddar cheese

- 4 large baking potatoes
- oil for brushing
- 8 rashers smoked streaky bacon
- 2.5ml (1/2tsp) paprika
- 50g (2oz) mature Cheddar cheese, grated
- 50g (2oz) mozzarella cheese, grated

onion

- 6 spring onions, chopped

Dip:

- 150ml (1/4pt) sour cream
- 60ml (4tsp) fresh chives

potatoes

Equipment

- fork
- pastry brush
- baking sheet
- knife
- chopping board
- wooden spoon
- frying pan
- 2 spoons
- small bowl

chopping board

wooden spoon

1 Preheat the oven to 200°C, 400°F, gas mark 6. Prick the potatoes with a fork and brush them with oil. Bake for 1 hour, until cooked. Cool slightly.

2 Cut up the bacon rashers into small pieces. Place the bacon in a frying pan and dry fry, until lightly browned.

3 Cut the potatoes in half and scoop out the flesh with a spoon, leaving a thin layer. Cut each potato in half lengthways to make boat shapes.

4 Place on a baking sheet, season and sprinkle over a little paprika. Top with half of the bacon pieces. Mix together the cheeses and spring onions and sprinkle over the potatoes. Top with the remaining bacon.

5 Return the potato skins to the oven until golden. Cool for 10 minutes. Mix together the dip ingredients and serve with the skins.

Helpful Hints

Make sure the potatoes get really crispy in the oven – it will be worth the wait!

These easy-to-make filled potato skins are a delicious option for a party!

Desserts

Desserts

Fruit Purée

Simple fruit sauces are a tasty and nutritious accompaniment to yoghurt, ice cream, and many other dishes. You need fruit with a soft, juicy texture such as mangoes, berries, or nectarines. Purée your fruit a blender, adding a little sugar if necessary.

Banana Custard

Mix together equal quantities of plain bio yoghurt and ready-made custard. Pile sliced bananas into a dish and pour over the yoghurt mixture. Stewed apples could be used instead.

Being healthy doesn't mean you have to avoid desserts – a balanced diet means that you can eat most things, in moderation. In fact, dessert is an ideal opportunity to get more fruit into your diet! Just remember desserts and cakes can be high in fat, so eat sensibly. There's something for everyone in this section, from fruity jelly to crunchy crumble and from lovely lollies to apple muffins. Here are some more simple ideas for tasty desserts to try.

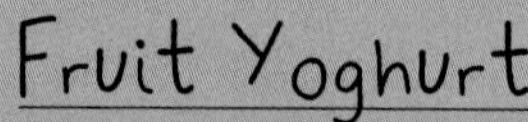

Fruit Yoghurt

Shop-bought yoghurts are often high in sugar and low in fruit so make your own healthy versions by stirring fresh fruit purée (see above) into thick plain bio or live yoghurt.

Mini Crumbles

Preheat the oven to 180°C (350°F/ Gas 4). Sprinkle 2 tbsp of the crumble mixture from p.186–187 over 3 peaches or nectarines (halved and stoned). Place the fruit on a baking dish. Pour a little water into the dish to prevent the fruit drying out. Cook in the oven for 20 minutes.

Homemade Fruit Spread

Put 110g (4oz) ready-to-eat dried apricots and 110g (4oz) ready-to-eat dried dates in a saucepan with 425ml (15fl oz) water. Bring to the boil, reduce the heat, cover, and simmer for 45 minutes. Transfer to a blender, add 5 tbsp of water and blend to a purée. Store in a jar in the fridge for up to 1 week.

Chocolate Banana

Preheat the oven to 180°C (350°F/ Gas 4). Slice a banana lengthways, but not all the way through. Press cubes of chocolate into the gap and then wrap the banana in a foil. Bake for 20 minutes, until the chocolate has melted.

Popcorn

Pour 1 tbsp sunflower oil into a medium saucepan. Heat the oil then add a thin layer of popcorn (one kernel deep). Put the lid on the pan and cook over a medium heat, shaking the pan occasionally, until the corn has popped. Caution – don't remove the lid until the sound of popping has stopped!

Warm Fruit Salad

Cook your favourite dried fruits in a little water over a low heat for about 20 minutes, or until soft and plump. Add a cinnamon stick and a little ground nutmeg if you like and serve with natural yoghurt.

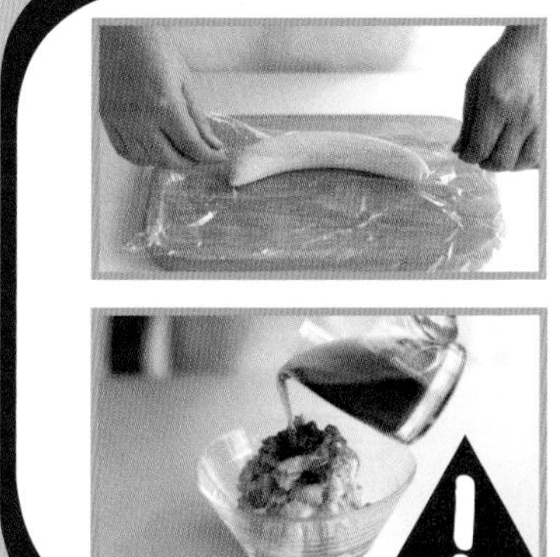

Banana Ice Cream

Wrap a peeled banana in cling film. Freeze for about 2 hours or until solid then remove the cling film and whiz in a food processor until roughly chopped. Serve in a bowl with a drizzle of maple syrup and a sprinkling of nuts.

• **Preparation** 10 mins • **Cooking** none • **Serves** 4–6

Melon Fruit Bowl

This colourful dessert is packed with the tasty goodness of fresh fruit. Best of all, you can eat the "bowl" afterwards!

Did you know?

There is more sugar in a lemon than in a strawberry! Strawberries are the only fruit whose seeds grow on the outside.

Ingredients

- 1/2 large Cantaloupe melon
- 150–200g (5–7oz) fruit such as chopped pums, apricots, grapes, strawberries, raspberries or blackberries, or slices of nectarine, peach, orange, apple, or kiwi
- 4 tbsp fresh orange juice

orange juice

strawberries

Equipment

- sharp knife
- chopping board
- melon baller or teaspoon
- large mixing bowl

melon baller

1 Scoop the seeds out of the centre of the melon and throw them away. Slice a sliver off the base of the melon so it stands up and place it on a serving plate.

Food Facts

Melons, especially those with an orange flesh, contain plentiful amounts of beta carotene. This is necessary for good vision, healthy skin, and growth. Vitamin C is also found in this juicy fruit.

melon

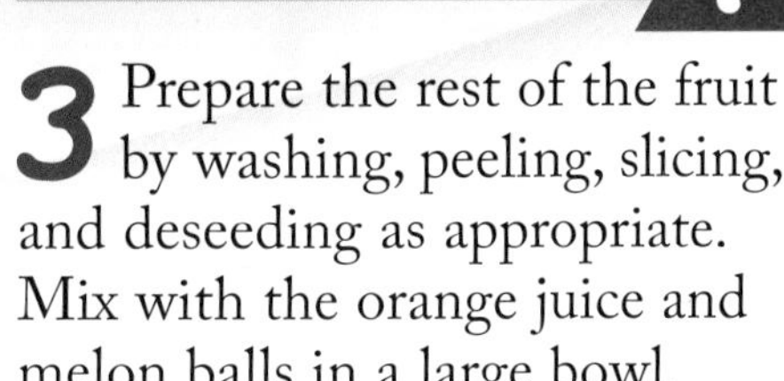

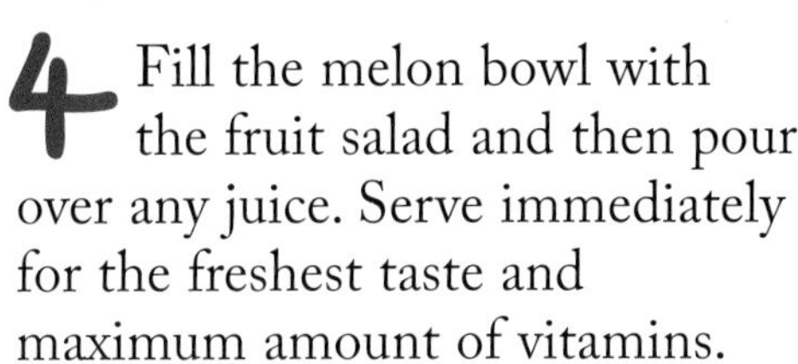

2 Use a melon baller or teaspoon to scoop out most of the melon flesh. Leave an even 1cm (½in) border in your hollowed out bowl shape.

3 Prepare the rest of the fruit by washing, peeling, slicing, and deseeding as appropriate. Mix with the orange juice and melon balls in a large bowl.

4 Fill the melon bowl with the fruit salad and then pour over any juice. Serve immediately for the freshest taste and maximum amount of vitamins.

• **Preparation** 15 mins • **Freezing** overnight (or at least 8 hours) • **Serves** 6–8

Tropical Yoghurt Ice

Bursting with vitamins from the fresh fruit, this cool and creamy yoghurt ice a healthy alternative to ice cream. Natural bio yoghurt has a smooth, creamy taste but is much lower in fat than cream. It contains beneficial bacteria that are good for your digestive system and is also rich in calcium.

Tasty Twists

Strawberries, plums, nectarines, raspberries and peaches taste just as good as the mango and banana. You will need about 450g (1lb) fruit.

Did you know?

More than 50% of the world's mangoes are grown in India. Mangoes belong to the same family as the cashew, pistachio, and poison ivy.

Ingredients

- 2 medium ripe mangoes
- 2 medium bananas, peeled
- 500g (1lb 2oz) thick natural bio yoghurt
- 3 tbsp icing sugar
- squeeze lemon juicex

bananas

yoghurt

Equipment

- sharp knife
- chopping board
- blender or food processor
- spoon
- plastic container with lid
- whisk or fork
- ice cream scoop

ice cream scoop

1 To prepare each mango, cut away the two sides close to the stone. Taking the two large slices, cut the flesh into a criss-cross pattern down to the skin.

2 Press each mango half inside out and carefully cut off the cubes of mango. Cut away any remaining mango near the stone. Repeat with the second mango.

3 Break the bananas into chunks and put them into a blender. Then add the mango, yoghurt, sugar, and a squeeze of lemon juice.

Remove the ice cream from the freezer 30 mins before you want to eat it.

4 Blend until the mixture becomes thick and creamy. Pour the mixture into a shallow container, securely attach the lid, and put it into the freezer.

5 After 2–3 hours whisk the mixture with a fork to break down any ice crystals. Freeze and repeat after 3 hours to give the yoghurt ice a creamy texture.

Food Facts

Mangoes are rich in vitamin C and beta carotene, and are also a good source of vitamins A and B. However, these nutrients are greatly reduced when mangoes are cooked.

• **Preparation** 10 mins • **Freezing** overnight (or at least 6 hours) • **Makes** 4–8

Peach and Orange Lollies

These refreshing ice lollies only take a few minutes to make and are a fun way to introduce fruit into your diet. Add thick natural yoghurt to make a frozen yoghurt lolly.

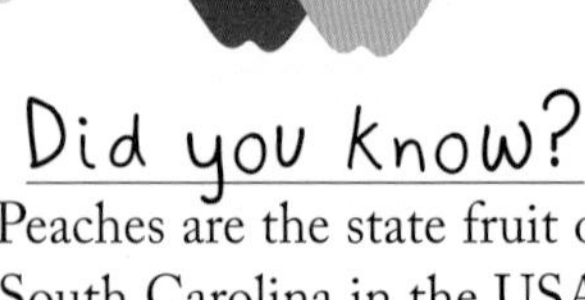

Did you know?

Peaches are the state fruit of South Carolina in the USA, while Georgia is known as the "Peach State".

Ingredients

- 3 ripe peaches or nectarines
- 300ml (10fl oz) fresh orange juice
- 1–2 tbsp icing sugar
- 4 heaped tbsp tinned fruit salad in natural juice, drained (optional)

glacé cherries

orange juice

Equipment

- small sharp knife
- chopping board
- large slotted spoon
- 2 bowls
- blender
- 4 ice lolly moulds

lolly moulds

1 Peaches can be tricky and messy to peel so here is a simple way to do it. Using a slotted spoon, lower the fruit into a bowl of boiling water.

2 After about 30 seconds, remove the fruit and then immediately plunge it into a bowl of cold water. The skin should peel away easily.

Tasty Twists

You could layer different fruits such as berries, mangoes, kiwis, oranges, or bananas but you must partially freeze each layer for 45 minutes before adding the next or they will all mix together.

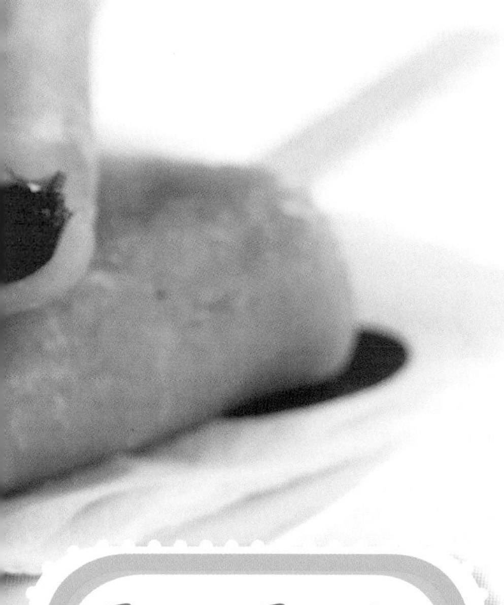

3 Carefully slice the fruit away from the stone and put it into a blender. Add the orange juice and 1 tablespoon of the icing sugar.

4 Blend the peaches, orange juice, and icing sugar until smooth and frothy. Taste the juice and add the rest of the icing sugar if necessary.

Food Facts

Peaches are full of vitamin C and are also a good source of potassium and fibre. They contain beta carotene, which the body converts to vitamin A. Nectarines are a smooth-skinned variety of peaches.

peaches

5 Spoon half of the fruit salad into the 4 moulds. Pour the juice over each mould until it is half full. Add the rest of the fruit salad and top up with fruit juice.

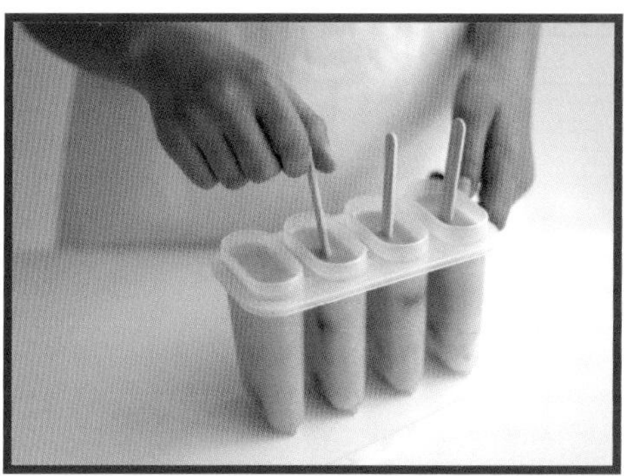

6 Insert the stick into the mould then freeze for at least 6 hours. Before eating, take the lollies out of the freezer and let them soften slightly.

• **Preparation** 20 mins • **Chilling** at least 6 hours but preferably overnight • **Serves** 4–6

Sunshine Jelly

Even though this healthier version of jelly is made with fruit juice and fresh oranges, it still contains sugar and should only be eaten as an occasional treat.

Tasty Twists

Mango, nectarine, peach, or cherry would all taste great in this recipe, but any fruity flavours of jelly would work well.

Did you know?

Jelly was first eaten in Ancient Egypt. In the UK, jelly and ice cream is a popular dessert, especially for children.

Ingredients

- 2 oranges
- 1 x 85g packet vegetarian real fruit lemon jelly granules
- 100ml (7fl oz) fresh orange juice

oranges

Equipment

sharp knife

- small sharp knife
- 600ml (1 pint) jelly mould or glass bowl
- jug
- serving plate

mixing bowl

1 Cut a thin slice off one end of an orange to help it stand up on a plate or chopping board. Carefully slice downwards to remove the skin and pith.

2 Cut the orange into thin, round slices. Arrange some of the orange slices on the base and sides of the jelly mould or glass bowl.

3 Pour the orange juice into a jug, add the jelly granules and carefully top up with boiling water to make 600ml (1 pint) in total.

4 Stir gently until the jelly granules dissolve. Carefully pour half of the warm liquid jelly into the jelly mould, on top of the orange slices.

5 Put the remaining orange slices on top of the jelly and then pour over the rest of the liquid jelly. Leave to cool, then chill for at least 6 hours to set.

Helpful Hint

Pineapple, kiwi, papaya, pawpaw, and figs are not suitable for this recipe because they contain enzymes which break down the jelly and stop it from setting.

6 Place a serving plate on top of the mould and then carefully turn it over so the plate is underneath – the jelly should slip out easily on to the plate.

Food Facts

Like all citrus fruits, oranges are a great source of vitamin C and they are full of natural sweetness and taste. It's better to use freshly squeezed fruit juice rather than one made from concentrates because a lot of the nutrients are lost during the manufacturing process

orange juice

• **Preparation** 20 mins • **Cooking** 2 mins • **Makes** 18

Fruit Sticks with Chocolate Orange Dip

This dessert is fun to make, and even more fun to eat! It is great for parties and works with any of your favourite fruits.

chocolate

Ingredients

- ½ cantaloupe melon (seeds scooped out)
- 1 small pineapple
- 3 kiwi fruit (peeled)
- 18 strawberries

Chocolate Orange Dip:

- 150ml (5fl oz) milk
- 100g (3½ oz) milk or plain chocolate (broken into tiny pieces)
- zest of 1 orange (grated)

strawberries

melon

Equipment

- medium saucepan
- wooden spoon
- sharp knife
- chopping board
- melon baller or teaspoon
- 18 wooden cocktail sticks

melon baller

1 Pour the milk into a saucepan, add the grated orange zest. Bring the milk to the boil. Carefully, remove the pan from the heat, and add the chocolate.

2 Gently stir the milk until the chocolate has melted. Pour the sauce into a bowl and leave it to cool slightly while your prepare the fruit sticks.

Tasty Twists

Use any of your favourite fruits in this recipe.The fruit sticks also taste delicious dipped into a yoghurt or fruit sauce.

1 Top and tail the pineapple using a knife. Hold the pineapple upright on a chopping board and cut downwards to remove the skin.

2 Slice the pineapple and quarter each slice. Cut off the core and eyes. Halve the melon and scoop out the flesh in balls, with a melon baller or teaspoon.

3 Top and tail each kiwi fruit. Holding the fruit upright, slice downwards, away from you, to remove the skin. Then cut it into large chunks

4 Thread some pineapple, a melon ball, a strawberry, and a chunk of kiwi onto a cocktail stick. Repeat for all 18 sticks and serve with the chocolate dip.

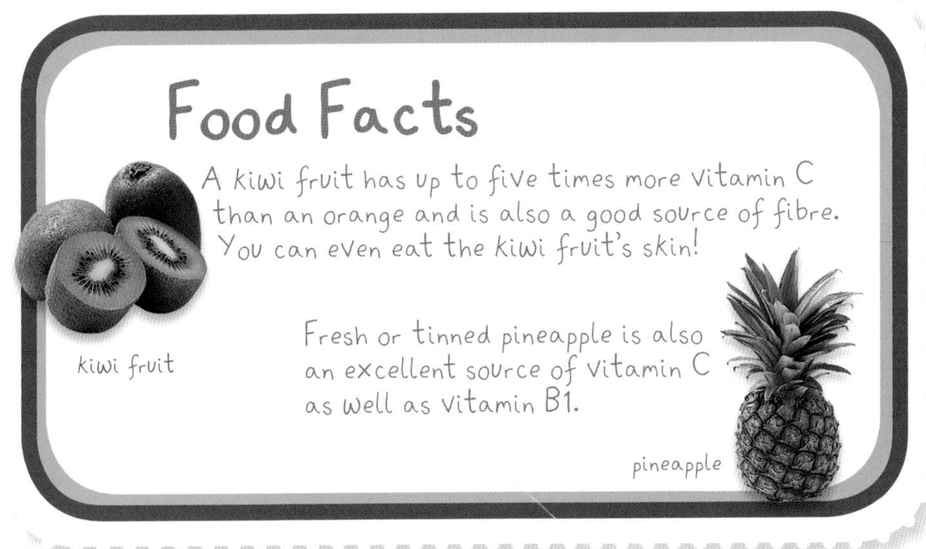

Food Facts

A kiwi fruit has up to five times more vitamin C than an orange and is also a good source of fibre. You can even eat the kiwi fruit's skin!

kiwi fruit

Fresh or tinned pineapple is also an excellent source of vitamin C as well as vitamin B1.

pineapple

Preparation 10 mins • **Cooking** none • **Serves** 4

Fruit Sundae

This fruity ice cream sundae is a refreshing, vitamin-filled treat. Any of your favourite fruits will taste great in this recipe and if you don't have time to make the Tropical Yoghurt Ice, you can use two extra scoops of vanilla ice cream instead.

Helpful Hints

Try to buy strawberries in season for the best, most nutritious fruit. The lemon juice enhances the flavour of the strawberries and also prevents the sauce oxidising or discolouring.

Ingredients

- 8 small scoops Tropical Yoghurt Ice (see p.176–177 for recipe)
- 4 small scoops vanilla ice cream
- a selection of fresh fruit, such as strawberries, mango, kiwi fruit or raspberries (the amount depends on size of your glasses)
- toasted flaked almonds (optional)

Strawberry Sauce:

- 350g (12oz) strawberries (hulled)
- squeeze of fresh lemon juice
- a little icing sugar

mango

raspberries

Equipment

- sharp knife
- chopping board
- sieve
- blender or food processor
- ice cream scoop
- 4 sundae glasses

kiwi

banana

1 First make the Strawberry Sauce. Slice the strawberries in half and then purée them in a blender until they form a smooth sauce with no lumps.

Press the strawberry purée through a sieve, using the back of a spoon, to remove the seeds. Stir in a little lemon juice and some icing sugar to sweeten.

2 Press the strawberry purée through a sieve, using the back of a spoon, to remove the seeds. Stir in a little lemon juice and some icing sugar to sweeten.

3 Put a scoop of Tropical Yoghurt Ice into the glass and add a spoonful of Strawberry Sauce. Add some fruit and a scoop of vanilla ice cream.

4 Add more sauce and fruit and then top the sundae with a scoop of Yoghurt Ice and a sprinkling of nuts. Repeat to make three more sundaes.

Food Facts

Strawberries are a good source of vitamin C, which is excellent for your skin, hair, and nails and also helps to boost your immune system.

strawberries

• **Preparation** 25 mins • **Cooking** 35 mins • **Serves** 6–8

Oaty Crumble

Fruit crumble is one of the great British puddings. It is easy to make but tastes so good it's very difficult to resist! Give this traditional dish a healthy twist by adding oats and seeds to the topping.

Tasty Twists

Try different varieties of fruit. Seasonal fruit tends to have the best flavour so in the summer months you could try nectarines, peaches, plums, or rhubarb, and in late summer/early autumn try apples, blackberries, or pears.

Ingredients

- 4 dessert apples
- 200g (7oz) blueberries, defrosted if frozen
- 4 tbsp fresh apple juice
- 1 tbsp light muscovado sugar

Topping:

- 75g (3oz) plain white flour
- 75g (3oz) wholemeal flour
- 75g (3oz) unsalted butter (cut into small pieces)
- 75g (3oz) light muscovado sugar
- 3 tbsp sunflower seeds
- 1 tbsp sesame seeds
- 3 tbsp rolled oats

sunflower seeds

muscovado sugar

Equipment

- large mixing bowl
- small sharp knife
- chopping board
- 900ml (2 pint) ovenproof dish
- small jug

sharp knife

mixing bowl

chopping board

1 Preheat the oven to 180°C (350°F/Gas 4). Put the plain white flour and wholemeal flour into a large mixing bowl and stir together with a spoon.

2 Add the butter. Rub the butter and flour together with your fingertips until they look like coarse breadcrumbs. Stir in the sugar, seeds, and oats.

3 Remove the skin from the apples and cut them into quarters. Then carefully remove the core and slice the fruit into bite-sized pieces.

You can leave the skin on the apples, if you like – it is very good fo you.

4 Put the pieces of apple into an ovenproof dish. Add the blueberries and pour over the apple juice. Sprinkle the sugar evenly over the top.

5 Spoon over the topping in an even layer then put the dish in the oven. Cook for 35 minutes until the top is crisp and beginning to brown.

Food Facts

For such a small fruit, blueberries pack a powerful health punch. According to recent research, they beat 40 other fruit and vegetables in helping to prevent certain diseases! They provide a high concentration of antioxidants which means they may help to prevent cancer and heart disease. What's more they may help to fight infections, boost memory and be anti-ageing.

blueberries

● **Preparation** 15 mins ● **Soaking** 30 mins ● **Cooking** 7 mins ● **Serves** 4

Fruit Bread Pudding

This is a quick version of the classic British dessert, summer pudding, which is usually made in a bowl and left overnight to allow the fruit juices to soak into the bread.

Did you know?

The word "companion" comes from the Latin words "com" meaning "with" and "panis" meaning "bread" so it originally meant one with whom bread is shared.

Ingredients

stale wholemeal bread

blackberries

- 8 slices wholemeal bread (preferably slightly stale)
- 600g (1lb 5oz) mixed fresh or frozen berries such as strawberries, blackberries, blackcurrants, and raspberries
- 125ml (4fl oz) water
- 100g (3½ oz) caster sugar

strawberries

medium saucepan

Equipment

sieve

- chopping board
- medium saucepan
- large pastry cutter or scissors
- bowl
- wooden spoon
- sieve
- large shallow dish
- tablespoon
- spatula or fish slice

wooden spoon

1 Cut the bread into your chosen shape using scissors or a large pastry cutter. (Use as much of the bread as possible to avoid waste.)

2 Put all but a handful of the berries, the water, and about two-thirds of the sugar into a saucepan. Stir and then bring to the boil. Reduce the heat.

3 Simmer the berries gently for about 7 minutes or until the fruit is soft and very juicy. Taste and add the remaining sugar if the fruit is too sharp.

4 Strain the juice from the fruit into a bowl. Press the fruit through a sieve into another bowl to make a purée.Throw away the seeds.

Food Facts

Bread is a staple food of many European, Middle Eastern, and Indian cultures and is prepared by baking, steaming, or frying dough. There are more than 200 different types of bread but for the healthiest diet, you should try and eat wholegrain varieties which contain more fibre and B vitamins.

bread

Tasty Twists

This delicious fruit purée would also taste great spooned over pancakes, yoghurt ice cream, or natural yoghurt.

5 Place 4 bread shapes in a large shallow dish and spoon over the fruit purée until the bread is completely covered with the fruit.

6 Add a second piece of bread on top of the first. Spoon over the remaining purée and the berry juice. Gently press the bread with the back of a spoon.

7 Leave for at least 30 minutes to allow the bread to soak up the juice. Carefully lift out of the dish and decorate with the leftover berries and a little juice.

• **Preparation** 20 mins • **Cooking** 5 mins • **Chilling** 2 h • **Serves** 10–12

Chocolate Fridgecake

This fridgecake looks great but it is actually very simple because unlike most cakes, it doesn't involve any baking! It is a tempting mixture of melt-in-your-mouth chocolate, crumbly biscuit, chewy cherries, and crunchy nuts.

Tasty Twists

You could miss out the cherries, raisins, and nuts if you want and replace them with the same quantity of puffed rice, marshmallows, or other dried fruits.

raisins

plain biscuits

Ingredients

- 200g (7oz) plain chocolate
- 125g (4oz) unsalted butter
- 1tbsp of golden syrup
- 150g (5oz) plain biscuits
- 90g (3oz) red glacé cherries (optional)
- 60g (2oz) shelled pistachio nuts (optional)
- 60g (2oz) raisins (optional)
- 30g (1oz) blanched almonds (optional)

chocolate

blanched almonds

pistachio nuts

Equipment

- cling film
- dessert spoon
- loaf tin (500g/1lb)
- 2 medium mixing bowls
- small saucepan
- wooden spoon
- chopping board
- sharp knife
- oven gloves
- rubber spoon spatula

1 Tear off a piece of cling film, at least double the size of the loaf tin. Loosely line the tin with the cling film and then put the tin to one side.

2 Break the chocolate into a bowl and add the butter and syrup. Place the bowl over a pan of barely simmering water and gently melt the contents.

3 Halve the cherries and break the biscuits into small pieces. If you would prefer a smoother fridgecake, break the biscuits into even smaller pieces.

When the fridgecake has softened, cut it into 10–12 equal slices.

4 Using oven gloves, remove the chocolate from the heat, and allow the bowl to cool slightly. Stir in the remaining ingredients until coated.

5 Spoon the mixture into the loaf tin and press it down with the back of a spoon. Loosely cover with the extra cling film and chill for 2 hours, to set.

6 Carefully turn the tin upside down on a chopping board. Remove the tin and unwrap the cling film. Leave the fridgecake to soften for a few minutes.

• **Preparation** 40 mins • **Cooking** 5 mins • **Chilling** 2½–3½ h • **Serves** 8–10

Mandarin Cheesecake

This scrumptious cheesecake looks amazing but is simple to make. The filling is a mixture of cream cheese, condensed milk, and lemon juice and the base is just made of crushed biscuits and a little melted butter. Best of all, this cheesecake does not need any baking, just chilling.

Tasty Twists

Other tinned fruits would taste great in this recipe. Try cherries, peaches, pineapple, or a combination of your favourite fruits.

Ingredients

lemons

- 200g (7oz) digestive biscuits
- 75g (2½oz) unsalted butter
- 200g (7oz) cream cheese, at room temperature
- 300g (10oz) sweetened condensed milk
- 5tbsp of fresh lemon juice
- 300g (10oz) tin mandarin segments in natural juice

digestive biscuits

mandarin segments

Equipment

- plastic food bag
- rolling pin
- medium saucepan
- wooden spoon
- flan tin (20cm/8in, loose bottomed and fluted)
- baking tray
- dessert spoon
- mixing bowl
- rubber spoon spatula
- balloon whisk
- colander
- chopping board
- knife

knife

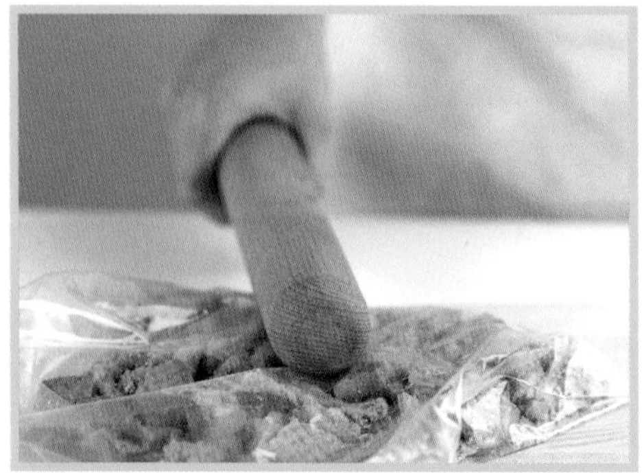

1 Break up the biscuits and put them into a food bag. Push the air out and seal. Crush the biscuits with a rolling pin until they are like fine breadcrumbs.

2 Gently melt the butter in a saucepan, over a low heat. Turn off the heat and stir in the crushed biscuits until they are completely coated with butter.

3 Put the flan tin on a baking tray and tip the biscuit mixture in. Spread the mixture out with the back of a spoon until it evenly covers the base and sides.

Tasty Twists

For a really naughty-but-nice dessert, sprinkle some grated chocolate on top of the cheesecake.

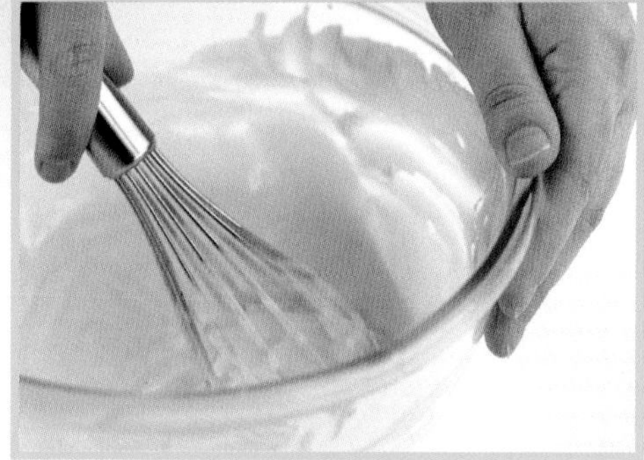

4 Chill the biscuit base for 30 minutes. Beat the cream cheese and then add the condensed milk and lemon juice. Whisk them all together, until smooth.

5 Thoroughly drain the mandarin segments. Roughly chop them into smaller pieces and then scatter them over the chilled biscuit base.

6 Pour the filling mixture over the base. Use a spatula to spread the mixture and smooth the top. Chill for 2–3 hours or overnight, to set.

• **Preparation** 10 mins • **Setting** 2 hours • **Serves** 8

Raspberry Cheesecake

This fruity cheesecake is so simple to make. The jelly adds flavour and also sets the cheesecake.

Ingredients

- 75g (3oz) unsalted butter
- 150g (5½oz) digestive biscuits
- 135g (5oz) pack of raspberry flavour jelly
- 200ml (7floz) evaporated milk, chilled
- 200g (7oz) soft cream cheese
- 100g (3½oz) raspberries
- a few raspberries for decoration

Equipment

- 20cm (8in) round loose-bottomed sandwich tin
- baking paper
- food bag
- rolling pin
- saucepan
- 3 metal spoons
- heatproof jug
- large bowl
- electric whisk

1 Line the base of a 20cm (8in) round loose-bottomed sandwich tin with baking paper.

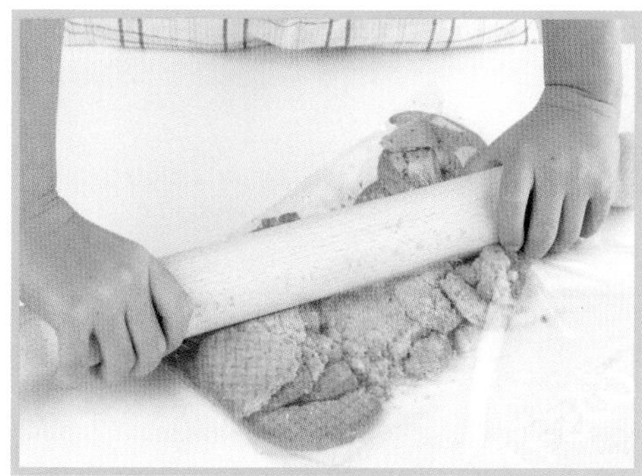

2 Place the biscuits in a food bag and crush with a rolling pin (or you can do this in a food processor).

3 Melt the butter in a saucepan and stir in the crushed biscuits. Press into the tin and chill.

4 Break the jelly into pieces. Then, in a heatproof jug, put the jelly in 100ml (3½floz) boiling water, stir until dissolved.

5 In a large bowl, whisk the milk until light and fluffy and doubled in volume. Whisk in the cream cheese, until the mixture is smooth. Whisk in the jelly.

6 Roughly chop the raspberries and stir into the mixture. Pour over the biscuit base and leave to chill for 2 hours. Serve decorated with extra raspberries.

- **Preparation** 40–45 mins
- **Cooking** 2 hours
- **Makes** 12

Tropical Fruit Meringues

Here's a handy tip – egg whites are easier to whisk when they are at room temperature. You should also use a clean, grease-free glass bowl when making meringues and ensure that the whites are completely free from any yolk.

Tasty Twists

You can use any of your favourite fruits in the salad – apple, peach, or banana would all taste great.

Add some meringue pieces in step 6 of the Fruit Ripple (p.206–207).

Ingredients

eggs

caster sugar

Ingredients for 12 meringues:

- 2 eggs
- 125g (4oz) caster sugar
- 1 pinch of salt

For the fruit salad:

- 1/2 small melon (quartered and deseeded)

- 1 kiwi fruit
- 30ml (2tbsp) fresh orange juice
- 1 small mango
- 10 green grapes (halved)
- 10 red grapes (halved)
- 1/2 small pineapple

small melon

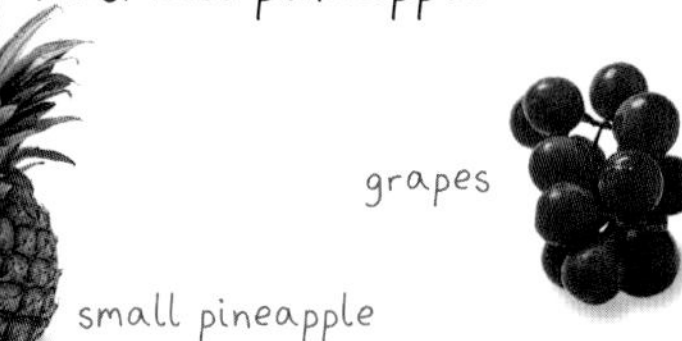

small pineapple

grapes

Equipment

baking sheet

- baking sheet
- non-stick baking sheet
- large bowl
- electric whisk
- tablespoon
- mixing bowl
- metal mixing spoon
- 2 dessert spoons
- chopping board
- sharp knife
- oven gloves

mixing bowl

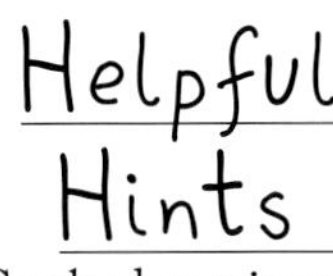

Helpful Hints

Cooked meringues will be dry and should peel off the baking parchment very easily.

1 Preheat the oven to 110°C (225°F/Gas 1⁄2) and line a baking sheet with non-stick parchment. Separate the egg whites from the yolks.

2 Whisk the egg whites and salt in a large bowl, until they form stiff peaks. Whisk 75g (5tbsp) of the sugar into the mixture, 15g (1tbsp) at a time.

3 Make sure the egg whites are stiff before adding each tablespoon of sugar. Fold the remaining sugar into the mixture, using a metal spoon.

4 Using 2 dessert spoons, put 12 spoonfuls of the meringue onto the baking sheet and bake on the bottom shelf of the oven for 2 hours.

5 Carefully slice the mango in half, around the stone. Slice the skin from the melon. Scoop out the mango and melon flesh and cut them into cubes.

6 Slice the pineapple and kiwi in the same way – first slice off the base and then the skin, working downwards. Remove the core from the pineapple.

7 Cut the kiwi into slices and the pineapple into cubes. Mix all the fruit together and stir in the orange juice. Chill until the meringues are ready.

• **Preparation** 20 mins • **Freezing** 5 hours • **Serves** 4

Blueberry Ice Cream

This ice cream is so simple to make! Just mix all the prepared ingredients together and freeze.

Cut into rectangles and serve between wafers for a sophisticated treat!

Ingredients

- 300g (10½oz) fresh blueberries
- 30ml (2tbsp) caster sugar
- grated zest and juice 1 unwaxed lemon
- 300ml (½pt) double cream
- 500g (1lb 2oz) natural bio milk yogurt
- 30ml (2tbsp) icing sugar

lemon

Equipment

wooden spoon

- saucepan
- wooden spoon
- bowl
- 2 spoons
- fine sieve
- large mixing bowl
- electric or hand whisk
- freezerproof container
- fork

1 Place the blueberries in a pan with the caster sugar and lemon zest and juice. Bring to the boil, then simmer for 4 to

2 Remove from the heat and press through a fine sieve into a bowl, to make a glossy purple coulis. Leave to cool.

Serving Tip

Place in the fridge for 15 minutes before serving to soften slightly.

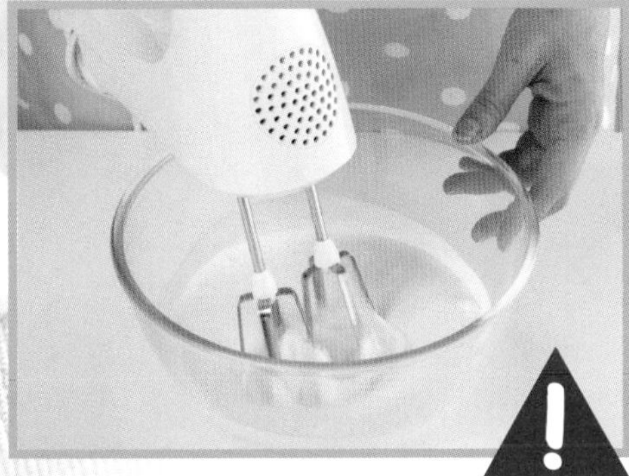

3 Place the cream in a large bowl and with an electric or hand whisk, lightly whip until just starting to thicken.

4 Using a metal spoon, fold in the yogurt and icing sugar until well combined and smooth, then stir in the blueberry coulis.

5 Transfer to a freezerproof container with a lid. Place in freezer for 4 to 5 hours until frozen. Remove every hour and break up the ice crystals with a fork.

Preparation 20 mins **Cooking** 15 mins **Serves** 4

Banana Fritters

These bananas are cooked in a light batter, coated with sesame seeds and served with a delicious warm fudge sauce. For extra indulgence add a scoop of vanilla ice cream.

Ingredients

bananas

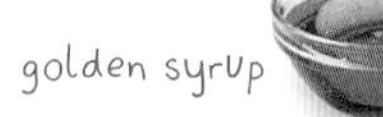

golden syrup

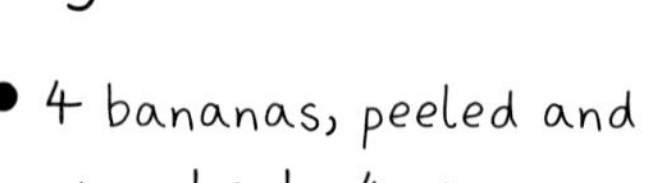

- 4 bananas, peeled and each cut into 4 pieces
- sunflower oil for frying

Fudge sauce:

- 75g (3oz) unsalted butter
- 150g (5$\frac{1}{2}$oz) light soft brown sugar
- 150ml ($\frac{1}{4}$pt) single cream
- 15ml (1tbsp) golden syrup

Batter:

- 125g (4oz) self-raising flour
- 30ml (2tbsp) caster sugar
- 175ml (6floz) milk
- 60ml (4tbsp) sesame seeds

milk

Equipment

- large saucepan
- wooden spoon
- large bowl
- large metal spoon
- teaspoon
- slotted spoon
- kitchen paper

wooden spoon

1 Place all the fudge sauce ingredients in a pan and cook gently for 2 to 3 minutes. Stirring continuously, bring to the boil for 3 minutes, until thickened.

2 Leave in the pan to cool slightly. Meanwhile, heat a pan $\frac{1}{3}$ of the volume full of oil, until a piece of bread goes golden brown when dropped in.

3 Mix all the batter ingredients together in a large bowl, reserving 30ml (2tbsp) of the sesame seeds. Add the bananas and turn to coat in the batter.

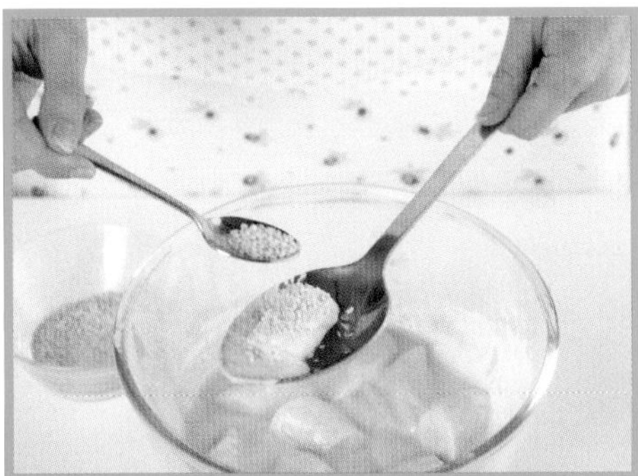

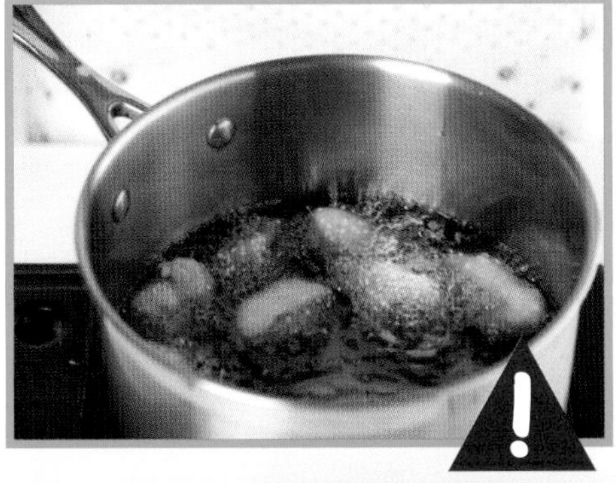

4 Using a slotted spoon, and holding over the bowl, remove the bananas, then sprinkle with some of the reserved sesame seeds.

5 Fry the banana in batches, in the oil for 3 to 4 minutes until golden brown. Remove and drain on kitchen paper. Serve immediately with the fudge sauce.

Helpful Hint

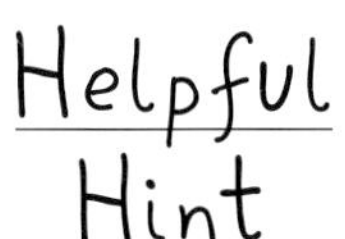

Eat these as soon as they are cooked as the batter will become soggy if you leavae them.

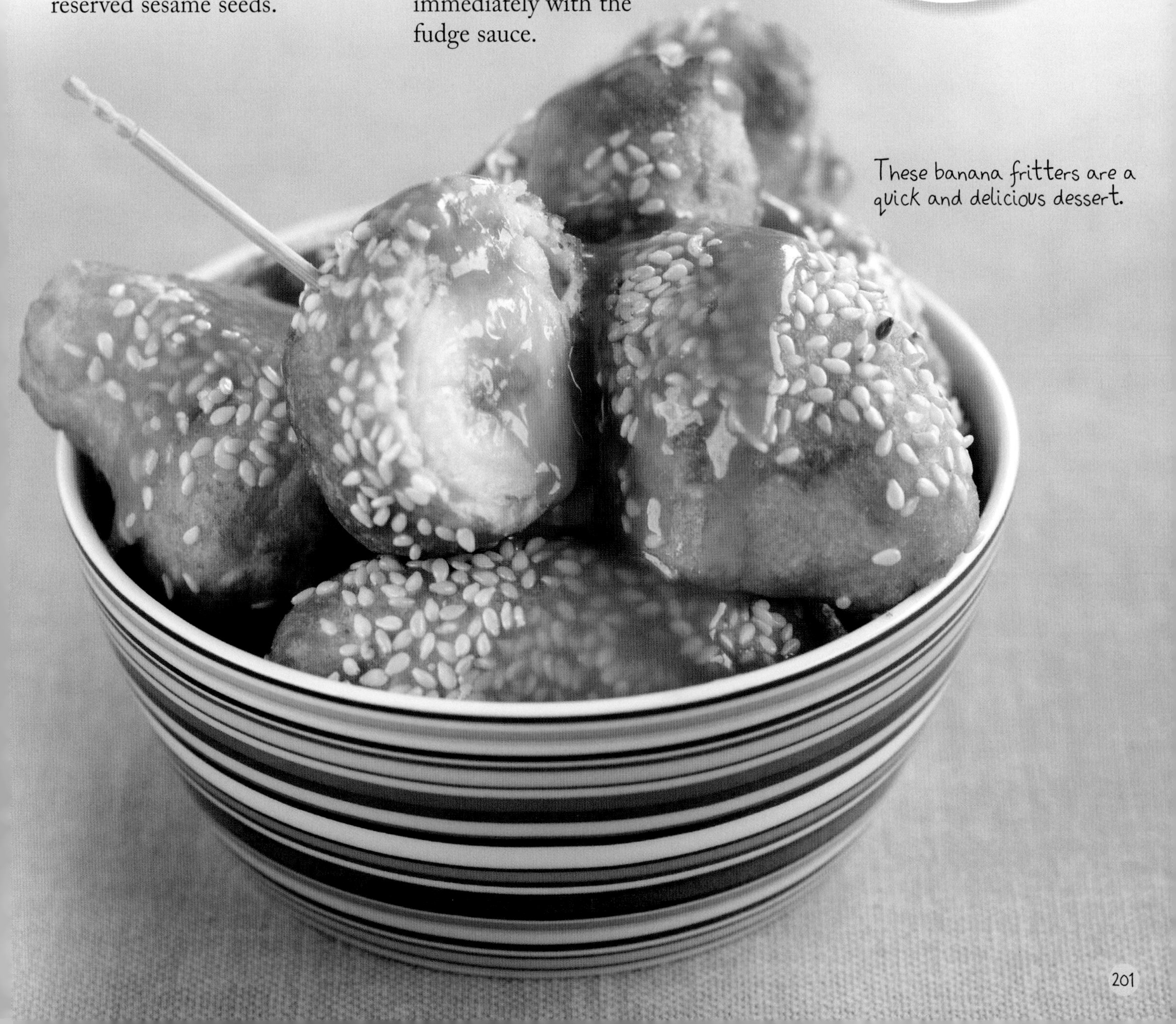

These banana fritters are a quick and delicious dessert.

- **Preparation** 10 mins
- **Cooking** 60 mins
- **Makes** 15

Strawberry Meringues

These delicious pretty meringues are crisp on the outside and soft in the middle. Fill with lightly whipped cream and sliced strawberries.

Helpful Hints

You can make vanilla sugar by leaving a vanilla pod in a jar of sugar.

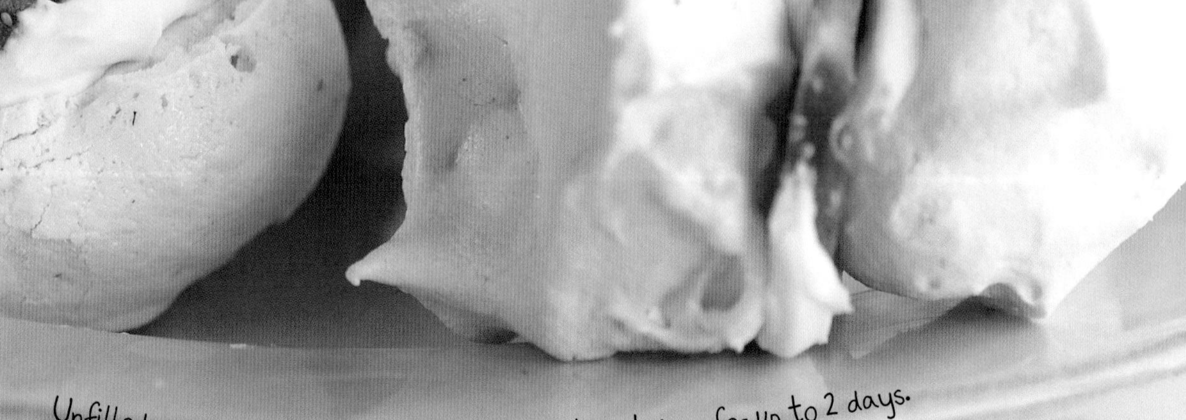

Unfilled meringues can be kept in an airtight container for up to 2 days.

Ingredients

- 2 large egg whites
- 100g (3½oz) caster sugar
- 150ml (¼pt) double cream
- 15ml (1tbsp) vanilla sugar
- 12 small strawberries (sliced)

caster sugar

Equipment

- 2 large baking sheets
- baking paper
- large mixing bowl
- electric whisk
- tablespoon
- teaspoon

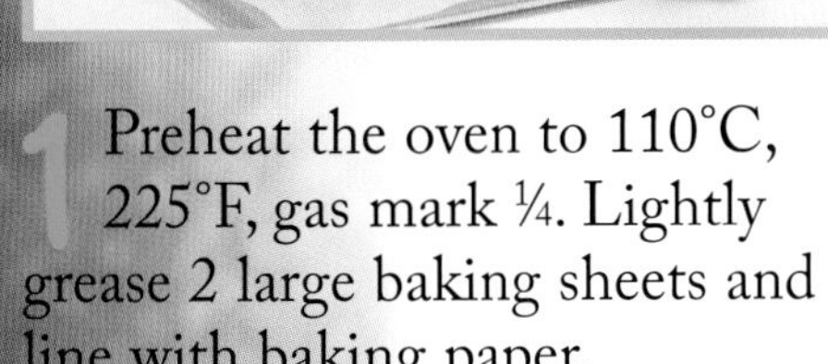

1 Preheat the oven to 110°C, 225°F, gas mark ¼. Lightly grease 2 large baking sheets and line with baking paper.

2 Place the egg whites into a large, spotlessly clean mixing bowl and whisk them until they form stiff peaks.

3 Add the sugar a tablespoon at a time, whisking well after each addition, until the mixture is smooth, thick and glossy.

4 Place heaped teaspoons of the mixture, spaced a little apart, onto the prepared baking sheets, until you have 30 meringues. Flatten slightly.

5 Bake in a preheated oven for one hour, or until they peel away from the baking paper. Leave to cool. Whisk the vanilla sugar into the cream until thick.

6 Spread some cream on the flat side of a meringue, put some strawberries on top, spread some cream on another meringue and sandwich together.

• **Preparation** 15 mins • **Cooking** 15 mins • **Makes** 4

Apple Crumble Sundae

Layers of apple, crunchy crumble, toffee sauce and ice cream are layered up in tall glasses to make a delicious sundae, which is a variation on an old favourite.

Helpful Hints

Use good quality vanilla ice cream – your sundaes won't be as delicious if you don't!

Serve these sundaes in traditional sundae glasses for a retro feel.

Ingredients

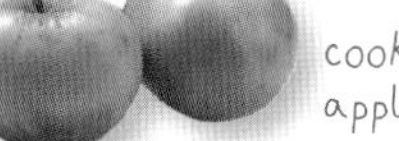

Crumble mixture:

- 100g ($3^{1}/_{2}$ oz) plain flour
- 50g (2oz) butter (diced)
- 50g (2oz) demerara sugar

Apple compote:

- 3 cooking apples, peeled, cored, and chopped
- 50g (2oz) caster sugar
- juice $^{1}/_{2}$ lemon
- 90ml (8tbsp) cold fudge sauce (see page 200) or ready made toffee sauce
- 8 scoops vanilla ice cream

Equipment

- medium bowl
- baking tray
- baking paper
- medium saucepan
- wooden spoon
- fork

1 Place the flour and butter in a bowl and rub them together with your fingertips until the mixture resembles fine breadcrumbs. Stir in the sugar.

2 Preheat the oven to 200°C, 400°F, gas mark 6. Line a baking tray with baking paper, and pour the mixture on top. Cook for 8 to 10 minutes until golden.

3 Meanwhile, place the apples, sugar and lemon juice in a medium pan. Cover and cook over a gentle heat for 12 to 15 minutes, stirring occasionally.

4 Leave the apple compote to cool with the lid off. Using your fingers or a fork, break up the cooled crumble topping.

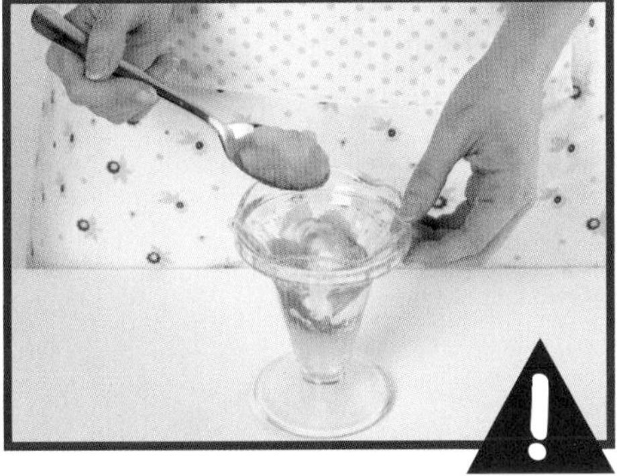

5 Layer each sundae glass with apple compote, crumble, ice cream and toffee sauce and serve with long spoons.

Tasty Twists

Serve warm with ice cream to get a deliciously different dessert!

- **Preparation** 20 mins
- **Cooking** none
- **Serves** 4

Summer Fruit Ripple

This creamy, light dessert looks great and tastes delicious! Although this recipe suggests fresh fruit, frozen fruit would be fine but you must thaw it completely before you begin. On a hot summer's day, you can freeze the finished ripple for at least 4 hours, to make a super-cool treat.

Tasty Twists

Try using tinned fruit such as mangoes and peaches but remember to set some fruit aside for decoration.

Ingredients

strawberries

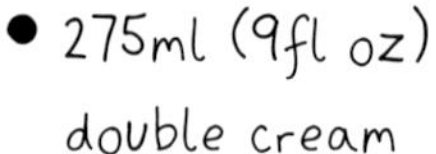

- 250g (8oz) ripe strawberries
- 125g (4oz) ripe raspberries
- 125g (4oz) ripe blueberries
- 4tbsp of fresh orange juice
- 275ml (9fl oz) double cream
- 2tbsp of clear runny honey
- 275ml (9fl oz) natural yoghurt
- 2tbsp of icing sugar (sieved)

blueberries

Equipment

- chopping board
- sharp knife
- food processor
- sieve
- 2 mixing bowls
- wooden spoon
- dessert spoon
- balloon whisk
- metal mixing spoon
- rubber spoon spatula

wooden spoon

1 Wash all the fruit and put a handful to one side. (They will be used to decorate the finished dessert.) Hull the strawberries and cut them into quarters.

2 Place the orange juice, icing sugar, and half of the fruit into the processor. Put the lid on securely and blend to make a smooth purée.

3 Sieve the blended fruit into a mixing bowl to separate the seeds and fruit pulp. Use a wooden spoon to press the liquid through.

If you don't have a food processor use a masher to crush the fruit in step 2.

Serving Tip

To serve, place the fruit set aside in step 1 on top of the rippled mixture in the serving glasses.

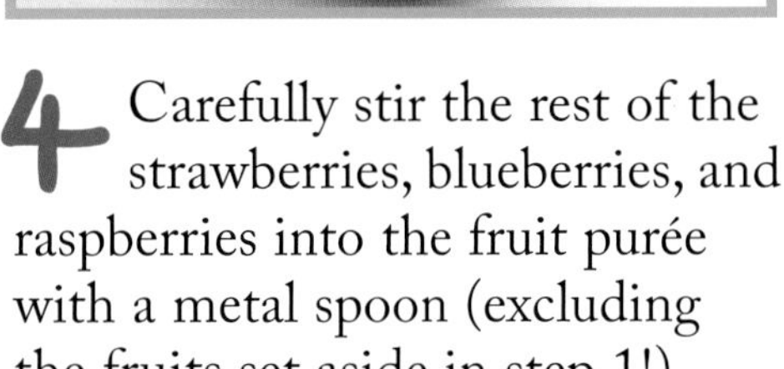

4 Carefully stir the rest of the strawberries, blueberries, and raspberries into the fruit purée with a metal spoon (excluding the fruits set aside in step 1!)

5 Lightly whip the cream in the large bowl. When it is ready, it will stand up in soft peaks. (You can use an electric whisk here, if you have one.)

6 Fold the yoghurt, honey, and half of the fruit mixture into the cream. Layer the marbled cream mixture with the rest of the fruit mixture, in serving glasses.

• **Preparation** 3 hours • **Cooking** 25 mins • **Makes** 25

Fondant Fancies

These gorgeous cakes take a while to prepare but are well worth the effort.

Ingredients

Cake:

- 200g (7oz) unsalted butter or margarine (softened)
- 200g (7oz) caster sugar
- grated zest 1 lemon
- 4 medium eggs, beaten
- 200g (7oz) self-raising flour

self-raising flour

Filling and icing:

- 75g (3oz) unsalted butter
- 175g (6oz) icing sugar (sifted)
- 90 to 120ml (6 to 8tbsp) water
- 15ml (1tbsp) milk
- 15ml(1tbsp) apricot jam
- 100g (3½oz) marzipan
- 1kg (2lb 4oz) icing sugar
- 2–3 drops pink food colouring

lemon

Equipment

- 2 bowls
- 2 spoons
- 20cm (8in) square tin
- baking paper
- electric whisk
- palette knife
- bread knife
- cling film
- rolling pin
- fork

palette knife

1 Preheat the oven to 180ºC, 350ºF, gas mark 4. Grease and line the cake tin. Cream together the butter, sugar and lemon zest.

2 Whisk in the eggs a little at a time, adding a little flour to prevent the mixture curdling. Fold in the rest of the flour. Spoon into the tin and smooth the top.

3 Bake for 20 to 25 minutes. Cool in the tin. Turn out and with a bread knife remove the top layer of the cake, to make it even then cut the cake in half horizontally.

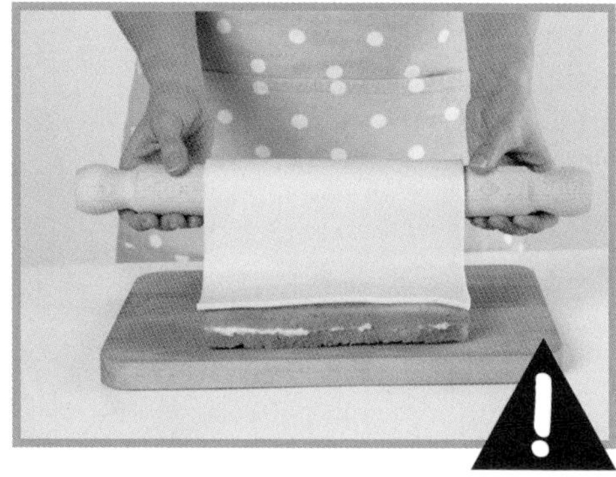

4 Cream together the butter and icing sugar, then add the milk and spread over one half of the cake. Sandwich together. Wrap in cling film and chill for at least 2 hours.

5 Warm the apricot jam and spread over the top. Roll out the marzipan to a 20cm (8in) square and place on top of the cake. Cut the cake into 25 cubes.

6 Mix the fondant icing sugar and water until smooth. Add the pink colouring. Holding over the bowl, drizzle over each cube and decorate as desired. Leave to set.

• **Preparation** 30 mins • **Cooking** 15 mins • **Makes** 20

Cupcakes

Cook these pretty cakes and decorate with pastel colour icings, sweets or crystallised flowers. Stack in a tower as an alternative way to celebrate a birthday party or get-together.

These cakes are easy and quick to make, and even quicker to eat!

Helpful Hint

These cakes can be made the day before and stored in an airtight container.

Ingredients

Cakes:

- 150g (5½oz) unsalted butter, softened
- 150g (5½oz) caster sugar
- 150g (5½oz) self-raising flour
- 3 medium eggs, whisked
- 2.5ml (½tsp) vanilla extract

sugar

Icing and decoration:

- 225g (8oz) icing sugar, sifted
- 30 to 45ml (2 to 3tbsp) hot water
- 3 different food colourings
- Edible crystallised flowers, sugar strands, hundreds and thousands, or sweets

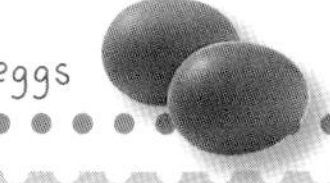

eggs

Equipment

- 2 x12 bun tins
- 20 paper cases
- 2 mixing bowls
- wooden spoon
- 2 metal spoons
- cooling rack
- knife
- 3 small mixing bowls

bun tin

mixing bowl

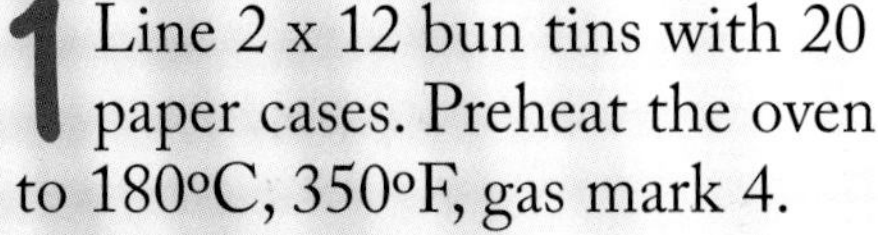

1 Line 2 x 12 bun tins with 20 paper cases. Preheat the oven to 180ºC, 350ºF, gas mark 4.

2 Place the butter, sugar, self-raising flour, eggs, and vanilla extract in a bowl and beat with a wooden spoon until pale and creamy.

3 Divide between the paper cases. Bake for 15 minutes until golden and just firm. Cool in the tin for 5 minutes, then transfer to a cooling rack to cool.

4 Trim any pointed tops to make a flat surface.

5 Place the icing in a large bowl, gradually beat in sufficient water to give a smooth thick icing, which coats the back of a spoon.

6 Transfer the icing mixture to 3 individual bowls and add a few drops of food colouring to each. Spoon onto the cakes and top with decorations. Allow to set.

Baking

Baking

Shop-bought cakes and biscuits are usually high in sugar and fat. Many of the recipes in this section contain fruit whose natural sweetness helps to reduce the amount of refined sugar needed, as well as adding vitamins. Nutritious wholemeal flour is also used to add extra fibre and B vitamins. Here are a few suggestions to get you started.

Apple Flapjacks

Preheat the oven to 180°C (350°F/Gas 4). Over a low heat, melt 125g (4½oz) butter with 150g (5½oz) soft brown sugar and 3 tbsp golden syrup. Add 250g (8oz) porridge oats, 1 apple (cored and grated), and 2 tbsp sunflower seeds into a mixing bowl and stir in the butter mixture. Pour it into a greased 20cm (8in) square cake tin and bake in an oven for 20–25 minutes. Leave to cool and then cut into squares.

Apple Tart

Preheat the oven to 180°C (350°F/Gas 4). Cut out 10cm (4in) circles of ready-rolled puff pastry. Arrange thinly sliced apples over the top, leaving a 1cm (½in) gap around the edge. Gently score the pastry around the fruit. Melt a littles jam or honey in a small pan and brush it over the top of the apples. Place on a baking sheet and bake for 20–25 minutes, or until the pastry becomes golden.

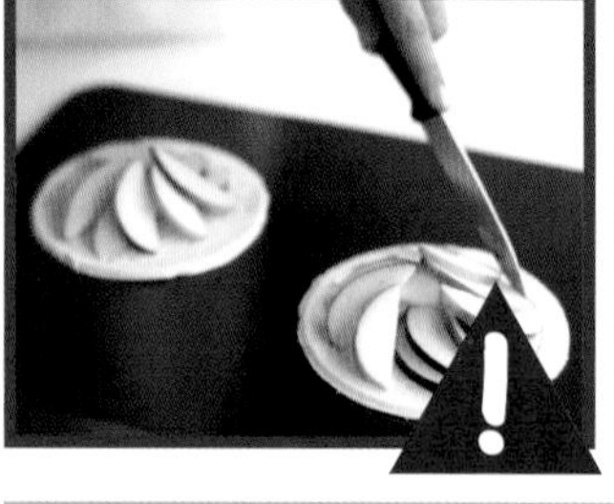

Oaty Bread

Carbohydrate foods, such as oats, help to boost serotonin levels in the brain which make us feel happy. Here's how to adapt the roll recipe on p.250–251 to make a loaf of bread: Replace 50g (12oz) of the wholemeal bread flour with 50g (12oz) oats in step 2. In step 6 make 1 large loaf instead of 10 rolls and sprinkle the loaf with oats before baking it in step 7.

Savoury Scones

Preheat the oven to 220°C (425°F/ Gas 7). Sieve 110g (4oz) each of wholemeal and white self-raising flour and ½ tsp salt into a bowl. Rub in 50g (2oz) butter until the mixture looks like breadcrumbs. Make a well in the centre and pour in 150ml (5fl oz) milk. (If you like add 50g/2oz of cheese, sun dried tomatoes, or ham.) Mix together to form a sticky dough and turn out onto a floured surface. Knead lightly until the dough is smooth and shape it into a circle about 2.5cm (1in) thick. Cut into smaller circles and brush the tops with milk. Place on a greased baking sheet and bake for about 20 mins.

Open Sandwich

Bread does not have to be made with wheat flour – you could use spelt flour, rye, corn flour, and buckwheat. Try an open sandwich with a new type of bread. Experiment with toppings such as lettuce, cottage cheese, and ham.

Fruity Muffins

Fresh and dried fruit add both sweetness and vitamins to your baking. On p.216–217 you could stir 125g (4oz) of your favourite fruits such as apples, bananas, apricots, or blueberries and raspberries into the mixture in step 4, instead of the dates.

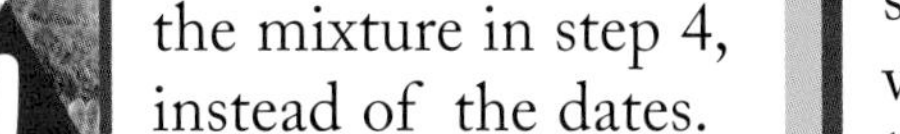

Seed Rolls

Nut and seeds give breads, biscuits, and cakes a delicious taste and texture. as well as adding important nutrients. For example in step 3 of the roll recipe on p.250–251, you could add 5 tbsp of chopped nuts and seeds instead of sprinkling sunflower seeds on the top.

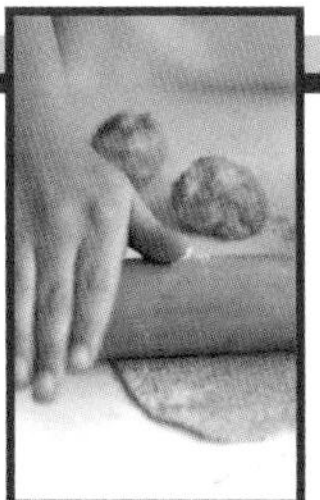

Flatbread

This flatbread makes a great sandwich wrap. Put 175g (6oz) wholemeal self-raising flour and ½ tsp salt into a bowl. Stir in 1 tbsp vegetable oil and 120ml (4fl oz) water to make a soft dough. Knead on a lightly floured surface and put the dough into a lightly oiled bowl. Cover with cling film and leave for 1 hour. Then, divide the dough into 8 pieces and roll each one into circles, about 2mm (1/12in) thick. Heat a lightly oiled, non-stick frying pan and cook for about 1½ minutes on each side, until golden and puffy.

• **Preparation** 15 mins • **Cooking** 20 mins • **Serves** 8

Sticky Date Muffins

These muffins taste light and luscious! The secret to good muffins is to not over-beat the batter otherwise they will be heavy and dense. For the perfect muffins give the mixture a gentle stir with a wooden spoon until the flour just disappears.

Did you know?

Dates are the fruit of the date palm tree, which can grow up to 25 metres (82 feet) tall. Egypt is the world's largest producer

Ingredients

caster sugar

- 200g (7oz) white or wholemeal plain flour
- 1 tbsp baking powder
- 125g (4oz) caster sugar
- 1 tsp ground cinnamon
- 1/2 tsp salt
- 125g (4oz) ready-to-eat dried chopped dates
- 1 tbsp orange juice
- 175ml (6fl oz) milk
- 1 large egg (lightly beaten)
- 140g (5oz) butter

egg

wholemeal flour

ground cinnamon

Equipment

- large muffin tin
- sieve
- large mixing bowl
- wooden spoon
- food processor or blender
- small saucepan
- jug
- fork
- wire rack
- paper cases

blender

large muffin tin

1 Preheat the oven to 200°C (400°F/Gas 6). Line the muffin tin with the paper cases. Sift the flour and baking powder into a bowl.

2 Stir the sugar, cinnamon, and salt into the flour and baking powder. Put the dates and orange juice in a blender and whiz until they form a smooth purée.

3 Melt the butter in a saucepan over a low heat. Pour the milk into a jug and add the egg, melted butter, and date purée. Beat together lightly with a fork.

Tasty Twists

Fresh fruit such as blueberries, raspberries, and strawberries make a delicious alternative to the puréed dates. Alternatively, try other dried fruits such as raisins, cherries, apricots, cranberries, or prunes.

4 Pour the date mixture into the flour mixture. Fold the ingredients together gently and evenly with a wooden spoon until the flour is just mixed in.

5 Spoon the mixture into the paper cases until it is almost to the top. Bake for 20 minutes until risen and golden. Transfer the muffins to a wire rack to cool.

Food Facts

Dates are one of the oldest cultivated fruits in the world and have been around since about 6000 BCE. They are soft and tasty and a natural sweetener. Dates are also a good source of iron, fibre, and potassium as well as being low in fat.

dates

• **Preparation** 30–35 mins • **Cooking** 25 mins • **Makes** 12

Crunchy Muffins

The secret of delicious, light muffins is not to over-mix the cake batter. A few lumps don't matter – if the batter is over-mixed, the muffins will have a heavy, dense texture.

Tasty Twists

Frozen raspberries would be fine for this recipe, as long as you thaw them completely. Try using other fresh or frozen fruits, such as strawberries, blueberries, or blackberries. Nuts, dried fruits, or chocolate chips would also taste great!

Ingredients

- 300g (10oz) plain flour
- 1tbsp of baking powder
- 1/2 tsp of salt
- 125g (4oz) granulated sugar
- 1 egg
- 2tbsp of corn oil or sunflower oil
- 275ml (9fl oz) milk
- 125g (4 oz) fresh raspberries
- 150g (5oz) white chocolate (chopped)
- 90g (3oz) crunchy oat cereal

chopped white chocolate

egg

raspberries

Equipment

- sieve
- mixing bowl
- wooden spoon
- jug
- whisk
- metal mixing spoon
- 12 paper muffin cases
- 12-hole muffin tray
- tablespoon
- teaspoon
- oven gloves
- cooling rack

wooden spoon

1 Preheat the oven to 200°C (400°F/Gas 6). Sieve the plain flour, baking powder, and salt into a mixing bowl and then stir in the sugar.

2 Crack the egg into a jug and add the oil. Beat the egg and oil together until they are light and fluffy. Add the milk and then whisk the mixture.

3 Fold the egg mixture into the flour mixture. The mixture will be lumpy but no flour should be visible. Then fold in the chocolate and raspberries.

Don't worry if the raspberries break up in step 3. The muffins will still taste delicious!

4 Put the muffin cases into the muffin tray and spoon the mixture into them. The easiest way is with a dessert spoon and the back of a teaspoon.

5 Sprinkle some of the crunchy oat cereal on top of each muffin. Bake the muffins for 25 minutes, or until risen and golden.

6 Remove the muffins from the oven and allow them to cool in the muffin tray before placing them on a wire rack. Then you can help yourself!

• **Preparation** 10 mins • **Cooking** 12 mins • **Makes** 48

Mini Muffins

These bite-sized treats are bursting with fruitiness. You will need to cook them in two batches.

These scrumptious muffins are a perfect teatime treat!

Ingredients

- 280g (10oz) plain flour
- 15ml (1tbsp) baking powder
- 2.5ml (1/2tsp) salt
- 125g (4oz) caster sugar
- 1 large egg
- 2 bananas, roughly chopped
- 240ml (8floz) milk
- 85g (3oz) melted butter
- 200g (7oz) blueberries

blueberries

Equipment

- 2 x 12 mini muffin trays
- sieve
- 2 mixing bowls
- fork
- jug
- metal spoon
- whisk

sieve

measuring jug

1 Preheat the oven to 200ºC, 400ºF, gas mark 6. Line 2 x 12 mini muffin trays with paper cases.

2 In a large bowl, sift together flour, baking powder and salt. Stir in the sugar.

3 In a small bowl, mash the bananas with a fork.

4 In a jug, whisk together the egg, milk and butter, then add to the mashed banana, stirring to combine.

5 Add all the wet ingredients to the dry. Stir to just combine, then fold in the blueberries.

6 Spoon into the cases and bake for 10 to 12 minutes or until lightly browned. Refill the muffin tins with paper cases and repeat with the remaining mixture.

- **Preparation** 15 mins
- **Cooking** 30 mins
- **Makes** 12–16 squares

Fruity Flapjacks

Traditional flapjacks are healthier than many other desserts because of the oats. These ones are even better for you because of the fruity layer in the middle.

Did you know?

In the US the word "flapjack" refers to a pancake! No one is really sure where the word originates from although it does appear in Shakespeare's play *Pericles* in the early 17th century.

Ingredients

- 225g (8oz) ready-to-eat dried apricots
- 2 tbsp water
- 285g (10 oz) wholemeal flour
- 150g (5½ oz) porridge oats
- ½ tsp salt
- 200g (7oz) unsalted butter
- 110g (4oz) muscovado sugar
- 2 tbsp golden syrup

muscovado sugar

unsalted butter

golden syrup

Equipment

palette knife

- scissors

- food processor or blender
- tablespoon
- large mixing bowl
- wooden spoon
- medium saucepan
- 18cm (7in) square cake tin
- baking paper
- palette knife

square cake tin

scissors

1 Preheat the oven to 200°C (400°F/Gas 6). Grease and line the bottom of the cake tin with baking paper. Add the apricots and water to a blender.

2 Process the apricots until they are a purée. Set aside. Put the flour, oats, and salt in a mixing bowl and stir with a wooden spoon until combined.

3 Melt the butter, sugar, and syrup in a saucepan over a low heat. Stir the mixture occasionally until the butter has completely melted.

4 Pour the butter mixture into the mixing bowl containing the flour, oats, and sugar. Stir until everything is combined in a sticky, oaty mixture.

5 Press half of the mixture into the bottom of the cake tin and smooth it to make an an even layer. Carefully spread the apricot purée over the oaty layer.

6 Press the rest of the oaty mixture over the apricot purée until it is covered. Bake for 25–30 minutes or until the flapjack is golden on top.

7 Remove from the oven and leave to cool for 5 minutes. Divide the flapjack into squares and leave it to cool completely in the tin before turning it out.

Preparation 20 mins • **Cooking** 50 mins • **Makes** 12–16 squares

Passion Cake

With no creaming or whisking, this is a deliciously simple cake recipe. Carrots give the cake a light and moist texture, as well as providing essential nutrients.

Helpful Hints

To test if the cake is cooked, insert a metal skewer into its centre. If it comes out clean, without cake mixture sticking to it, the cake is ready to take out of the oven.

Decorate the cake with slivers of orange peel.

Ingredients

self-raising wholemeal flour

- butter (for greasing)
- 125g (4½ oz) wholemeal self-raising flour
- 125g (4½ oz) white self-raising flour
- 2 tsp ground mixed spice
- 250g (9oz) light muscovado sugar
- 250g (9oz) carrots (peeled and grated)
- 4 free-range eggs
- 200ml (7fl oz) sunflower oil
- 125g (4½ oz) reduced-fat cream cheese
- 1 tsp vanilla extract
- 5 tbsp unrefined icing sugar

free-range eggs

Equipment

- 20cm (8in) square cake tin
- baking paper
- sieve
- large mixing bowl
- wooden spoon
- measuring jug
- skewer
- palette knife

measuring jug

sieve

1 Preheat the oven to 180°C (350°F/Gas 4). Lightly grease a 20cm (8in) square cake tin and then carefully line the base with baking paper.

2 Sift both types of flour into a bowl, adding any bran left in the sieve. Stir in the mixed spice, sugar, and carrots until they are thoroughly combined.

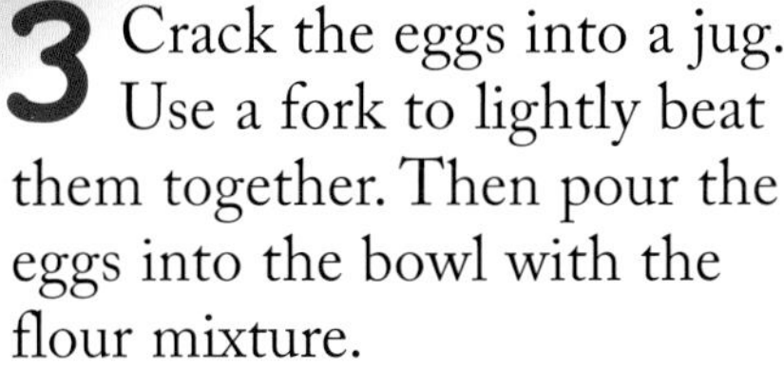

3 Crack the eggs into a jug. Use a fork to lightly beat them together. Then pour the eggs into the bowl with the flour mixture.

4 Add the oil and then stir until all the ingredients are mixed together. Pour the mixture into the tin and smooth the top with the back of a spoon.

Food Facts

Not all fats are bad. Vegetable oil is a type of unsaturated fat which is a good source of energy and helps your body to absorb some vitamins.

Vegetable oil

5 Bake the cake for 50 minutes until it is risen and golden. Remove it from the oven and leave to cool in the tin for 10 minutes before turning it out.

6 Carefully turn the cake out on to a cooling rack. Put the cream cheese and icing into a bowl and beat together until smooth and creamy.

7 Stir in the vanilla extract. Put the icing in the fridge for 15 minutes to harden slightly. Spead the icing over the cake and smooth using a palette knife.

• **Preparation** 15 mins • **Cooking** 15 mins • **Makes** 10

Fruit & Nut Cookies

These yummy cookies are full of energy-boosting ingredients such as oats, dried fruit, and nuts. They are much healthier than shop-bought ones and taste better too!

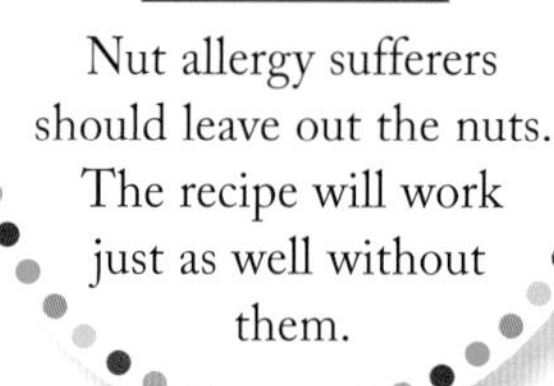

Nut allergy sufferers should leave out the nuts. The recipe will work just as well without them.

Ingredients

- 75g ($2\frac{3}{4}$ oz) dried apricots
- 100g ($3\frac{1}{2}$ oz) plain flour, wholemeal or white
- 60g (2oz) whole porridge oats
- 50g ($1\frac{3}{4}$ oz) chopped hazelnuts (optional)
- 125g ($4\frac{1}{2}$ oz) unsalted butter
- 75g ($2\frac{3}{4}$ oz) soft light brown sugar
- 2 tbsp runny honey

apricots

Equipment

- 2 baking trays
- scissors
- mixing bowl
- wooden spoon
- sharp knife
- small saucepan
- dessert spoon
- cooling rack

1 Preheat the oven to 180°C (350°F/Gas 4) and lightly grease 2 baking trays with butter. Cut the apricots into small pieces and put them in a mixing bowl.

2 Add the flour, oats, and hazelnuts to the bowl. Mix together with a wooden spoon. Cut the butter into small chunks and put into a saucepan.

3 Add the sugar and honey to the saucepan. Heat them over a low heat. Stir gently with a wooden spoon, until the butter and sugar have melted.

4 Add the butter mixture to the bowl and mix. Put 5 dessert spoonfuls of the cookie dough onto each baking tray, leaving space between each one.

5 Flatten the cookies a little so they are about 5cm (2 in) diameter and 1cm (½ in) thick. Bake for 15 minutes or until they are light golden.

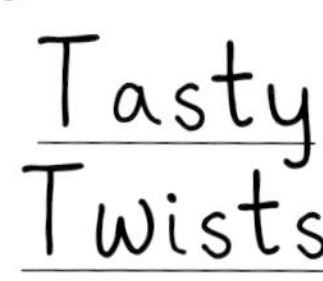

Tasty Twists

Chopped dried cherries, raisins cranberries, peaches, or dates can be used instead of apricots and any other nuts, such as walnuts, can be used instead of hazelnuts.

6 Remove the trays from the oven and leave the cookies to cool slightly. Then transfer the cookies to a cooling rack to cool and become crisp.

Food Facts

Flour is made by grinding grain, usually wheat. Wholemeal flour is made from the whole wheat grain with nothing added or taken away. It is higher in fibre and B vitamins than white flour, which is refined and processed until only about 75% of the grain is left. B vitamins are essential for producing energy, while fibre helps your digestive system work more efficiently.

Wheat

These tangy biscuits just melt in your mouth! They can be served with icing for a tasty treat or plain for a simple homemade biscuit.

Tasty Twists

When slicing the dough in step 5, turn the log 90° after each slice to produce evenly-shaped biscuits. If the dough breaks, you can just re-shape it.

If you don't have a piping bag, use a spoon to drizzle the icing.

Ingredients

- 125g (4oz) self-raising flour
- 60g (2oz) unsalted butter (diced) + extra for greasing
- 60g (2oz) soft dark brown sugar

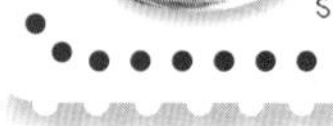

icing sugar

- ½ egg yolk (beaten)
- 15ml (1tbsp) clear runny honey
- 5g (1tsp) orange zest

For the icing

- 225g (7½oz) icing sugar (sieved)
- 45ml (3tbsp) fresh orange juice

Equipment

- sieve • table knife
- 2 mixing bowls
- cling film • knife
- 2 baking sheets
- cooling rack
- wooden spoon
- oven glove
- piping bag and nozzle or teaspoon

1 Preheat the oven to 180°C (350°F/Gas 4). Sieve the flour into a bowl and rub the butter into the flour, until you have a breadcrumb texture.

2 Using a table knife, stir the sugar, orange zest, honey, and egg into the flour and butter, until the mixture starts to come together in lumps.

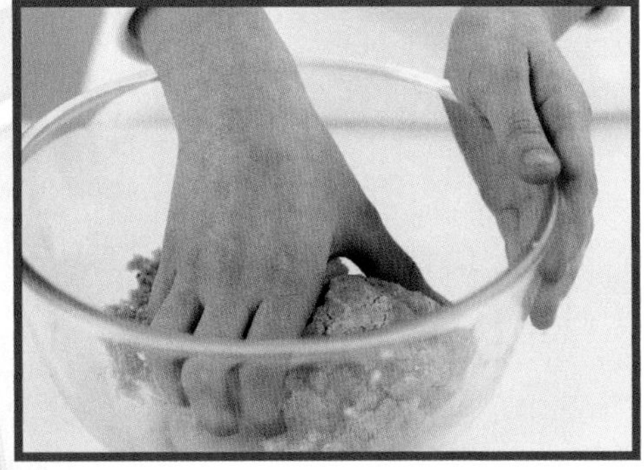

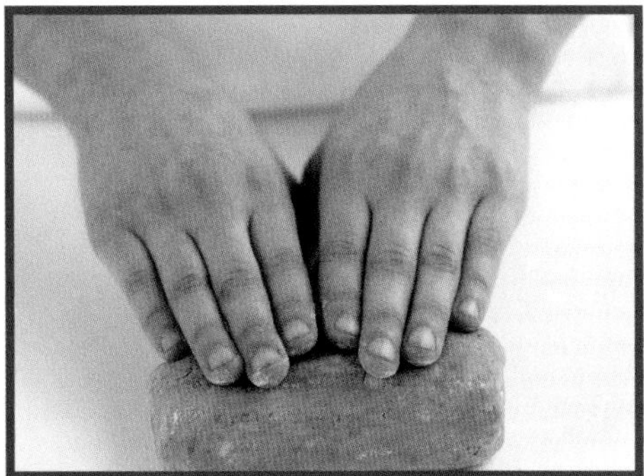

3 Use your hands to bring the lumps together to form a smooth ball of dough. Briefly knead the dough and then lightly flour the work surface.

4 Roll the dough into a log, about 5cm (2in) in diameter and 10cm (4in) long. Wrap the log in cling film and chill it for 1 hour 30 minutes, or until firm.

Tasty Twists

Try using 5g (1tsp) lemon zest or ground ginger instead of orange zest in step 2 and use 45ml (3tbsp) water instead of orange juice to make the icing in step 6.

5 Lightly grease 2 baking sheets with butter. Slice the log into 20–24 thin discs and place the biscuits on the baking sheets. Bake for 7–9 minutes.

6 Carefully remove the biscuits from the oven and allow to set and cool. Beat the icing sugar and orange juice together in a bowl, to form a smooth paste.

7 Carefully transfer the biscuits to a cooling rack. Put the icing into a piping bag and then drizzle it over the cool biscuits in your favourite patterns.

• **Preparation** 10 mins • **Cooking** 20 mins • **Makes** 12

Banocolate Cookies

These banana-flavoured biscuits are combined with chunks of chocolate. They are best eaten on the day they are made, but can be stored in an airtight container for up to 2 days.

Try using different types of chocolate such as milk, white, dark, or flavoured.

Ingredients

- 1 large ripe banana
- 100g ($3^1/_2$oz) unsalted butter, cut into pieces
- 100g ($3^1/_2$oz) soft light brown sugar
- 1 medium egg, beaten
- 100g ($3^1/_2$oz) plain flour
- 2.5ml ($^1/_2$tsp) baking powder
- 50g (2oz) whole porridge oats
- 100g ($3^1/_2$oz) plain chocolate, broken into small chunks

chocolate

Equipment

- 2 baking sheets
- knife
- food processor
- mixing bowl
- metal spoon
- cooling rack

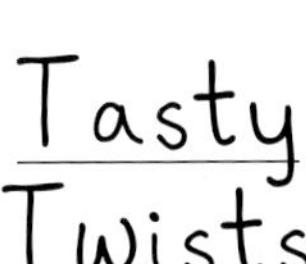

Tasty Twists

If you don't like banana, leave it out and add 30ml (2tbsp) of cocoa powder instead.

1 Preheat the oven to 180ºC, 350ºF, gas mark 4 and grease two baking sheets with butter. Peel and slice the banana, then place in a food processor.

2 Add the butter, sugar, and egg and process until smooth. Add the flour, baking powder, and oats and pulse until combined.

3 Transfer the mixture to a bowl and stir in the chocolate chunks.

4 Drop heaped dessertspoons of the mixture onto the sheets. Flatten them then bake for 15 to 20 minutes. Cool for 5 minutes, then transfer to a cooling rack.

• **Preparation** 30 mins • **Cooking** 20 mins • **Chilling** 15 mins • **Makes** 12

Strawberry Shortbreads

These strawberry shortbreads are perfect for afternoon tea. What do you mean, you don't have afternoon tea? Well now you have no excuse! The shortbread can be stored in an airtight container until you are ready to serve them.

Tasty Twists

Add a generous dollop of whipped cream to each biscuit and top with a spoonful of the strawberries.

Ingredients

strawberries

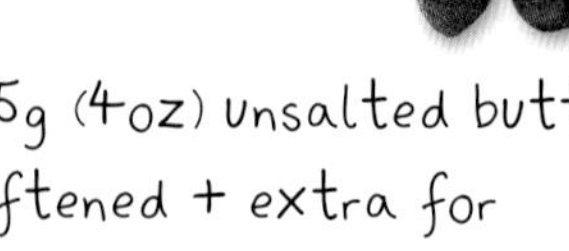

- 125g (4oz) unsalted butter, softened + extra for greasing
- 60g (2oz) caster sugar
- 125g (4oz) plain flour
- 60g (2oz) cornflour

unsalted butter

raspberry jam

For the topping:

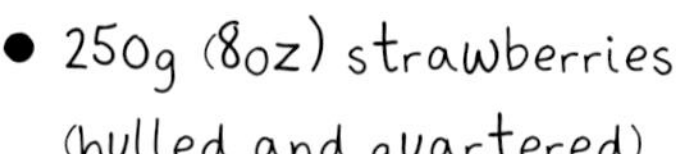

- 250g (8oz) strawberries (hulled and quartered)
- 60g (2oz) raspberry jam

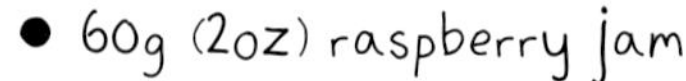

- 300ml (1/2pt) double cream (whipped)
- 140g (5oz) butter

double cream

Equipment

- mixing bowl

- electric whisk
- fork • sieve
- cling film • rolling pin
- greaseproof paper
- cookie cutter • oven gloves
- large baking tray
- small saucepan
- dessert spoon • cooling rack

measuring jug

1 Preheat the oven to 170°C (325°F/Gas 3). Place the butter and sugar in a bowl and cream together until light and fluffy using an electric whisk.

2 Sieve the plain flour and cornflour into the creamed butter. Mix together with a fork until all the ingredients are combined.

3 Form the dough into a smooth, round disc, using your hands. Wrap the dough in cling film and leave it to chill in the fridge for 15 minutes.

Experiment with different shaped cookie cutters eg. hearts, flowers, or stars.

Tasty Twists

Experiment with other fruit toppings, such as blueberries, blackberries, or raspberries. Or add 5g (1 tsp) of orange zest to the biscuit mixture in step 2 and miss out the topping.

4 Place the dough between 2 pieces of greaseproof paper. Roll it out to form a circle which is about 20cm (8in) in diameter and 1cm (½in) thick.

5 Cut out 12 shortbreads and place them onto a greased baking tray. (You will need to gather and re-roll the dough a few times.) Bake for 20 minutes.

6 Warm the jam in a saucepan, fold in the strawberries, and leave to cool. Remove the shortbread from the oven and leave them to set and cool.

● **Preparation** 40 mins ● **Cooking** 32 mins ● **Makes** 24

Caramel Shortbread

Caramel shortbread is also known as millionaires' shortbread. It is more like a biscuit than a cake and is definitely for those with a sweet tooth!

Ingredients

Base:
- 50g (2oz) soft brown sugar
- 125g (4oz) butter (softened)
- 150g (5½oz) self- raising flour

Caramel topping:
- 397g (14oz) can sweetened condensed milk
- 125g (4oz) butter (diced)
- 75g (3oz) soft light brown sugar
- 50ml (2tbsp) golden syrup

Chocolate topping:
- 75g (3oz) white chocolate
- 75g (3oz) plain chocolate

chocolate

self-raising flour

Equipment

- 8 x 28cm (7 x 11in) baking tin
- baking paper
- electric whisk
- mixing bowl
- wooden spoon
- saucepan
- 2 bowls
- metal spoon

mixing bowl

saucepan

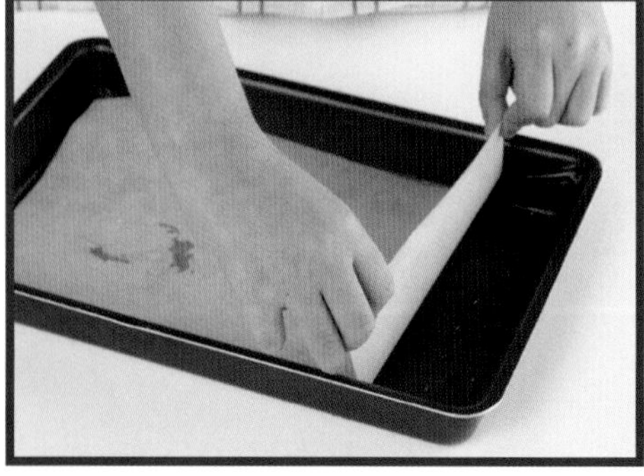

1 Preheat the oven to 180ºC, 350ºF, gas mark 4. Grease and line a 18 x 28cm (7 x 11in) tin with baking paper.

2 Cream together the butter and sugar until light and fluffy. Stir in the flour and mix until combined.

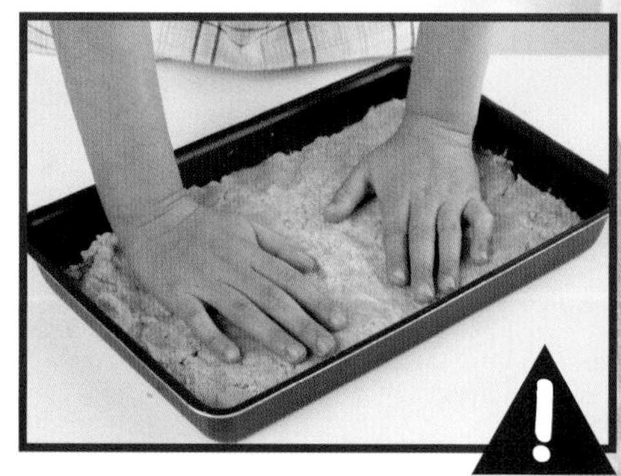

3 Press the mixture over the base of the tin and bake for 15 to 20 minutes until golden. Leave to cool.

4 Place the caramel topping ingredients in a saucepan. Place over a low heat until dissolved and bring to the boil. Continue to boil, stirring continuously, for 10 to 12 minutes.

5 Pour the caramel topping over the base. Leave to cool completely. Melt the chocolate in separate bowls over a pan of simmering water.

6 Pour the dark and white chocolate over the caramel and swirl together with the back of a spoon. Leave to set, then cut into squares.

These shortbread bites are lots of fun to make. What patterns can you create?

- **Preparation** 25 mins
- **Cooking** 30 mins
- **Makes** 6

Cherry and Apple Pies

Cherries and apples are combined in this variation of the American classic. This type of pie is called a free-form pie because it is not cooked in a dish and the sides of the pastry are simply gathered up to encase the filling.

Helpful Hints

Ground almonds, semolina, or fine polenta help to soak up the fruit juices and prevent the pastry from going soggy. Ground almonds also add extra flavour but nut allergy sufferers should use semolina or fine polenta instead.

Ingredients

- 75g ($2^{1}/_{2}$oz) unsalted butter (plus extra to glaze)
- 2 tbsp caster sugar
- 1 large egg (lightly beaten)
- 220g ($7^{1}/_{2}$oz) plain flour (plus extra for dusting)
- 1 tbsp water

Filling:

dessert apples

- 2 tbsp caster sugar
- 300g ($10^{1}/_{2}$oz) pitted canned cherries (drained weight)
- 2 dessert apples
- 50g ground almonds, semolina, or fine polenta

Glaze:

- 1 large egg (lightly beaten)

Equipment

cling film

- 2 large baking sheets
- baking paper
- scissors
- mixing bowl
- food processor or blender
- cling film
- sieve
- vegetable peeler
- rolling pin

food processor

1 Line the baking sheets. Put the butter, 75g (3oz) of the sugar, and 1 egg into a food processor and process until smooth and creamy.

2 Add the flour and 1 tablespoon of water to the processor and whiz until the mixture comes together in a ball. (The pastry will be quite soft.)

Did you know?

Perhaps rather appropriately, cherries date back to the Stone Age. Cherry stones have been found in many Stone Age caves in Europe.

3 Turn the dough out on to a lightly floured work surface and gather it until it forms a smooth ball. Cover with cling film and chill for 30 minutes.

4 Preheat the oven to 200°C (400°F/Gas 6). While the pastry is chilling, drain the cherries in a sieve and mix with the apples, sugar, and almonds.

Food Facts

Tinned fruit is used in this recipe because cherries are seasonal and therefore only widely available at certian times of the year. Choose fruit tinned in natural juices rather than with added sugar or syrup.

tinned cherries

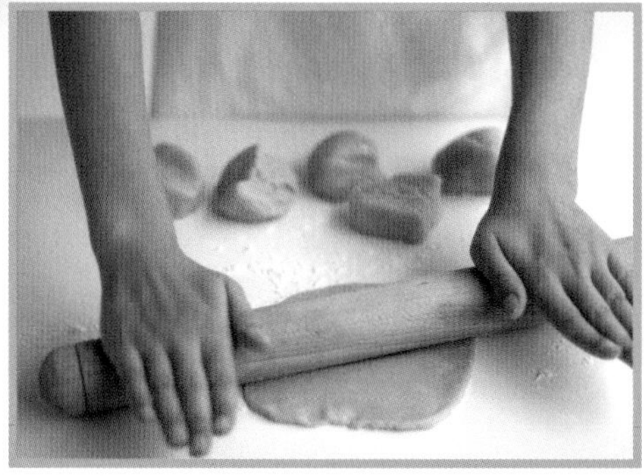

5 Divide the pastry into 6 pieces. On a lightly floured surface, roll the pastry into thin circles about 13cm (5in) in diameter. Put on the baking sheet.

6 Brush the pastry with egg and sprinkle on the almonds. Add the fruit leaving a 2.5cm (1in) border. Gently gather the pastry to make open-topped pies.

7 Brush the outside of the pies with egg. Place a small piece of butter on top of the fruit. Bake the pies for 25 mins or until the pastry is light golden.

• **Preparation** 25 mins • **Cooking** 50 mins • **Makes** 1 loaf

Banana and Pineapple Cake

This rich, moist cake is the tastiest fruit cake around! It is the perfect addition to a picnic or school lunchbox or it makes a great after-dinner treat.

Did you know?

Banana plants have been around for a long time. One of the first records dates back to Alexander the Great's conquest of India where he discovered bananas in 327 BCE!

Ingredients

self-raising wholemeal flour

bananas

- 125g (4oz) unsalted butter, cut into small pieces (plus extra for greasing)
- 5 small bananas (about 450g/1lb peeled weight)
- 75g (3oz) ready-to-eat dried pineapple
- 175g (6oz) self-raising white flour
- 50g (2oz) self-raising wholemeal flour
- 1 tsp baking powder
- pinch of salt
- 125g(4oz) unrefined caster sugar
- 2 large free-range eggs
- 50g (2oz) chopped walnuts (optional)

free-range eggs

Equipment

scissors

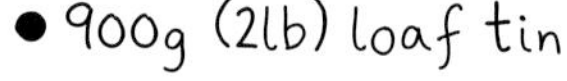

- 900g (2lb) loaf tin
- baking paper
- small bowl
- fork
- scissors
- sieve
- large mixing bowl
- wooden spoon

mixing bowl

loaf tin

1 Preheat the oven to 180°C (350°F/Gas 4). Trace around the loaf tin onto baking paper and cut it out. Lightly grease the tin with butter and then line.

2 Put the bananas in a bowl and mash them with a fork. Cut the pineapple into very small pieces. Set the bananas and pineapple aside.

Helpful Hint

If the pineapple is very dry, it's best to soak it in hot water for about 1 hour or until it is tender.

3 Sift the flour, baking powder, and salt into a mixing bowl. Stir and then add the butter. Rub the butter into the flour mixture until it looks like fine breadcrumbs.

4 One at a time, crack the eggs into a small bowl. Lightly beat the eggs together with a fork until the white and yolk are mixed together.

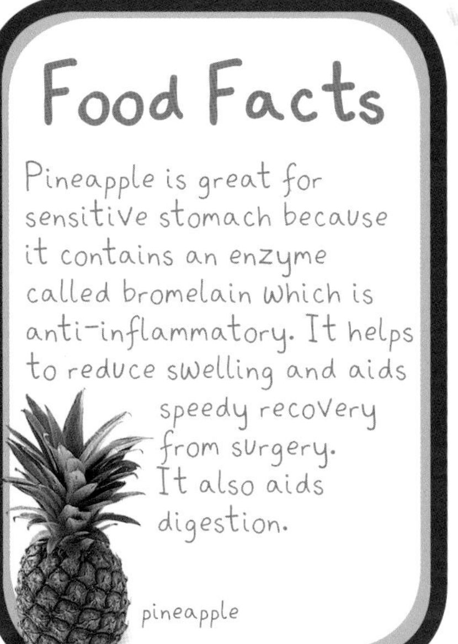

Food Facts

Pineapple is great for sensitive stomach because it contains an enzyme called bromelain which is anti-inflammatory. It helps to reduce swelling and aids speedy recovery from surgery. It also aids digestion.

pineapple

5 Pour the beaten eggs into the mixing bowl, add the sugar, bananas, and pineapple and mix together. Pour the cake mixture into the prepared cake tin.

6 Make sure the mixture is level and then sprinkle over the walnuts. Cook in the centre of the oven for about 50 minutes until risen and golden.

7 Remove from the oven and place on a cooling rack for 10 minutes. Carefully turn the cooled cake out of the tin, cut into slices, and serve.

• **Preparation** 35–40 mins • **Cooking** 25–30 mins • **Makes** 1

Chocolate Cake

When baking a cake make sure that the oven is at the right temperature before you put the cake in. When the cake is in the oven, don't open the door to check on it until the cooking time has passed, otherwise it will sink!

For a flat top, put the second cake on upside down!

Food Facts

The beaten eggs used in step 1 should be at room temperature and added slowly, otherwise the cake mixture may curdle. If the mixture does start to curdle, mix in a little flour.

eggs

Ingredients

beaten eggs

- 3 beaten eggs (at room temperature)
- 175g (6oz) unsalted butter (softened)
- 175g (6oz) caster sugar
- 150g (5 oz) self raising flour
- 1/2 tsp of baking powder
- oil (for greasing)
- 3tbsp of cocoa powder

For the topping

- 100g (3 1/2 oz) milk chocolate
- 200ml (7fl oz) double cream (at room temperature)
- 100g (3 1/2 oz) plain chocolate

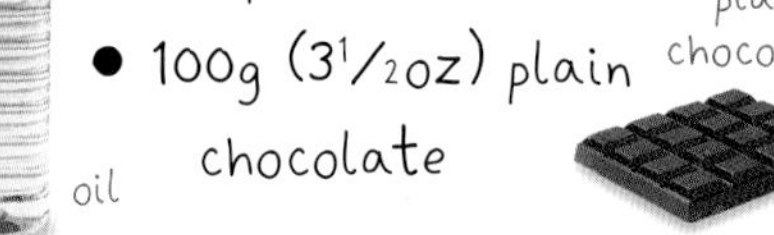

oil

cocoa powder

plain chocolate

Equipment

- 2 20cm/8in round cake tins
- small saucepan
- serving plate
- baking parchment
- large mixing bowl
- electric whisk
- oven gloves
- sieve
- cooling rack
- metal mixing spoon
- step palette knife
- small mixing bowl

Tasty Twists

For a tasty topping, melt 100g ($3^1/_2$ oz) white chocolate (see step 4) and pour it into a wax paper-lined tray. Leave it to set. Break the set chocolate into small pieces and use it to decorate the top of the cake.

1 Grease the cake tins and line the bases. Cream the butter and sugar together in a bowl until they are light and fluffy. Gradually beat in the egg.

2 Preheat the oven to 180°C (350°F/Gas 4). Sieve the flour, cocoa powder, and baking powder into the bowl and fold them into the creamed mixture.

3 Divide the mixture equally between the two greased and lined cake tins, smoothing the tops with a palette knife. Bake for 20–25 minutes or until firm.

4 Turn the cooked cakes out onto a cooling rack. Break the plain and milk chocolate into a bowl and gently melt them over a pan of simmering water.

5 Remove the bowl from the pan. Allow the chocolate to cool for 5 minutes and then stir in the cream. Leave the mixture to thicken for a few minutes.

6 Make sure the cakes are completely cool before putting on the topping. Put one cake on a serving plate and spread a quarter of the topping over it.

7 Put the other cake on top and spoon over the rest of the topping. Spread it over the top and the sides until the cake is evenly coated. Leave to set.

• **Preparation** 1.5 hours • **Cooking** 12 mins • **Serves** 10

Gingerbread House

For an extra surprise, fill the centre of the house with more sweets before attaching the roof.

Try making gingerbread men, women and children to live in your house.

Ingredients

Dough:

- 250g (9oz) unsalted butter (softened)
- 150g (5½oz) soft brown sugar
- 2 medium eggs, beaten
- 175ml (6floz) golden syrup
- 30ml (2tbsp) ground ginger
- 625g (1¼lb) plain flour
- 10ml (2tsp) bicarbonate of soda

For decoration:

- 1 egg white
- 225g (8oz) icing sugar (sifted)
- marshmallows, halved, for the roof and sweets of your choice

eggs

flour

Equipment

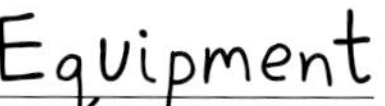

- two 18 x 10cm (7 x 4in) rectangles for the roof
- two 15 x 10cm (6 x 4in) rectangles for the sides. Add windows
- two 10cm (4in) squares for the ends, extending 7½cm (3in) from the top edge of the squares to a point. Add a door
- food processor
- cling film
- rolling pin
- baking paper
- knife
- mixing bowl
- spoon
- cooling rack

food processor

1 Place the butter and sugar in a food processor and blend until creamy. Add the eggs, golden syrup, ginger, bicarbonate of soda, and half the flour and process.

2 Add the remaining flour and process until the mixture forms a ball. Wrap in cling film and chill for 30 minutes. Meanwhile, cut out the templates.

3 Preheat the oven to 180ºC, 350ºF, gas mark 4. Roll out the dough between 2 pieces of baking paper to 5mm (¼in) thick. Use the templates to cut the dough.

4 Chill for 10 minutes, then bake for 12 minutes. Leave to cool for 2 minutes, then transfer to a cooling rack. Beat the egg white and icing sugar together.

5 Join the front and sides of the house together with a little of the icing and allow to dry. Add the back and roof in the same way. Decorate with icing and sweets.

• **Preparation** 20–25 mins • **Cooking** 25 mins • **Makes** 12–16

Chocolate Brownies

Here are a few tips on baking brownies – melt the chocolate gently over a low heat and make sure that the bowl does not touch the water in the pan. You must fold, not stir, the mixture in step 5, and you should always line the tin to prevent the brownies sticking to it.

Ingredients

- 90g (3oz) plain chocolate
- 150g (5oz) unsalted butter + extra for greasing
- 125g (4oz) plain flour
- 15g (1/2oz) cocoa powder
- 1/2 tsp of baking powder
- 1tsp of vanilla extract
- 1 pinch of salt
- 300g (10oz) soft light brown sugar
- 2 eggs
- 100g (3 1/2oz) chopped pecan nuts (optional)

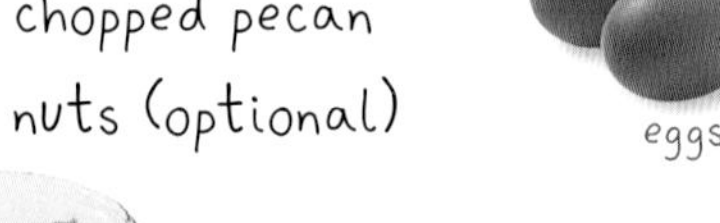

Equipment

- baking tin (20x15cm or 8x6in)
- scissors • pencil
- baking parchment
- 3 medium bowls • sieve
- small saucepan
- rubber spoon spatula
- palette knife
- oven gloves

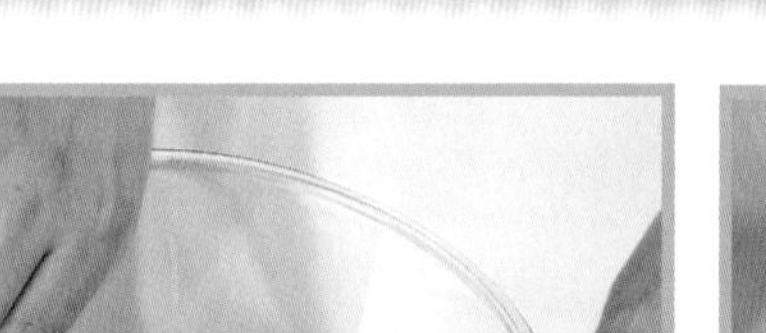

1 Preheat the oven to 180°C (350°F/Gas 4). Grease and line the base of the baking tin with non-stick baking parchment.

2 Break the chocolate into a bowl and add the butter. Melt the butter and chocolate over a saucepan of barely simmering water, stirring occasionally.

3 Remove the bowl from the heat and allow the chocolate to cool slightly. Sieve the flour, cocoa powder, baking powder, and salt into a separate bowl.

Tasty Twists

If you don't like nuts or are allergic to them, you can leave them out. These brownies taste just as delicious without nuts.

4 In a third bowl, beat the eggs and then add the sugar and vanilla extract. Stir the ingredients together until they are just combined.

5 Fold the melted chocolate into the beaten egg mixture. Then fold in the flour mixture and nuts. There should be no visible flour.

6 Spoon the mixture into the tin, smooth the top with a palette knife, and bake for 25 minutes. Allow it to cool in the tin before cutting into squares.

- **Preparation** 30–35 mins
- **Cooking** 30–35 mins
- **Rising** 2½ hours
- **Makes** 2 loaves

Homemade Bread

It is simple to create a light, airy loaf of bread. All you need are a few basic ingredients – flour, yeast, salt, and water. The most important thing is to learn special bread-making skills, such as kneading and knocking back. These are all explained in the glossary on p.298.

Helpful Hints

The dough needs to be put in a warm, but not hot, place to rise. Places such as an airing cupboard or near a warm oven are perfect!

Ingredients

water

- 250ml (8fl oz) lukewarm water
- 15g (½oz) fresh yeast
- 1tsp of caster sugar
- 2tsp of salt
- 1tbsp of olive oil + extra for greasing
- 450g (14½oz) strong plain white bread flour, plus extra for kneading

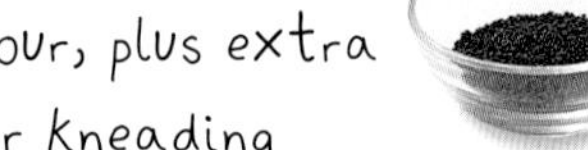

For the topping:

- 2tsp of poppy seeds (optional)
- 1 egg (beaten)
- 2tsp of sesame seeds (optional)

beaten egg

Equipment

- ramekin
- sieve
- mixing bowl
- 2 loaf tins (500g/1lb)
- wooden spoon
- large bowl
- cling film
- pastry brush
- oven gloves

wooden spoon

Helpful Hints

If you don't have fresh yeast, you can use 7g (1/3 oz) of easy-blend dry yeast instead. Miss out step 1 and stir the dry yeast and 1tsp of caster sugar into the sieved flour in step 2.

1 Using your finger, mix 3tbsp of the water with the yeast and sugar. Leave it in a warm place for 10 minutes or until it begins to bubble.

2 Sieve the flour and salt into a bowl and stir in the yeast mixture. Stir in the oil and then enough of the remaining water to make a soft dough.

3 Lightly flour your hands and the work surface. Knead the dough for about 10 minutes or until it becomes smooth and elastic. (See p.298 for tips.)

4 Put the dough in a lightly-greased bowl and cover it with greased cling film. Put it in a warm place for 1½ hours, until the dough has doubled in size.

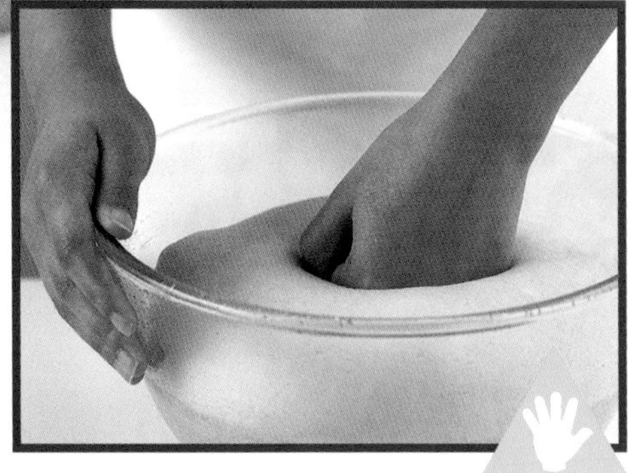

5 Preheat the oven to 220°C (425°F/Gas 7). Knock back the risen dough and then knead it on a lightly-floured surface for a further 5 minutes.

6 Shape the dough into 2 rectangles. Place each piece into a lightly-greased loaf tin, cover and place in a warm place until they have doubled in size.

7 Glaze the loaves with egg and sprinkle with seeds. Bake for 30–35 minutes. A cooked loaf will look golden and sound hollow if tapped on the base.

• **Preparation** 15 mins • **Cooking** 35 mins • **Makes** 1 loaf

Raisin Soda Bread

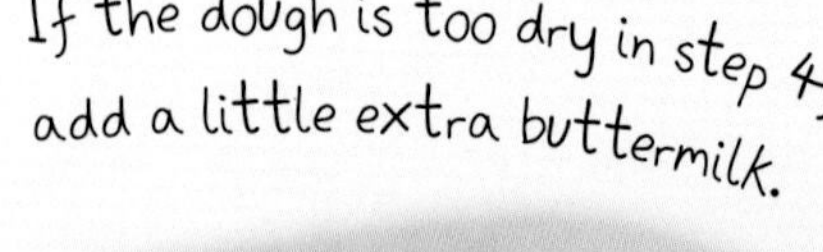

Soda bread is the perfect starting point for anyone who hasn't made bread before. It doesn't contain yeast so it doesn't need as much kneading or rising as ordinary bread, but it's every bit as tasty.

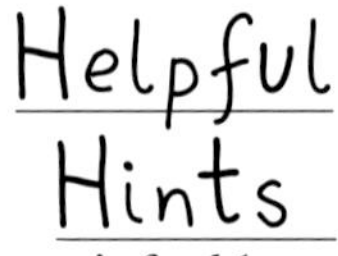

If you can't find buttermilk in the shops, use the same quantity of low fat natural yoghurt or milk combined with 1 tablespoon lemon juice.

Ingredients

- 200g (7oz) wholemeal plain flour
- 200g (7oz) white plain flour, plus extra for dusting
- 1 tsp salt
- 1 tsp bicarbonate of soda
- 50g (2oz) porridge oats
- 1 heaped tbsp caster sugar
- 125g (4½oz) raisins
- 1 egg (lightly beaten)
- 300–350ml (10–12fl oz) buttermilk

Equipment

- baking sheet
- sieve
- large mixing bowl
- wooden spoon
- knife

wooden spoon

large mixing bowl

Food Facts

Traditionally, buttermilk is the liquid remaining after the cream has been churned into butter. It is low in fat and is often used to make pancakes and scones as well as soda bread. When combined with bicarbonate of soda it acts as a raising agent. However, if you can't get buttermilk, natural yoghurt is a great alternative.

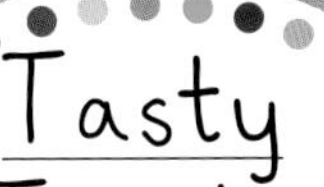
buttermilk

Tasty Twists

Chopped dried dates, cranberries, blueberries, or cherries could be used instead of raisins – or you could try a mixture of dried fruits.

1 Preheat the oven to 200°C (400°F/Gas 6). Sprinkle a baking sheet with flour until it is lightly covered. This will prevent the loaf sticking to the sheet.

2 Sieve the wholemeal and white flour, salt, and bicarbonate of soda into a mixing bowl. If there is any bran left in the sieve, add it to the bowl.

3 Add the oats, sugar, and raisins to the bowl and stir. Make a well in the centre of the mixture and pour in the egg and 300ml (10fl oz) of the buttermilk.

4 Mix together with a wooden spoon. When the mixture starts to come together, use your hands to form a soft, slightly sticky ball of dough.

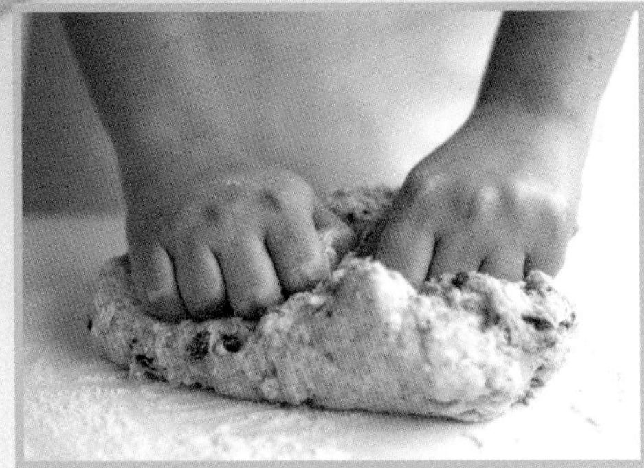

5 Put the dough onto a lightly floured work surface and gently knead, once or twice, until the dough is smooth. Don't over-knead or the dough will toughen.

6 Form the dough into a flattish circle, about 18cm (7in) round and 4cm (1½ in) thick. Put the dough on the floured baking sheet.

7 Sieve over a little extra flour. Cut a large, deep cross, almost to the bottom of the dough. Bake for 30–35 minutes, or until risen and golden.

● **Preparation** 20 mins + 2 hours 10 mins rising ● **Cooking** 25–30 mins ● **Makes** 10 rolls

Sunflower Seed Rolls

There's nothing like the aroma of fresh bread! All you need is a handful of basic ingredients to make these seedy rolls. You could also make a single loaf instead of the rolls.

Healthy Hints

Instead of sprinkling the seeds over the top of the rolls, you could mix them into the dough in step 2. Sesame, pumpkin, or poppy seeds also taste great.

To test if the rolls are cooked, lightly tap the base – if it sounds hollow, it is cooked!

Ingredients

- 350ml (12fl oz) tepid water
- 2 tsp dried yeast
- 50g (12oz) strong white bread flour
- 150g (5½ oz) strong wholemeal bread flour
- 1½ tsp salt
- 1 egg (beaten)
- 5 tbsp sunflower seeds

sunflower seeds

wholemeal bread flour

Equipment

- small bowl
- large mixing bowl
- wooden spoon or tablespoon
- baking sheets
- pastry brush
- jug

mixing bowl

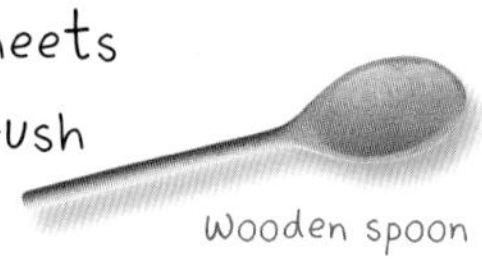

wooden spoon

1 Pour 100ml (3½ fl oz) of the water into a small bowl. Sprinkle in the yeast and stir until dissolved. Set aside for 5 minutes.

2 Put both types of flour and the salt into a large mixing bowl and mix together. Make a well (a large hole) in the centre of the flour.

3 Pour the yeast and most of the remaining water into the well and gently stir in the flour. Stir in the rest of the water, if necessary, to make a soft dough.

4 Turn the dough out on to a floured work surface. Knead for 10 minutes until smooth and shiny. Put the dough in a clean bowl and cover with a tea towel.

5 Leave the rise for 1½–2 hours, until it has doubled in size. Preheat the oven to 220°C (425°F/Gas 7). Knock back the risen dough with your knuckles.

6 Divide the dough into 10 pieces. Dust your hands with flour and shape the dough into rolls. Cover the rolls and set aside for 10 minutes.

7 Brush each roll with beaten egg and gently press the sunflower seeds into the tops. Bake for 25–30 minutes or until risen and golden.

Food Facts

Yeast is a single-celled micro-organism that is part of the fungus family and can be bought fresh or dried. It is used in bread-making to make the dough rise and give the bread a light, airy texture. To work, the yeast needs warmth and moisture. It ferments and produces tiny bubbles of gas which make the dough rise and give it a light, spongy texture.

fresh yeast

• **Preparation** 40-45 mins • **Rising** 1 h • **Cooking** 4-6 mins • **Makes** 4

Naan Bread

The dough will be sticky in step 3 so rub a little flour on your hands.

Naan is a special type of flatbread from India that is usually eaten with curry. Unlike the loaf of bread on p.246–247, naan bread is grilled not baked. As the naan cooks, a hollow pocket forms inside which is perfect for adding a tasty filling.

Helpful Hints

If you are using dry yeast, miss out step 1 and stir in 5g (1/4 oz) of easy-blend dry yeast in step 2.

Ingredients

cumin seeds

- 3tbsp of warm milk
- 2tsp of fresh yeast
- 200g (7oz) strong plain white bread flour
- 1/2 tsp of salt
- 2tsp of cumin seeds (optional)
- 1 egg (beaten)
- Vegetable oil (for greasing)
- 3tbsp of natural yoghurt
- 30g (1oz) unsalted butter (melted)

beaten egg 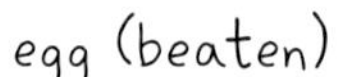

milk

Equipment

- ramekin
- sieve
- wooden spoon
- 2 large bowls
- cling film
- table knife
- rolling pin
- baking tray
- pastry brush
- oven gloves

rolling pin

Helpful Hint

The milk in step 1 should be lukewarm, not hot. If it is too hot, it will kill the yeast and the bread will not rise.

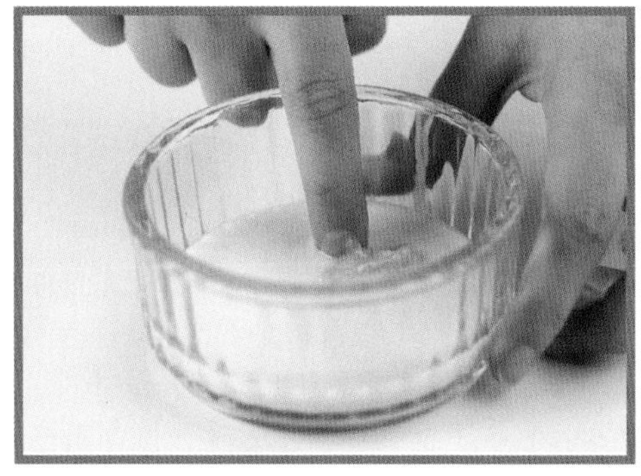

1 Using your finger, mix the milk and fresh yeast together in a ramekin. Leave the mixture in a warm place for 10 minutes or until it bubbles slightly.

2 Sieve the flour and salt into a bowl. Using a wooden spoon, gradually stir the yeast mixture, egg, and yoghurt into the flour until you have a soft dough.

3 On a lightly floured surface, knead the dough for 5 minutes or until it is smooth and elastic. Lightly grease a bowl with oil and then add the dough.

4 Cover the bowl with lightly greased cling film and leave it in a warm place for about 1 hour or until the dough has doubled in size.

5 Remove the cling film and knock back the dough. Divide the dough into 4 equal pieces and knead some of the cumin seeds into each piece (optional).

6 Roll each piece into a teardrop shape. Don't be afraid to stretch the dough to get the right shape! Preheat the baking tray under a hot grill.

7 Place the naan breads on the hot baking tray and glaze both sides with melted butter. Grill each side on high for 2 minutes or until risen and golden.

Party Food

- **Preparation** 60 mins
- **Rising** 1–1½ hours
- **Cooking** 20–25 mins
- **Makes** 2 mins

Pizza

The pizza base is made in the same way as the bread on p.246–247. However, the dough only needs to rise once in this recipe, rather than twice, like the bread.

Ingredients

For the base:

- 250g (8oz) plain flour
- 5g (¼oz) fresh yeast
- 150ml (¼ pint) water
- 1 tsp of caster sugar
- ½ tsp of salt
- olive oil, for greasing

For the topping:

- 1 small tin of chopped tomatoes
- 1tbsp of tomato purée
- salt and pepper
- 1tsp of dried oregano
- 1 small tin pineapple pieces
- 2 slices of ham
- 1 ball mozzarella (drained and sliced)

chopped tomatoes

Equipment

- ramekin
- 2 sieves
- mixing bowl
- 2 wooden spoons
- large bowl
- cling film
- small bowl
- small saucepan
- teaspoon
- chopping board
- rolling pin
- baking tray
- dessert spoon
- oven gloves

chopping board

mixing bowl

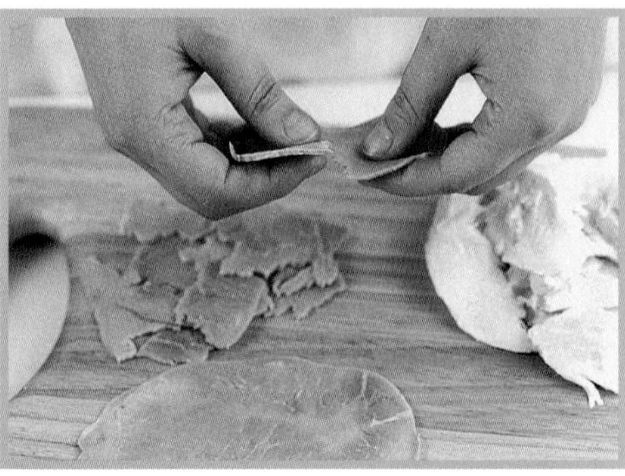

1 To make the base, follow steps 1–4 on p.246–247. While the dough is rising in step 4, use a sieve to drain the excess liquid from the tomatoes.

2 Put the tomatoes into a small saucepan and add the tomato purée, oregano, salt, and pepper. Gently warm them over a low heat for 2 minutes.

3 With your fingers, tear the ham and mozzarella into bite-sized pieces. Drain the pineapple pieces. Preheat the oven to 220°C (425°F/Gas 7).

Pesto is a tasty alternative to tomato sauce on a pizza. (See p. 86–87 for a recipe.)

Tasty Twists

To prevent sticking and to make 2 equal-sized circles in step 4, turn the dough 45° after each roll.

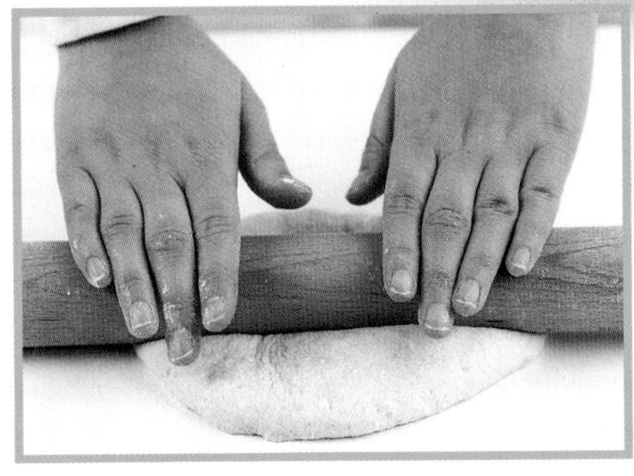

4 Knock back the risen dough and put it onto a lightly floured work surface. Roll it out into 2 equal circles, about 15cm (6in) in diameter.

5 Place the pizza bases on a lightly greased baking tray. Spread half of the tomato sauce onto each base leaving a 2cm (¾in) rim around the edge.

6 Add the toppings and bake the pizzas for 20–25 minutes. Let the pizzas cool a little before cutting and eating as the cheese will be very hot!

• **Preparation** 1 h 15 mins • **Chilling** 1 h 15 mins • **Cooking** 1 hour 5 mins • **Makes** 1

Vegetable Tart

This is a simple introduction to making savoury shortcrust pastry. Here's a top tip – when making savoury or sweet pastry, make sure that your hands are not too hot and the butter and water are also cool to give the pastry a lighter texture.

The technique used in step 6 is called baking blind.

Tasty Twists

Other fillings, such as bacon, peppers, broccoli, onion, or mushrooms would taste great in this recipe.

ham

Ingredients

- 225g (7½oz) plain flour + extra for rolling
- 1 pinch of salt
- 90g (3oz) unsalted butter (diced)
- 30g (1oz) vegetable fat or lard (cubed)
- 2tbsp of water

For the filling

- 2 eggs (beaten)
- 100ml (3½fl oz) cream
- 125g (4oz) sweetcorn
- 125g (4oz) peas
- 100g (3½oz) ham (cubed)
- 100ml (3½fl oz) milk
- 30g (1oz) cheese (grated)
- 1 small leek (sautéed)

peas

sweetcorn

Equipment

- sieve
- mixing bowl
- fork
- tablespoon
- cling film
- rolling pin
- flan tin, loose-bottomed and fluted (approx. 20cm/8in in diameter)
- table knife
- greaseproof paper
- baking beans or dried kidney beans
- oven gloves
- jug
- whisk

mixing bowl

Helpful Hints

Sprinkle the cheese over the top and bake the tart for 45 minutes. Allow the tart to set and cool before serving.

1 Sieve the flour and salt into a bowl. Using a fork, gently stir the diced butter and vegetable fat into the flour until they are completely coated.

2 Rub the butter and fat into the flour with your fingertips, until it looks like coarse breadcrumbs. Preheat the oven to 200°C (400°F/Gas 6).

3 Add the water, drop by drop, and stir into the crumbs with a table knife. When the crumbs start to stick together in lumps, gather the pastry in your hands.

4 Shape the pastry into a smooth disc and wrap it in cling film. Chill it for 1 hour, or until firm. Lightly flour the work surface.

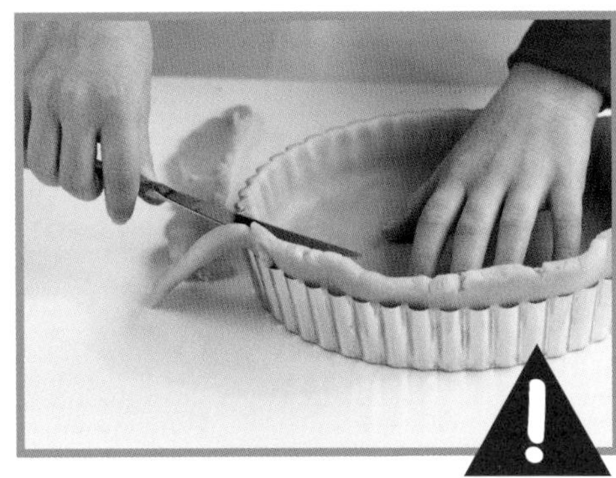

5 Roll out the pastry so that it is slightly bigger than the tin. Gently press it into the tin and trim off the excess. Prick the base and chill it for 15 minutes.

6 Cover the tart with 2 layers of greaseproof paper and add the baking beans. Bake for 15 minutes, remove the paper and beans and bake for 5 minutes.

7 Reduce the oven to 180°C (350°F/Gas 4). Scatter the ham and vegetables over the base. Whisk the eggs, milk, and cream together and pour into the tart.

• **Preparation** 10 mins • **Cooking** 10 mins • **Serves** 4

Red Pepper Houmous

This roasted red pepper houmous makes a perfect dip for snacking with toasted pitta or crudités. Alternatively, spread onto tortillas with some crumbled feta cheese for an easy wrap.

Ingredients

- 2 red peppers, deseeded and each cut into 4
- 400g (14oz) can chickpeas, drained and rinsed
- 2 cloves garlic, peeled
- 30ml (2tbsp) tahini (sesame seed paste)

lemon

garlic

- juice 1/2 lemon
- 45ml (3tbsp) olive oil
- a little paprika

red peppers

Equipment

- knife
- food processor
- plastic bag
- bowl

food processor

1 Place the red peppers under a hot grill. Grill until the skins have blackened. Place in a plastic bag and when cool, peel off the blackened skin.

2 Place the skinless peppers with the remaining ingredients in a food processor and blend until smooth and creamy.

3 Transfer the houmous to a bowl and sprinkle with a little paprika. Serve with grilled pitta breads or vegetable crudités.

This healthy snack is great served with vegetable dippers like carrot and cucumber.

Helpful Hints

Wait until the peppers are cool before you peel the skin off – you don't want burnt fingers!

• **Preparation** 10 mins • **Cooking** 6 mins • **Serves** 4

Griddled Fruit & Honey

You will love this fruit griddled – it helps bring out the sweetness. If you don't have a griddle pan, place the fruit under a hot grill.

Ingredients

- 3 peaches
- 4 apricots
- 30ml (2tbsp) caster sugar
- 2.5ml (1/2tsp) ground cinnamon
- 200ml (7floz) Greek yogurt
- 30ml (2tbsp) clear honey

Equipment

- knife
- chopping board
- 2 mixing bowls
- 2 metal spoons
- griddle pan
- tongs

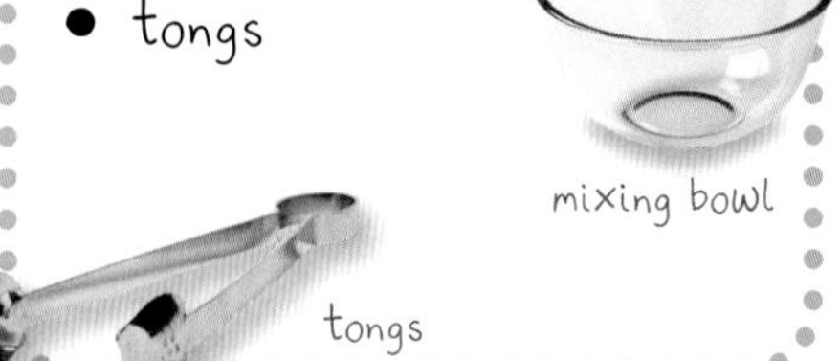

1 Cut each peach in half and remove the stone. Then cut each into quarters. Halve the apricots and remove the stones.

2 In a large bowl, mix together the sugar and cinnamon, then add the fruit. Toss to coat in the sugar mixture.

3 Preheat a griddle pan and add the peaches, flesh side down. Cook for 2 to 3 minutes. Add the apricots, and turn over the peaches. Cook until caramelised.

4 Meanwhile, place the yogurt in a bowl and pour over the honey. Stir to create a rippled effect. Serve the warmed griddled fruit with the yogurt and honey dip.

Tasty Twists

If you don't like Greek yogurt, try this with ice cream or crème fraîche.

Slices of mango and pineapple are also delicious griddled.

• **Preparation** 25 mins • **Cooking** 15 mins • **Serves** 30

Cheese & Pesto Straws

Flavoured with pesto and cheese, these light crisp straws are perfect for dipping.

These moreish cheese & pesto straws are great for parties and picnics.

Ingredients

- 200g (7oz) plain flour
- 125g (4½oz) chilled butter, cut into small cubes
- 50g (2oz) Gruyère or Cheddar cheese, finely grated
- 50g (2oz) Parmesan cheese, finely grated
- 1 whole medium egg, plus 1 yolk
- 30ml (2tbsp) pesto sauce (red or green)

Equipment

- sieve
- mixing bowl
- metal spoon
- rolling pin
- knife
- baking paper
- baking sheet
- cooling rack

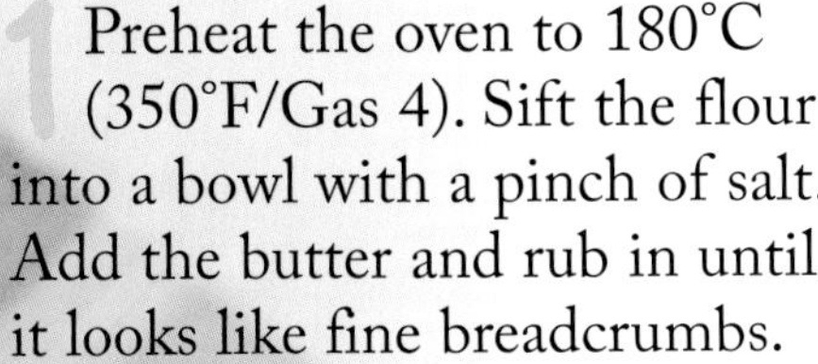

1 Preheat the oven to 180°C (350°F/Gas 4). Sift the flour into a bowl with a pinch of salt. Add the butter and rub in until it looks like fine breadcrumbs.

2 Stir in 75g (3oz) of the cheeses. Beat together the egg and egg yolk and stir into the flour with the pesto sauce. Mix to a dough.

3 The mixture should be of the consistency where you can roll it into a ball.

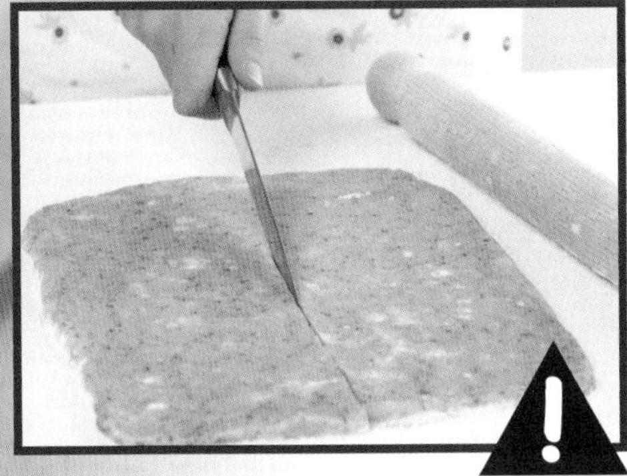

4 Roll out on a lightly floured surface into a rectangle about 28 x 23cm (11 x 9in). Cut in half down the longest length, then cut each into about 15 straws.

5 Line a baking sheet with baking paper. Transfer the straws to the baking sheet, leaving a gap between each.

6 Sprinkle over the remaining cheese and chill for 15 min. Bake for 12 to 15 minutes. Cool for 5 minutes on the sheet, then transfer to a cooling rack.

• **Preparation** 5 mins • **Cooking** 4 mins • **Serves** 4

Nachos & Salsa

Make this quick tomato salsa and spoon over tortilla chips with cheese for a tasty snack.

Tasty Twists

Add some cooked diced chicken or kidney beans to make this snack more filling.

Ingredients

- 1 x 200g (7oz) pack plain tortilla chips
- 50g (2oz) mozzarella cheese (grated)
- 50g (2oz) mature Cheddar cheese (grated)

tomatoes

Salsa:

- 350g (12oz) tomatoes
- 1/2 red onion (finely chopped)
- 2 cloves garlic (crushed)
- juice 1/2 lime
- (60ml) 4tbsp freshly chopped coriander
- 2.5ml (1/2tsp) sugar
- 1 green chilli (deseeded and chopped)

Equipment

- chopping board
- knife
- mixing bowl
- metal spoon
- baking tray

mixing bowl

baking tray

1 Cut the tomatoes in half and remove the seeds, then dice. Place in a bowl and stir in all the remaining salsa ingredients.

2 Place the nachos on a large baking tray or shallow ovenproof dish and spoon over the salsa.

3 Scatter over the cheese. Place under a preheated grill for 3 to 4 minutes until the cheese has melted.

Serving Tip

Serve with sour cream and guacamole to dip your delicious nachos into.

• **Preparation** 10 mins • **Cooking** 35 mins • **Serves** 4

Spicy Potato Wedges

These spiced potato wedges can be eaten as a snack, served with a cooling sour cream and chive dip. Alternatively, they make a great accompaniment to burgers.

Ingredients

potatoes

- 3 medium baking potatoes, (about 650g or 1lb 4oz)
- 30ml (2tbsp) olive oil
- 15ml (1tbsp) paprika
- 10ml (2tsp) ground cumin
- 10ml (2tsp) dried mixed herbs
- 2.5ml (1/2tsp) cayenne pepper (optional)
- 2.5ml (1/2tsp) salt

paprika

Equipment

- knife
- chopping board
- large saucepan
- mixing bowl
- metal spoon
- non-stick baking tray
- pastry brush

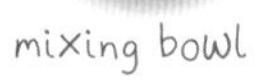

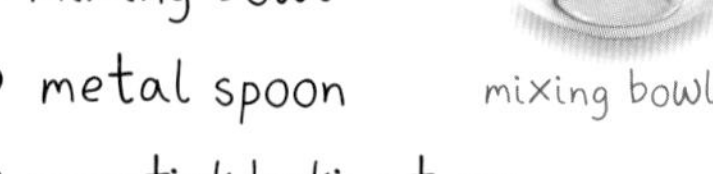

mixing bowl

saucepan

1 Preheat the oven to 200°C, 400°F, gas mark 6. Cut each potato into 8 wedges.

2 Bring a pan of water to the boil, add the potatoes and simmer for 8 minutes. Drain and return to the pan. Allow to cool slightly.

3 In a bowl, mix together all the remaining ingredients; add the potatoes and toss gently to coat in the spice mixture.

4 Place on a non-stick baking tray, skin side down, and brush with any remaining spice mixture. Cook for 20 to 25 minutes until golden.

These spicy potato wedges are a healthy and delicious alternative to chips.

Helpful Hints

Make sure the wedges get nice and crispy in the oven before taking them out.

Preparation 20 mins • **Cooking** 5 mins • **Serves** 4

Vegetable Tempura

These vegetables are cooked in a light, crisp batter and served with dipping sauce. Choose a selection of your favourite vegetables.

Ingredients

caster sugar

Peanut dipping sauce:

- 15ml (1tbsp) sesame seeds
- 30ml (2tbsp) smooth, unsalted peanut butter
- 15ml (1tbsp) dark soy sauce
- 15ml (1tbsp) rice wine vinegar
- 15ml (1tbsp) cold water
- 10ml (2tsp) caster sugar
- 2.5ml (1/2tsp) chilli powder
- vegetable oil, for frying

chilli powder

Tempura batter:

- 200g (7oz) self-raising flour
- 5ml (1tsp) cornflour
- 2 egg yolks
- 350ml (12floz) ice-cold water
- 450g (1lb) mixed vegetables

cornflour

Equipment

- frying pan
- wooden spoon
- 2 bowls
- whisk
- measuring jug
- chopstick
- saucepan
- slotted spoon

whisk

1 Prepare the dip. Place the sesame seeds in a frying pan and cook over a moderate heat until lightly toasted.

2 Place the sesame seeds in a bowl and whisk in all the remaining dressing ingredients, until well combined and smooth.

3 Place the flours in a bowl. Whisk the egg yolks with the chilled water. Add this to the flour and mix using a chopstick. The mixture should be lumpy.

4 Fill a saucepan ⅓ full of oil and heat to 180ºC (350ºF). Dip the vegetables in the batter and fry them for 2 to 3 minutes. Remove with a slotted spoon.

Tasty Twists

Button mushrooms, small cauliflower florets, courgettes, red pepper, or carrots cut into thin strips all work well in this recipe.

Drinks and
Treats

• **Preparation** 5 mins • **Serves** 4

Milkshake

Make your own delicious milkshakes with fresh fruit. This simple drink is healthy and full of natural goodness.

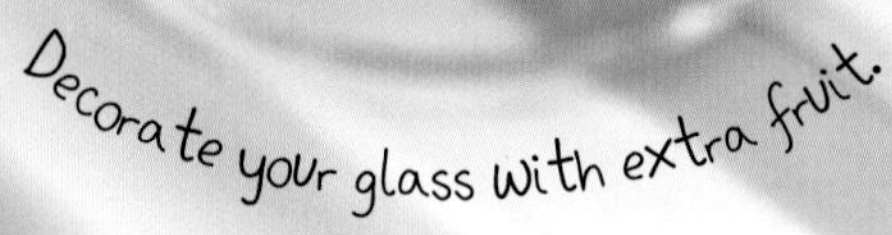

Ingredients

- 400g (14oz) fresh strawberries or 4 bananas
- 600ml (1pt) cold milk
- 8 scoops vanilla ice cream

strawberries

Equipment

- knife
- chopping board
- blender

blender

1 Remove the stalks from the strawberries/peel and chop the banana. Place in a liquidiser or blender and blitz to a purée.

2 Add the milk and ice cream and blend for 1 minute until frothy. Pour into 4 tall glasses and serve. For the banana one, try adding 4tbsp of toffee sauce or try chocolate ice cream instead of vanilla.

• **Preparation** 5 mins • **Cooking** 4 mins • **Serves** 4

Hot Chocolate

This simple recipe uses good quality chocolate instead of drinking chocolate – the taste is so much better!

Deliciously flavoured hot chocolate!

Ingredients

chocolate

- 100g ($3^1/_2$oz) good quality plain, milk, or white chocolate
- 600ml (1pt) milk
- few drops of mint, orange or vanilla extract
- 12 marshmallows
- cocoa powder, for dusting

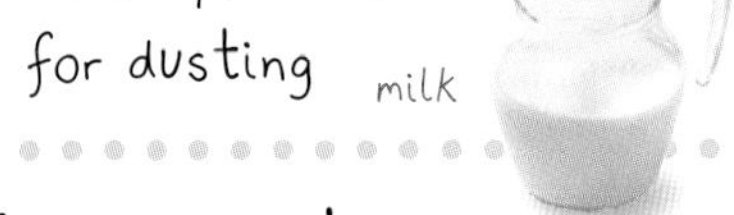

milk

Equipment

- grater
- whisk
- saucepan

saucepan

1 Coarsely grate the chocolate. Place the milk and chocolate in a saucepan and whisk over a moderate heat for 3 to 4 minutes until the chocolate has dissolved.

2 Add a few drops of flavouring. Pour the hot chocolate into 4 mugs and top each with 3 marshmallows. Dust with the cocoa powder.

• **Preparation** 30 mins • **Cooking** 20 mins • **Makes** 20 drinks

Cherry Cordial

Make this cordial when cherries are in season. Top with chilled sparkling water and ice for a refreshing drink.

This cherry cordial is a refreshing drink for a hot summer's day!

Ingredients

- 1kg (2lb 2oz) fresh red cherries
- 600ml (1pt) cold water
- 350g (12oz) caster sugar
- chilled still or sparkling water and ice, to serve

sugar

Equipment

wooden spoon

- knife
- chopping board
- 2 large saucepans
- wooden spoon
- food processor
- sieve
- metal spoon
- sterile jars
- measuring jug

measuring jug

saucepan

1 Cut each cherry in half and remove the stone. Place the cherries in a medium pan with the cold water.

2 Bring to the boil and simmer over a gentle heat for about 15 minutes until the fruit has softened.

3 Leave to cool for 10 minutes, then place in a food processor and blend. (You may need to do this in batches.)

4 Mash through a sieve into a clean pan, pressing the pulp left in the sieve. Add the sugar and, over a low heat, stir until dissolved.

5 Simmer for 5 minutes. Pour into sterilized jars and store in a cool place. Pour a little of the cordial into a glass and top with chilled water and ice.

Tasty Twists

To make a blackcurrant cordial replace the cherries with the same weight of blackcurrants.

• **Preparation** 20 mins • **Serves** 4

Watermelon Punch

This pretty red punch is made from watermelon and raspberries.

This delicious drink is full of goodness.

Ingredients

orange

- 1 small watermelon
- 300g (10½oz) fresh raspberries
- 1 orange, sliced
- 20 fresh mint leaves
- 20 ice cubes
- extra raspberries, to serve

raspberries

Equipment

- knife
- large bowl
- chopping board
- blender
- sieve

sieve

1 Cut the watermelon into wedges and remove the skin. Cut the flesh into chunks – you need about 1kg (2lb 2oz). Place in a blender with the raspberries and blend until liquified.

2 Strain the mixture through a sieve over a bowl. Pour into a jug or punch bowl and add the orange slices, mint and ice cubes. Add the extra raspberries. Serve immediately.

Smoothies

Fruit smoothies not only make a nutritional drink, but can also be served as a healthy snack, or with cereal or toast for breakfast.

Choose which flavour you like the best!

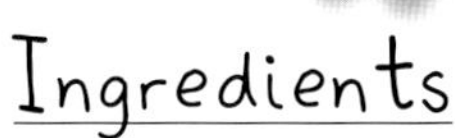

blueberries

Ingredients

- 350g (12oz) mixed berries
- 1 ripe banana
- 500g (1lb 2oz) low fat or fat free vanilla bio live yogurt
- 300ml (1/2pt) semi-skimmed milk

bananas

Equipment

- knife
- blender

blender

1 Peel the banana and roughly break into small pieces. Place in a blender with the berries, yogurt and milk. Whizz until the mixture is thick and smooth.

2 Pour into glasses and serve at once. For a banana and mango smoothie, substitute the berries for 1 large ripe mango and add another banana.

• **Preparation** 15 mins • **Serves** 5

Pink Lemonade

There is nothing more refreshing than a cool glass of homemade lemonade. Pink lemonade was traditionally dyed with a little beetroot juice, but this recipe uses cranberry juice for flavour and colour.

Ingredients

- 4 unwaxed lemons
- 100g ($3^1/_2$oz) caster sugar
- 600ml (1pt) boiling water
- 200ml (7floz) cranberry juice (chilled)
- 200ml (7floz) water (chilled)
- ice and lemon slices

lemon

Equipment

chopping board

- potato peeler
- knife
- chopping board
- wooden spoon
- heatproof jug
- mini-sieve
- serving jug

mini-sieve

1 Using a potato peeler, peel the zest from the lemons, leaving as much of the white pith on the lemons as possible. Squeeze the juice from the lemons.

2 Pour the lemon juice into a large heatproof jug, add the sugar and lemon zest. Pour over the boiling water and stir until the sugar has dissolved.

3 Leave to cool. Then strain the lemonade into a serving jug.

4 Stir in the cranberry juice and chilled water. Sweeten with extra sugar if desired and serve in glasses with ice and a slice of lemon.

This decorative drink is very pretty and tastes great!

• **Preparation** 10 mins • **Cooking** 5 mins • **Makes** 24

Marshmallow Squares

These delicious squares of marshmallow and toasted rice are so easy to make and will keep in an airtight container for up to a week.

Ingredients

- 250g (9oz) marshmallows
- 2.5ml (1/2tsp) vanilla extract
- 100g (3 1/2oz) butter, diced
- 175g (6oz) toasted rice cereal

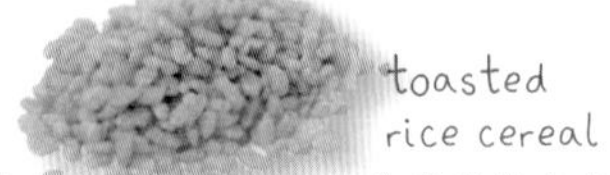
toasted rice cereal

Equipment

- 18 x 28cm (7 x 11in) oblong tin
- saucepan
- wooden spoon
- metal spoon
- knife

wooden spoon

saucepan

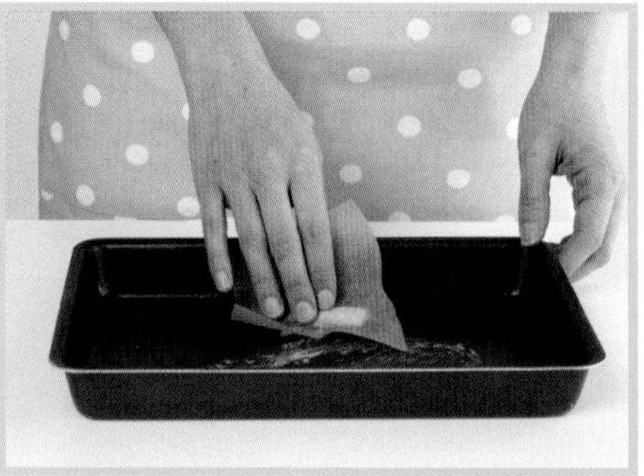

1 Grease a 18 x 28 cm (7 x 11 in) oblong tin. Place 200g (7oz) of the marshmallows, with the butter and vanilla extract in a medium saucepan.

2 Place over a medium heat and cook until the butter and marshmallows have melted. Roughly chop the remaining marshmallows.

3 Mix the toasted rice with the marshmallow mixture, then stir in the extra marshmallows. Spoon the mixture into the tray and press down with the back of a spoon.

4 Allow to cool in the tray and then cut into squares.

Tasty Twists

Use different coloured marshmallows to make your squares look more colourful.

These are perfect to make if you don't have much time as they are so quick & easy!

Toffee Popcorn

Homemade popcorn is great fun to make and tastes much better than shop-bought.

Tasty Twists

If you prefer salted popcorn, just leave out the toffee sauce and sprinkle over some salt.

Ingredients

- 30ml (2tbsp) corn oil
- 100g (3½oz) popping corn
- 50g (2oz) butter
- 50g (2oz) soft brown sugar
- 75ml (3tbsp) golden syrup

Equipment

- 2 medium saucepans
- large mixing bowl
- spoon

wooden spoon

saucepan

1 Heat the oil in a saucepan. Add the corn and, with the lid on, shake to coat in the oil. Over a medium heat, shake the pan occasionally until the corn pops.

2 Remove from the heat. Place the butter, sugar and syrup in another pan. Stir together over a medium heat until the butter has melted and the sugar has dissolved.

3 Put the popcorn into a large mixing bowl and drizzle the toffee sauce over the top.

4 Stir until the popcorn is coated. Stop stirring when the sauce has cooled and is setting. Leave until cool enough to eat.

This recipe makes the perfect accompaniment to your favourite movies!

Helpful Hint

Wait until there are 3 to 5 seconds between each "pop" before you turn off the heat.

• **Preparation** 20 mins • **Makes** 60

Peppermint Creams

These sophisticated sweets make a gorgeous gift for a friend – or maybe for yourself!

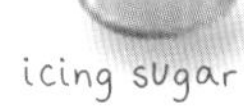
icing sugar

Ingredients

- 450g (1lb) icing sugar, sifted
- 120 to 135ml (8 to 9tbsp) sweetened condensed milk
- few drops peppermint extract or essence
- few drops green food colouring
- 150g ($5^1/_2$oz) plain chocolate

chocolate

rolling pin

Equipment

- mixing bowl
- metal spoon
- rolling pin
- small circular cookie cutter
- baking paper
- heatproof bowl
- saucepan

heatproof bowl

1 Place the icing sugar in a large bowl and add the condensed milk. Stir until you have a crumbly mixture.

2 Add a few drops of the peppermint extract or essence, and a few drops of green food colouring. Knead until you have a smooth firm mixture.

3 Lightly dust the work surface with a little icing sugar and roll out to 5mm (½in) thick. Cut into rounds with a small cutter. Leave to dry on a piece of baking paper.

4 Melt the chocolate in a heatproof bowl over a pan of simmering water, then dip each cream into the melted chocolate. Leave to set.

The combination of chocolate and mint flavours is scrumptious!

• **Preparation** 5 mins • **Cooking** 30 mins • **Makes** 36

Ultimate Fudge

Homemade sweets make wonderful gifts or treats. This basic recipe can be adapted to make chocolate or raisin fudge.

Helpful Hint

Like all sweets and treats, eat fudge in moderation or you will feel ill!

Ingredients

- 450g (1lb) caster sugar
- 50g (2oz) unsalted butter, diced
- 170g (6floz) can evaporated milk
- 150ml (1/4pt) milk
- 2.5ml (1/2tsp) vanilla extract

sugar

milk

square tin

Equipment

- 18cm (7in) shallow non-stick square tin
- medium heavy-based saucepan
- sugar thermometer
- wooden spoon
- knife

saucepan

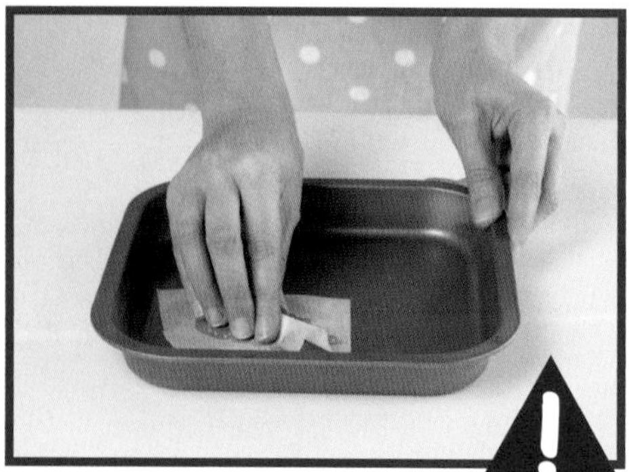

1 Grease an 18cm (7in) shallow non-stick square tin.

2 Gently heat the sugar, butter and milks in a saucepan, stirring with a wooden spoon until all the sugar has dissolved.

3 Bring to the boil and simmer gently, stirring continuously, for about 20 to 25 minutes.

4 A sugar thermometer should reach a temperature of 116°C (240°F). Remove from the heat, add the vanilla extract.

5 Beat until the mixture is thick and paler in colour. Pour into the prepared tin and leave to cool. When cold, cut into squares.

Tasty Twists

For chocolate fudge stir in 150g (5½oz) melted plain chocolate in place of the vanilla. For raisin fudge, stir in 75g (3oz) chopped raisins.

Give fudge as a gift, beautifully presented in a homemade giftbox.

• **Preparation** 25 hours • **Cooking** 5 mins • **Makes** 20

Chocolate Truffles

You can flavour these truffles with vanilla, orange, or peppermint extract and roll them in cocoa powder, chocolate sprinkles, or chopped nuts.

Ingredients

chocolate

- 200g (7oz) milk chocolate
- 100ml (3½floz) double cream
- 15g (½oz) unsalted butter
- few drops of orange, vanilla, or peppermint extract (optional)

To decorate:

- sifted cocoa powder
- grated milk, plain, and white chocolate
- chopped nuts, e.g. pistachios

double cream

Equipment

- medium-sized bowl
- small saucepan
- wooden spoon
- plate

bowl

saucepan

1 Break the chocolate into small pieces in a medium-sized bowl. Put the cream in a small saucepan with the butter and bring slowly to the boil.

2 Immediately pour over the broken chocolate. With a wooden spoon, stir until the mixture is smooth and all the chocolate has melted.

3 Stir in a few drops of orange or peppermint extract if using. Cover and allow the mixture to cool for about 30 minutes at room temperature.

4 Chill in the refrigerator for about 2 hours. Using a teaspoon, scoop out bite-sized pieces. Dust your hand lightly with cocoa powder and roll into balls.

5 Immediately roll the truffles in sifted cocoa powder, grated chocolate or nuts. Place in individual foil sweet cases and chill. They will keep for up to 10 days.

Tasty Twists

Alternatively, you can dip the truffles in melted milk, dark or white chocolate.

For a pure and simple hit of chocolate, these truffles are just the thing!

• **Preparation** 15 mins • **Makes** 72

Coconut Ice

This coconut ice recipe requires no cooking – just mix all the ingredients together and leave to set.

Try using different food colourings instead of the traditional pink and white.

Ingredients

- 397g (14oz) can sweetened condensed milk
- 500g (1lb 2oz) icing sugar, sifted
- 350g (12oz) desiccated coconut
- few drops pink food colouring

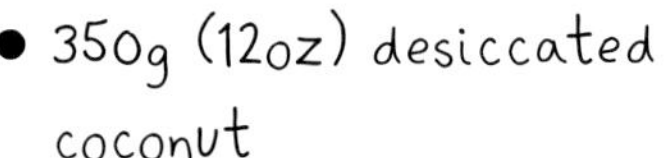

Equipment

- 20cm (8in) square cake tin
- baking paper
- mixing bowl
- metal spoon

Helpful Hints

If stored in an airtight container, the coconut ice will keep for up to 3 weeks.

1 Line a 20cm (8in) square cake tin with baking paper.

2 In a large bowl, combine the condensed milk with the icing sugar, then stir in the coconut, to form a stiff mixture.

3 Divide the mixture in half and using your hands, press half into the tin.

4 Knead the remaining mixture with a few drops of pink colouring and dusted with a little icing sugar.

5 Press this over the white layer. Refrigerate until set, then cut into squares.

Tools

Here is a handy guide to all equipment used in this book. Each recipe has a tools checklist so that you can gather everything you need before you begin cooking:

Miscellaneous Tools

pie dish

small ovenproof dish

ovenproof dish

wooden kebab skewers

lolly mould and sticks

bamboo rolling mat

Glossary

This is the place to find extra information about the cookery words and techniques used in this book. Key terms are explained simply, plus there are chef's tips to give you even more handy hints.

Cutting Words

Food is often cut into smaller pieces to make it easier to cook with and eat. Here are some cutting words:

Chopping – cutting into smaller pieces with a knife.
Coring – removing the core of a fruit. The core is the hard central part of some fruit, such as apples.
Crushing – breaking food up into very small pieces e.g. with a garlic crusher.
Cubing – cutting food into cubes about 2.5cm (1in).
De-seeding – removing the seeds of fruit and vegetables, such as peppers, tomatoes, and cucumber.
Dicing – cutting into small cubes.
Grating – rubbing food against a grater to make coarse or fine shreds.
Hulling – cutting off the green stalks and leaves of fruit, such as strawberries.
Juicing – squeezing the liquid from fruit or vegetables.
Mashing – crushing food, such as bananas or cooked potatoes, to make a smooth mass.
Peeling – removing the skin or outer layer of vegetables and fruit, by hand or with a knife. Some vegetables, such as onions and garlic, are always peeled first.
Roughly chopping – cutting into pieces of varying sizes.
Scoring – making long, shallow cuts in food, to reduce cooking time or allow flavour to be absorbed.
Slicing – cutting food into thick or thin pieces.
Stoning – removing the large stone at the centre of some fruit, such as peaches or mangoes.
Strips – long, thick or thin pieces.
Tailing – removing the stalk of a vegetable.
Trimming – cutting off the unwanted parts (such as roots or leaves) of fruit, vegetables, meat, or fish.
Zesting – finely grating the peel of oranges, lemons, or limes to make zest, which is used as a flavouring.

★ Chef's Tips

How to Dice an Onion

First cut the onion in half through the root and then peel off the skin. Place one half flat-side-down and firmly hold the onion so that the root is near your little finger. Carefully cut parallel slices, horizontally towards the root (step 1). Turn the root of the onion away from you and slice, downwards from the root (Step 2). Turn the root back towards your little finger and slice across so that the onion falls away in small cubes (Step 3). To chop an onion, just follow steps 2 and 3.

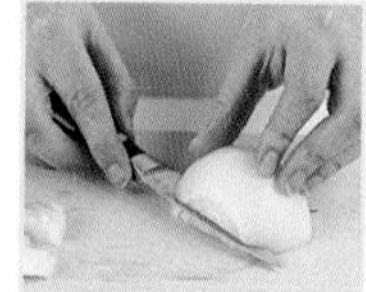
Step 1

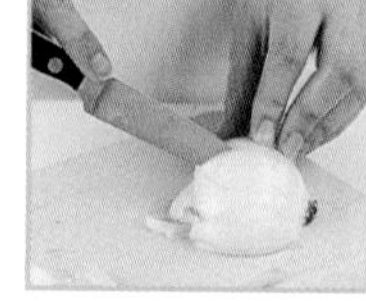
Step 2

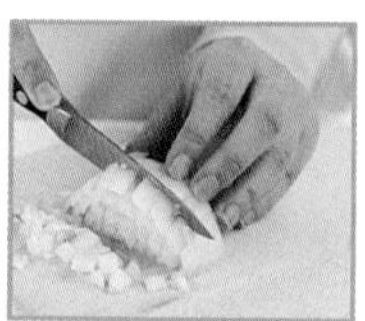
Step 3

How to Crush Garlic

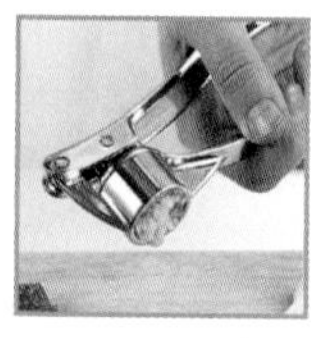
crushing garlic

Break open the garlic bulb and remove the cloves. Peel each clove and place them in a garlic crusher, one at a time. Squeeze the handle to crush the garlic and press it through the holes.

How to De-seed a Pepper

Cut the top off the pepper. Inside you will see the core and the seeds. Carefully cut any parts attached to the side of the pepper and pull out the core and seeds.

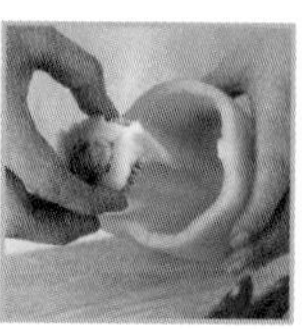
de-seeding

How to Juice an Orange

juicing

Cut an orange in half. Hold each half in turn over a bowl and press a reamer or juicer into the centre. Twist the orange or reamer so that the juice drips into the bowl and then remove any pips.

Cooking Words

Many of the recipes ask you to **preheat** the oven or grill, which means to heat it to the correct temperature before you begin. This helps the food to cook thoroughly and evenly. Here are some other words to help you:

Baking – cooking food in an oven with dry heat (without any liquid). The outside will become brown.
Basting – spooning hot fat or a marinade during cooking to prevent drying out.
Boiling – when a liquid, such as water reaches boiling point it bubbles and is very hot.
Dry-frying – frying without oil or fat.
Frying – cooking in a frying pan or saucepan with a little oil, over direct heat.
Griddling – cooking or browning in a griddle pan, on a hob.
Grilling – cooking or browning under intense heat.
Par-boiling – boiling for half the normal cooking time to soften, not completely cook.
Poaching – cooking in gently simmering liquid.
Reducing – simmering a liquid, such as a sauce, so that it thickens and reduces in quantity.
Roasting – cooking in the oven at a high temperature.
Sautéing – frying quickly in a little oil or fat.
Shallow-frying – frying in about 1.25cm (½") or more of oil so that the food becomes golden and crispy.
Simmering – cooking over a low heat so the liquid or food is bubbling gently but not boiling.
Stir-frying – frying quickly in a little oil or fat over a high heat, stirring constantly.
Toasting – browning and crisping food under a grill, in a toaster, or in the oven.
Warming – heating gently over a low heat, without boiling.

How to Roast a Red Pepper

Pre-heat the oven to 220°C (425°F/Gas 7). Brush a pepper with oil and place it on a roasting tin. Roast for 30 minutes or until the skin starts to blacken. Allow the pepper to cool before peeling and de-seeding.

How to Check That Meat is Cooked

It is really important that you always check that meat is cooked thoroughly. Although meat sometimes looks cooked on the outside, you should check that the centre is not pink or bloody. To check a roast chicken, stick a skewer into the centre or thickest part of the meat. If the juices that run out are clear (not bloody or pink), then the meat is thoroughly cooked.

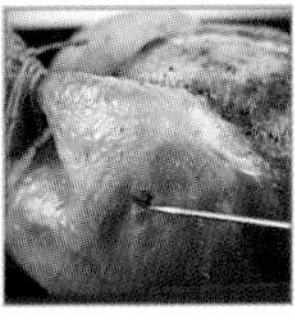
roast chicken

Mixing Words

Mixing means to combine ingredients together. There are lots of mixing words.

Beating – stirring or mixing quickly until smooth, to break down or add air.
Blending – mixing ingredients together using a blender or food processor, to form a liquid or smooth mass.
Creaming – beating butter and sugar together to incorporate air.
Folding – a gentle way of mixing ingredients together, to retain as much air in the mixture as possible.
Whipping – beating ingredients, such as cream or egg whites, to add air and make them thicker.
Whisking – evenly mixing ingredients, with a whisk; another word for whipping.

How to Beat an Egg

To beat an egg, crack the egg into a bowl and stir vigorously with a fork or whisk.

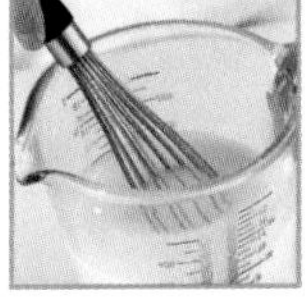
beating

How to Cream Butter and Sugar

creaming

Dice the butter and then allow it to soften a little. Whisk the butter and sugar together or beat them with a wooden spoon to incorporate air and make a light and fluffy mixture.

How to Fold Ingredients

Use a metal spoon or rubber spatula to gently lift and turn the ingredients until they are just about mixed together, to avoid losing precious air in the mixture.

folding

whipping

How to Whip Cream

Use a hand or electric whisk to vigorously whip the cream until it forms soft, firm peaks. Do not over-whip as this will make the cream curdle.

Bread-Making

Bread-making is a lot of fun but you'll need a lot of energy for all that kneading! Here are some useful bread-making terms:

Kneading – pressing and folding the dough with your hands until it is smooth and stretchy. This distributes the yeast and helps it to rise.
Knocking back – deflating the dough with a gentle punch. This evens out the texture of the bread.
Proving – this is the correct name for the process of rising in bread-making.
Rising – the time it takes for the dough to increase in size.

Chef's Tips

How to Knead Dough

Lightly sprinkle flour on the work surface and use one hand to hold the dough. With the heel of the other hand, gently push the dough away from you and then lift the dough back over. Repeat for about 10 minutes until the dough is smooth and stretchy, rotating frequently for even kneading.

kneading

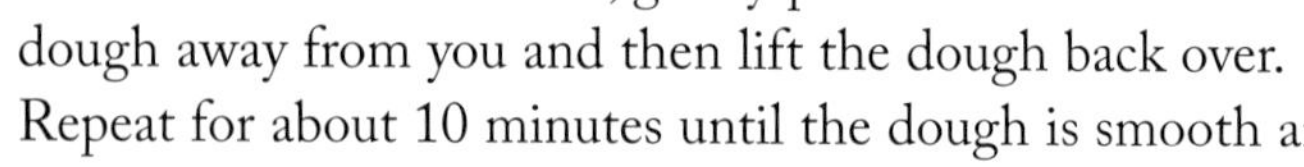

How to Knock Back Dough

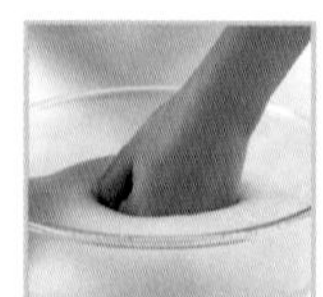

knocking back

After the dough has risen and doubled in size, it will need to be knocked back. Press down firmly with your knuckles and the dough will deflate.

Pastry-Making

Shortcrust pastry is the type usually used for pies or tarts. **Puff** pastry is light and flaky. Here are some useful pastry words:

Baking blind – weighing down pastry with baking beans to stop it rising or changing shape during baking.
Crimping – sealing or decorating the edges of pastry with a fork or by pinching with your fingers.
Glazing – brushing egg yolk or milk on to pastry (or dough) to make it look shiny when cooked.
Rolling – flattening the pastry with a rolling pin to make a bigger, thinner sheet.
Rubbing – mixing fat into the flour with your fingertips until it resembles breadcrumbs.

Chef's Tips

How to Roll Pastry or Dough

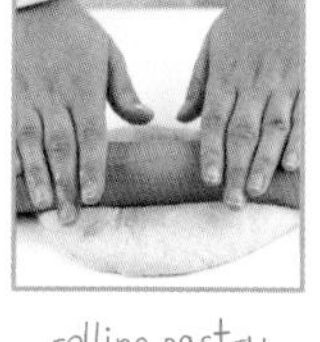

rolling pastry

Sprinkle some flour onto the work surface and rolling pin. Roll the rolling pin across the pastry, away from you. Rotate the pastry and sprinkle more flour, if needed. Keep rolling and rotating until you get the right shape and thickness. Always roll the pastry slightly bigger than you need.

How to BakeBlind

baking blind

Cover the pastry with a double layer of greaseproof paper and weigh it down with baking beans or dried beans. Bake blind for 15 minutes, or as directed in the recipe and then remove the paper and beans.

Cake-Making

Here are some useful cake-making words:

Greasing – lightly coating the inside of a cake tin or other surface with oil or fat to prevent sticking.
Lining – covering the insides of a cake tin with parchment paper to prevent sticking.
Melting – heating a solid, such as chocolate or butter, to turn it into a liquid.
Sieving – to put a powdery ingredient, such as flour, through a sieve to remove lumps and aerate the mixture.

Chef's Tips

How to Grease and Line a Cake Tin

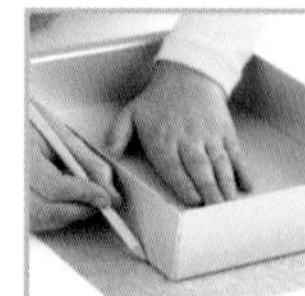

lining

greasing

With a pencil, draw around the cake tin onto some parchment or greaseproof paper. Cut around the outline with scissors. Grease the tin by rubbing butter or oil all over the inside, using a small piece of parchment paper. Lay the paper on the bottom of the tin.

How to Test thaat a Cake is Cooked

testing a cake

Insert a skewer or knife into the centre of a cake. If it comes out clean (without any cake mixture) the cake is cooked. If the skewer comes out with mixture on it, bake for a few more minutes.

Egg Words

All the recipes in this book use medium-sized eggs, which should be at room temperature. The names for the parts of an egg are:

Shell – the hard outer covering of the egg.
White – the clear, runny part of the egg that turns white when cooked.
Yolk – the yellow ball in the centre of the egg.

How to Check for Freshness

fresh egg test

Most eggs have a "use-by" date on them but here is a handy tip: place an egg in a glass of water – if it is fresh (good), the egg will lie horizontally on the bottom, but if it is stale (bad), it will stand upright and pop up to the top of the glass. You should never use a stale egg.

cracking an egg

How to Crack an Egg

Tap the egg firmly on the side of a bowl or jug, gently pull the sides apart, and let the insides drop into the container. It is best to crack an egg into a separate dish before adding it to your mixture, in case bits of the shell fall in as well!

How to Separate an Egg

Crack the egg over a bowl and break it open gently. Don't let the yolk fall into the bowl – tip it carefully from one half of the shell to the other until all the white has dropped into the bowl. Put the yolk into a separate bowl.

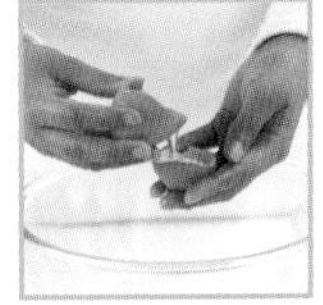
separating an egg white from the yolk

Useful Words

Here are some more words that you will learn in this book:

Absorb – to soak up, usually during cooking.
Batter – a runny mixture made of flour, eggs, and milk.
Caramelizing – turning brown and sticky when heated; this happens if the food has a sweet coating or sauce.
Chill – to cool in a refrigerator.
Coat – to cover with a layer of something, such as flour.
Curdle – when the liquid and solid parts of an ingredient or mixture separate. Milk curdles when over-heated and cakes curdle if the eggs are too cold or added too quickly.
Dash – a small quantity.
Defrost – to thaw frozen food.
Dollop – a large spoonful of a soft food.
Drain – to remove unwanted liquid, sometimes with a colander or sieve.
Drizzle – to pour slowly, in a trickle.
Drop – a single splash of liquid.
Freeze – to turn a liquid into a solid by storing it in an extremely cold place (freezer).
Knob – a small lump of a solid ingredient, such as butter.
Marinade – a mixture of oil, herbs, spices, and other flavourings in which food is soaked to add flavour.
Marinate – to soak meat, fish, or vegetables in a marinade in order to add flavour or tenderize.
Paste – a soft, thick mixture.
Pinch – as much of a powdery ingredient as you can hold between your finger and thumb.
Prick – to make small air holes, usually with a fork.
Purée – a thick pulp produced by blending or sieving.
Refresh – to rinse a just-cooked food, such as pasta, in cold water to prevent further cooking.
Rest – to set aside cooked food for a short time, such as roasted meat, to allow it to become tender and moist.
Rinse – to wash in running water from the tap.
Ripe – when a fruit is soft and ready to be eaten.
Scatter – to roughly sprinkle pieces of an ingredient or food over something with your hands.
Seal – to join up or encase a food to prevent anything getting in or out.
Season – to add salt and pepper to a food to balance and enhance its natural flavour.
Set – to turn from a liquid into a solid.
Shape – to use your hands to turn a soft food or mixture into a particular shape.
Sieve – to use a sieve to drain liquid, remove lumps, or add air.
Sprinkle – to scatter a food lightly over something.
Stand – to set a food aside for a while to cool, finish cooking, or improve the flavour.
Stock – a flavoured liquid in which meat, fish, or vegetables are cooked.
Thicken – to add an ingredient, such as flour, to make a liquid less thin.
Wedges – thick slices with a pointed or thin edge.

Index

Acknowledgements

The publisher would like to thank: Photography assistants Jon Cardwell, Michael Hart, and Ria Osborne. The following children for being fantastic hand models and trainee chefs – Latoya Bailey, Efia Brady, Hannah Broom, Ella Bukbardis, Eleanor Bullock, Nakita Clarke, Megan Craddock, Elise Flatman, Eliza Greenslade, George Greenslade, Mykelia Hill, Hannah Leaman, Toby Leaman, Rozina McHugh, Eva Mee, Grace Mee, Louis Moorcraft, Hannah Moore, Shannon O'Kelly, Lily Sansford, Sadie Sansford, Gabriella Soper, Olivia Sullivan-Davis, James Tilley, Rachel Tilley, Charlotte Vogel, and Hope Wadman.